# FINANCIAL TIMES
# MANAGEMENT

## Knowledge   Skills   Understanding

Financial Times Management is a new business created to deliver the knowledge, skills and understanding that will enable students, managers and organisations to achieve their ambitions, whatever their needs, wherever they are.

Financial Times Pitman Publishing, part of Financial Times Management, is the leading publisher of books for practitioners and students in business and finance, bringing cutting-edge thinking and best practice to a global market.

To find out more about Financial Times Management and Financial Times Pitman Publishing, visit our website at:

www.ftmanagement.com

This bo

CHA

# FRAMEWORKS

Each book in the Frameworks series is a
comprehensive and concise introduction to
the subject. The books are well structured
and provide a step-by-step guide to essential
principles. They develop a basic framework
of understanding to underpin further study
of core business, financial and legal subjects
in the higher education curriculum.

# FRAMEWORKS

# Consumer Law

## Fourth Edition

## Malcolm Leder

LLB, Solicitor

*Head of School of Law
and Professor of Consumer Law
Middlesex University*

## Peter Shears

BA, LLB, LLM

*Director of Legal Studies
Plymouth Business School
University of Plymouth*

**FINANCIAL TIMES**
**PITMAN PUBLISHING**

LONDON · HONG KONG · JOHANNESBURG
MELBOURNE · SINGAPORE · WASHINGTON DC

FINANCIAL TIMES MANAGEMENT
128 Long Acre, London WC2E 9AN
Tel: +44 (0)171 447 2000
Fax: +44 (0)171 240 5771
Website: www.ftmanagement.com

*A Division of Financial Times Professional Limited*

Fourth edition published 1996

ISBN 0 273 63412 7

*British Library Cataloguing in Publication Data*
A CIP catalogue record for this book can be obtained from the British Library.

10 9 8 7 6 5 4

Printed and bound in Great Britain by Bell and Bain Ltd, Glasgow

*The Publishers' policy is to use paper manufactured from sustainable forests.*

# CONTENTS

**Part One**
**PRIVATE LAW REMEDIES**

## Part Two
## ADMINISTRATIVE REMEDIES AND CRIMINAL LAW SANCTIONS

# PREFACE

Consumer protection has moved on since the original and second editions of *Consumer Law* were written by the first-named author. Nevertheless the basic aim of the text remains the same: to deal succinctly with consumer law, bringing together all its diverse elements.

Consumer transactions may be broadly defined as the business supply of goods or services to the private individual. The expression 'consumer' is becoming overworked, but even so there are many different types of consumer transaction properly so-called. This book does not purport to delineate every byway of consumer law, but concentrates on the legal principles applicable to those areas thought to be of most concern to traders, consumers, and their legal advisers.

This fourth edition records significant developments in consumer law since the date of the previous edition. Indeed, the last year in particular has seen a veritable flurry in the law. For instance, the Sale of Goods (Amendment) Act 1994 has finally abolished market overt. The term 'merchantable quality' has been found not fit for its purpose and under the Sale and Supply of Goods Act 1994 has been replaced by the modern, more extensively defined (albeit anodyne) term 'satisfactory quality'. Consumer remedies have been enhanced and clarified at the same time. Deriving from the European Union, the General Product Safety Regulations 1994 have imposed an expanded general safety requirement, which disapplies the version in the Consumer Protection Act 1987 to the extent that the respective provisions overlap. Also deriving from the EU are the Unfair Terms in Consumer Contracts Regulations 1994, which come into force on 1 July 1995 and which, if they do not amount to a universal regime against unconscionability in consumer contracts, at least mark a significant step forwards in that direction. A new chapter has been added on package holidays, reflecting the increased regulation of this area under the awkwardly named Package Travel, Package Holidays and Package Tours Regulations 1992 (yet another development emanating from the EU). Advertising is now treated in a separate chapter, which includes reference to the 1995 editions of the British Codes of Advertising and Sales Promotion Practice.

These landmark changes apart, opportunity has been taken in the new edition to augment and update the text generally and to rearrange material as seemed indicated. Pointers are given to likely future developments.

*Consumer Law* is intended primarily for the use of undergraduates on LLB programmes or majoring in law, and for prospective solicitors on a Legal Practice Course, as well as for intending 'para legals'. In addition, business studies and accountancy students who are studying the legal obligations of the business enterprise will find the book helpful, since consumer rights and business obligations are simply the obverse and reverse of the same coin. In our experience, those whose work involves a consideration of the legal aspects of consumer problems will also find the book useful. Some acquaintance with general legal principles is assumed, but where a particular principle is central to an understanding of consumer law the principle in question is itself reviewed.

Our thanks are due to our editor, John Cushion, whose understanding and efficiency characterized his role as he progressed this new edition through to publication.

The law is stated as including unfair terms in consumer contracts at 1 July 1995 and otherwise as we believe it to be in the Spring of 1995, with a few additional points of later date also included. The likely enactment of the Sale of Goods (Amendment) Bill later in 1995 is anticipated in the text.

*Malcolm Leder*
*Peter Shears*
May 1995

**Note**: a reference in the text such as *see* **12** refers to numbered section 12 of that particular chapter; a reference such as *see* 6:**20** refers to section 20 of chapter 6.

# TABLE OF CASES

# TABLE OF STATUTES

# TABLE OF STATUTORY INSTRUMENTS

# PRIVATE LAW REMEDIES

## Introductory note

In a sense there is still no such creature as 'consumer law'. English law has never developed a fully coherent body of law designed to protect the consumer. The consumer and his advisers have instead been obliged to utilize a hotchpotch of common law concepts and doctrines designed primarily for other purposes. Even the recent statutory consumer protection developments have been piece-meal, and do not amount to a comprehensive code. This is true, too, of EU Law. Although the initiative in consumer protection has passed to the institutions of the European Union, no general unifying normative structure has emerged. The chapter dealing with the implementation of the EC Directive on Unfair Terms in Consumer Contracts underlines this point – the new rules are incorporated but not truly *integrated* in English law.

The upshot of this empirical approach is that consumer law is a hybrid creation. The student accordingly needs to study a number of disparate categories of law, but at the same time needs to be constantly aware of their inter-relationships from the consumer viewpoint. This book draws attention to the interrelationships in its discussion of the law.

Part One of the text considers the consumer's rights and remedies under private (or civil) law. The text deals not only with the law of sale of goods as it relates to consumers, but also with analogous contracts and with contracts involving the supply of a service, including package holidays. After a review of product liability, attention is directed at the consumer credit dimension.

For various reasons indicated in the text, private law remedies do not by themselves afford adequate consumer protection. Part Two of this book there-fore deals with intervention in the consumer interest by administrative remedies, backed by criminal law sanctions. It may well be that administrative remedies and criminal law sanctions now play a more significant role in consumer protection as a whole than does private law. Nevertheless, the individual con-sumer with a particularised complaint lives, so to speak, in a mixed legal economy; private law is not obsolete and the consumer's adviser must know its details.

# 1

# CLASSIFICATION OF CONSUMER CONTRACTS

## 1. Introductory

The law relating to the sale of goods has long been largely regulated by statute. For most practical purposes, so too have hire-purchase agreements. Contracts of hire, on the other hand, and contracts for the transfer of goods analogous to contracts of sale (e.g. exchange, or supply of work and materials – defined below) have until recent times been left to be regulated by the common law.

The enactment of the Supply of Goods and Services Act 1982, which complements the Sale of Goods Act 1979 and the Supply of Goods (Implied Terms) Act 1973, has in considerable measure rationalized the position. That is to say, whatever the type of contract under which goods are supplied, there is a basic package of consumer protection implied into the transaction. In this respect it is really a question of asking 'where do I find the law?', a question which this chapter answers through classification of the various types of contract into which consumers enter.

It must be emphasized that unlike the Sale of Goods Act, the 1982 Act regulates only the implied terms. Other aspects (e.g. formation, performance, remedies) of contracts falling within the scope of the Act remain to be governed by the common law, reference to which will be made where appropriate. Chapter 5 will deal with the implied terms themselves, as imposed under the Sale of Goods Act 1979, the Supply of Goods (Implied Terms) Act 1973, and the 1982 Act respectively – all as amended by the Sale and Supply of Goods Act 1994.

## CONTRACTS FOR THE SALE OF GOODS

### 2. Sale of Goods Act 1979

The law relating to the sale of goods was codified in the Sale of Goods Act 1893. This Act and the amendments made to it from time to time were consolidated in the Sale of Goods Act 1979 (SGA). The legislation was in its origins more concerned with regulating commercial relations than with protecting consumers, but consumers must nevertheless have regard to its provisions. Common law rules, however, continue to apply save in so far as they are inconsistent with the Act: s. 62(2). Moreover, subject to the Unfair Contract Terms Act 1977 and the new rules on unfair consumer contract terms (*see* Chaps. 6, 7), both the Act and common law rules may be negatived or varied by usage, or by express agreement or a previous course of dealing between trader and consumer: s. 55.

### 3. Definitions

Only contracts for the *sale* (not e.g. hire) of *goods* (not services) are governed by the Sale of Goods Act. The Act defines a contract for the sale of goods as 'a contract by which the seller transfers or agrees to transfer the property in goods to the buyer for a money consideration, called the price': s. 2(1). The contract of sale may be absolute or conditional: s. 2(3). The definition covers both a sale, where the ownership of goods is transferred to the buyer, and an agreement to sell, where the ownership is to be transferred at some future time or subject to some condition yet to be fulfilled: s. 2(5). A sale of 'future goods' (goods to be manufactured, such as a suit, or grown, such as a crop, or acquired by the seller after making the contract of sale) operates as an agreement to sell: s. 5. The interpretation section of the Act (s. 61) throws further light on the definition of a contract for the sale of goods: a seller is a 'person who sells or agrees to sell goods' and likewise a buyer is a 'person who buys or agrees to buy goods'; 'property' means ownership and 'goods' are defined to include 'all personal chattels other than things in action and money'.

### 4. The price

This can be either money or goods and money. It cannot, however, be goods alone, which would make the arrangement amount to a contract of exchange (*see* 8). Where the price is not fixed by the contract or by a previous course of dealing between the parties, the buyer has to pay a reasonable price: s. 8. So the consumer who orders (say) central heating fuel without inquiring about the price cannot thereafter claim the contract to be void for uncertainty: the price payable will be the current market price.

## CONTRACTS FOR THE TRANSFER OF GOODS

### 5. Contracts for the transfer of property in goods

Part I of the Supply of Goods and Service Act 1982 (SGSA) regulates 'a contract for the transfer of goods', defined as being 'a contract under which one person transfers or agrees to transfer to another the property in goods': s. 1. A contract may be a contract for the transfer of goods whatever the nature of the consideration for the transfer and whether or not the supply of services is included.

### 6. The excepted contracts

Certain contracts are excepted from the above definition because statutory implied terms already exist in regard to goods supplied thereunder. The excepted contracts are:

(a) contracts of sale

(b) hire-purchase agreements (*see* 13)

(c) contracts involving the supply of goods on the redemption of trading stamps (*see* 12).

> *Note*: Also excepted (for reasons of policy) are transfers or agreements to transfer made by deed for which there is no consideration other than the presumed consideration imported by the deed; and contracts intended to operate by way of security.

## 7. Work and materials

Contracts for the supply of work and materials pre-eminently fall within the definition of a contract for the transfer of goods and consequently are governed by the SGSA and not the SGA. They are analogous to contracts for the sale of goods because ownership in goods is transferred, yet they are distinct. Contracts for *services* alone (e.g. insurance, a package holiday, or cleaning curtains) may be easily recognized and distinguished from the sale of goods. The difficulty of classification arises where there is involved a combination of services and goods. Is this sale of goods or work and materials? The test for classifying the contract is: what is the essence of the transaction, the production of something to be sold (sale of goods) or the expenditure of skill and labour (work and materials)? Painting a portrait, repairing a car, applying a hair dye, roofing a house – all have been held to be contracts for work and materials. Likewise, contracts for the installation of double glazing or central heating would be contracts for work and materials. But a meal in a restaurant is regarded as a contract for the sale of goods.

## 8. Exchange or barter

It has already been noted that the Sale of Goods Act defines a contract for the sale of goods as a contract for the transfer of property 'for a money consideration, called the price'. It follows that a simple exchange of goods (barter) is not a sale of goods, because no money is payable. The nature of a contract of exchange is not purely a matter of theoretical interest to the consumer. The promotion of products through the distribution of coupons, vouchers, wrappers, labels, etc., may amount to a contract of barter on redemption by the consumer. Likewise barter, perhaps, is the part-exchange transaction whereby used goods are traded in as part-consideration for new. Once it is established that a contract is one of exchange or barter it comes within the definition of a contract for the transfer of goods and is governed by the SGSA. Redemption against trading stamps is governed by another statute (*see* 12).

## 9. Free gifts

'Free gifts' agreed to be supplied with products (e.g. 'free cassette with every VCR purchased') are not, it seems, supplied on a contract of sale but on a collateral contract: cf. *Esso Petroleum Ltd* v. *Commissioners of Customs and Excise* (1976), in which judicial opinion in the House of Lords on the status of 'free gifts' (World Cup coins) was divided. If it is correct that a free gift is supplied on a collateral contract, then it will be a contract for the transfer of goods within the SGSA.

On the other hand, if the gift is merely a free sample distributed as part of the promotion of a product without any connection with a contract of supply so that there is technically no consideration for the gift, then there can be no contract at all and no implied terms will be applicable. (In such a case the consumer might have a remedy in the tort of negligence if the free sample turned out to be a dangerous product: *see* Chap. 11.)

## CONTRACTS FOR THE HIRE OF GOODS

### 10. The nature of hire

Hire is a contract for the bailment of goods in consideration of a rental whereby the hirer obtains possession of the goods for an agreed time and purpose. Hire is legally quite distinct from sale in that a hirer obtains possession only, not ownership.

> *Note*: An agreement for hire to an individual which is capable of subsisting for more than three months and does not require the hirer to make payments exceeding £15,000 is a 'consumer hire agreement' and is regulated under the Consumer Credit Act 1974 (*see* Chap. 13 *et seq.*).

### 11. Hire under the Supply of Goods and Services Act

Part I of the SGSA implies similar terms, *mutatis mutandis*, in contracts of hire to those it does in contract for the transfer of goods (*see* Chap. 5). The SGSA s. 6, defines 'a contract for the hire of goods' as being 'a contract under which one person bails or agrees to bail goods to another by way of hire'. Excepted from this definition are hire-purchase agreements (*see* 13), and contracts involving the bailment of goods on the redemption of trading stamps (*see* 12). The fact that services may be supplied under a contract will not prevent it from being a contract for the hire of goods; nor is the nature of the consideration relevant.

## OTHER CONTRACTS UNDER WHICH GOODS PASS

### 12. Trading stamps

The supply of goods on the redemption of trading stamps is not a sale of goods (*see* 4), nor is it a contract within the SGSA (*see* 6, 11). In fact, special legislation protects the consumer. The Trading Stamps Act 1964 regulates the use of trading stamps, by providing that they must be marked with their cash value; that they must be redeemable for cash at the consumer's option; that retailers must display information enabling consumers to calculate the number of stamps they should receive; and prohibiting misleading advertising as to the value of trading stamps. Section 4 of the 1964 Act (as amended by the Sale and Supply of Goods Act 1994) also imposes implied obligations as to title and quality 'notwithstanding any terms to the contrary'. These obligations correspond to the Sale of Goods Act provisions as to title and quality in contracts of sale (*see* Chap. 5).

## 13. Hire-purchase

This is a contract of hire which grants the debtor (i.e. the hirer) the option to purchase the goods if the terms of the agreement are complied with by him. But the debtor is not bound to exercise the option to purchase. Accordingly he is not someone who 'agrees to buy' goods, and so the transaction does not fall within the scope of the Sale of Goods Act. However, a consumer who enters into a hire-purchase agreement is in reality, if not in law, acquiring goods, albeit on credit. Since the passing of the Supply of Goods (Implied Terms) Act 1973, the policy of the law has been to assimilate the implied obligations of the supplier in sale and hire-purchase transactions (*see* 5:**13**). As will be seen later, the Consumer Credit Act includes hire-purchase contracts under its umbrella, and, indeed, makes certain special provisions concerning them.

> *Helby* v. *Matthews* (1895): the owner of a piano let it on hire at a rent of 10s. 6d. a month. Under the agreement the hirer could return the piano at any time, the hirer remaining liable for all arrears of hire. It was agreed that the hirer would become owner of the piano on paying all the stipulated instalments, but that meanwhile the piano should continue in the sole ownership of the original owner.
> HELD: These arrangements amounted to what is now called a hire-purchase agreement. The hirer had not 'agreed to buy' and the contract did not fall within the provisions of the Sale of Goods Act (House of Lords).

# CONTRACTS FOR THE SUPPLY OF SERVICES

## 14. Services under Part II of the Supply of Goods and Services Act

Whilst Part I of the SGSA 1982 regulates contracts for the transfer of goods and contracts of hire, as outlined above, it is Part II which deals with the supply of services. Part II implies certain terms into contracts for the supply of services. Details are given in Chapter 5. For present purposes of classification, however, it is sufficient to note that s. 12 SGSA defines a 'contract for the supply of a service' as being 'a contract under which a person ("the supplier") agrees to carry out a service'. Contracts of service or apprenticeship are expressly excluded from this definition. The fact that a contract also provides for the transfer or hire of goods does not prevent it from being a contract for the supply of a service if otherwise within the definition.

> *Note*: It will be observed that the various categories of contract which the consumer (or firms, for that matter) may enter into are capable of overlapping.

## Progress test 1

1. To what extent may (a) common law principles; and (b) special stipulations agreed between the parties, be applied to a contract for the sale of goods?

2. Define a contract for the sale of goods and distinguish a sale from an agreement to sell. Is a house 'goods' within the meaning of the Sale of Goods Act? What are 'future goods'?

3. D fills up the boot of his car with logs which he has obtained from a timber merchant. Nothing has been said about the price. How much must D pay for the logs?

4. Define a contract for the transfer of goods. Give examples.

5. Consider whether the following are contracts for the sale of goods or for work and materials:
   (a) F eats a meal at E's restaurant.
   (b) G repairs H's car and puts a new engine in it.
   (c) I, a hairdresser, applies a hair-dye to J's hair.
   (d) K buys a fitted carpet, which is fitted by the retailer.

6. Does the distribution of 'free gifts' involve the making of any contract? If so, what type?

7. L redeems several books of trading stamps for a radio. The radio does not work. Can L sue for breach of contract?

8. Define a contract for the hire of goods and distinguish between (a) a contract of hire; (b) a contract of hire-purchase; and (c) a contract for the sale of goods.

9. Define a contract for the supply of a service.

# 2

## OWNERSHIP AND RISK

## TRANSFER OF PROPERTY AND RISK

### 1. Ownership and risk

In this chapter we turn to contracts for the sale of goods, as defined and governed by the Sale of Goods Act (*see* 1:3). The essence of the contract is the transfer of ownership in the goods. The point of making the contract is that the buyer will become the owner of the goods (obtain the property in them) and that the seller will be paid money (a money consideration called the price). In English law the transfer of the risk of loss of the goods from trader to consumer is closely connected with the transfer of ownership. This aspect of the law – the transfer of risk – is the subject of this chapter.

### 2. Property, ownership, title

The Sale of Goods Act uses the expressions 'transfer of property' or 'property passes', meaning transfer of ownership. 'Title' is another word which can be used synonymously with ownership. The reader should note this use of the word 'property' with particular care. It is very easy to become confused and wrongly interpret 'property' as meaning possession.

### 3. Risk

Section 20 of the Sale of Goods Act provides that risk passes with property, that is the risk of loss or damage to the goods passes to the consumer when ownership passes to him. There are three exceptions to this rule:

**(a)** the parties may expressly or impliedly agree otherwise

**(b)** where delivery has been delayed through the fault of one party, the party at fault takes the risk of any loss which might not otherwise have occurred

**(c)** the party in possession, being a bailee of the goods (i.e. in possession of goods he does not own), is liable at common law if he is negligent.

It follows from s. 20 that the transfer of ownership is frequently crucial to the transfer of risk. The consumer would be unlikely to appreciate the point. He would probably assume that he becomes owner of the goods when delivery is effected and that he bears the risk of loss only after delivery. The time of transfer of ownership and (usually) risk can be very important. The buyer may, for example, wish to insure against the risk he then assumes.

## 4. Goods must be ascertained

The rules as to the transfer of ownership are highly technical. A fundamental rule is that where there is a contract for the sale of unascertained goods, i.e. goods described but not yet *identified* at the time of sale, no property can pass until the goods have subsequently become ascertained, in other words identified and agreed upon: s. 16. But if, as expected, the Sale of Goods (Amendment) Bill [before Parliament in June 1995] is duly enacted, then an important exception will allow certain buyers to become co-owners of unascertained goods. This exception concerns the sale of a specified quantity of goods out of an identified bulk. In such cases, ownership (in common with others) of an undivided share in the bulk will pass to the buyer if and when the buyer has paid the whole or part of the price. Pre-paying buyers will thus gain protection, crucially against insolvency of the seller.

## 5. Intention

Given that the goods are not unascertained, the fundamental and deceptively simple rule concerning the transfer of property is that property in goods passes when the parties intend it to pass: s. 17.

The contract will generally be silent as to the parties' intention (assuming they have one), and the circumstances surrounding the contract may be equally indecisive. The Sale of Goods Act, s. 18, therefore lays down five rules for ascertaining the parties' intention. It is important to note that these rules only apply in the absence of any apparent contrary intention.

## 6. Specific goods: Rule 1

In an unconditional contract for the sale of specific goods, in a deliverable state, property passes when the contract is made, even though the time of payment and/or delivery is postponed: s. 18, Rule 1. Note the following points:

**(a)** The Rule only applies to 'specific goods', defined in s. 61(1) as 'goods identified and agreed upon' at the time the contract is made (e.g. 'this television set', 'that one there').

**(b)** Similarly the Rule only applies when the goods are in a 'deliverable state', defined in s. 61(5) as meaning that they 'are in such a state that the buyer would under the contract be bound to take delivery of them', so they are not, for example, cemented to the floor.

**(c)** Postponement of delivery or payment, or both, does *not* make the contract conditional and outside the scope of Rule 1.

Rule 1 is inimical to consumer interests, providing as it does that property (and therefore risk: s. 20) passes when the contract is made. Suppose a consumer were to select a specific piece of consumer hardware from a retailer's, but before delivery of that piece was due it was damaged by a fire in the retailer's show-rooms. By virtue of s. 20 and s. 18, Rule 1, the consumer would have to bear the loss, unless the retailer had been negligent in causing the fire, or alternatively as a matter of goodwill he did not stand upon his strict legal rights. In view of the strict legal position, it seems likely that the courts will strive to construe a different intention whenever possible: '. . . . in modern time very little is needed to give rise to the inference that property in specific goods is to pass only on delivery or payment' (Diplock LJ in *R.V. Ward* v. *Bignall* (1967)). Often, of course, Rule 1 will not apply on the facts. Thus, where consumers do not take goods away with them immediately on making the purchase, because they have chosen goods from a showroom model and delivery will be made later from another source, Rule 1 will not apply since the goods are not specific – not identified at the time of sale.

> *Dennant* v. *Skinner and Collom* (1948): a rogue successfully bid for a car at an auction. He tendered a cheque and was allowed to drive the car away on signing a form that no property in the car would pass until the cheque was cleared. The rogue resold that car, which was resold in turn to the defendant. The rogue's cheque was dishonoured and the original owners sought to recover the car from the defendant. HELD: As an auction is complete when the hammer falls, under s. 18 Rule 1 property thereupon passes. The form the rogue had signed had no legal effect because property had already passed. The rogue could accordingly pass good title to subsequent purchasers and the original owners could not recover the car.

## 7. Specific goods: Rules 2 and 3

By Rule 2, if the retailer is bound to do something to put specific goods into a deliverable state, property passes when the act is done and the consumer has notice. For example, if an antique dealer has undertaken to treat certain furniture he has sold for woodworm before delivery, property will not pass until the treatment has been carried out and the consumer has been so informed.

By Rule 3, in a contract for the sale of specific goods, in a deliverable state, if the retailer is bound to do something to the goods to ascertain the price (e.g. weigh, measure or test them), property passes when the act is done and the consumer has notice.

## 8. Goods on approval

By Rule 4, when goods are delivered to the consumer on approval or on sale or return or similar terms property passes:

**(a)** when the consumer approves the transaction either by telling the seller, or by doing any other act adopting the transaction; *or*

**(b)** when, without giving notice of rejection, the consumer retains the goods for the agreed time, or if no time has been agreed, for a reasonable time (a question of fact).

An example of the operation of these rules would be where the consumer takes bottles of wine on sale or return terms for a party. Once a bottle is opened, even if the contents are not touched, property in the wine will pass, as an act inconsistent with the retailer's ownership will have been done.

## 9. Mail order

Property in goods sent on approval by a mail order firm would under Rule 4 (*see* 8) pass when the consumer adopts the transaction, or pass after the lapse of the time specified by the firm for the return of the goods, or if no time had been specified, after the lapse of a reasonable time.

Rule 4 will govern the majority of mail order transactions since the consumer will generally be allowed a short period in which to return unwanted goods, as provided under the Mail Order Traders' Association's Code of Practice (where the consumer buys from a catalogue) and the British Code of Advertising Practice (where the consumer buys in response to a magazine or newspaper advertisement) respectively. Should there be no approval period, however, then it seems that unless a contrary intention can be construed, property would pass under Rule 5 (*see* 10) as soon as the goods are posted by the seller (cf. *Badische Anilin* v. *Basle Chemicals* (1898) HL).

Unsolicited goods sent by a mail order firm or other business are dealt with differently by the law. Under the Unsolicited Goods and Services Act 1971 and 1975, the consumer may treat unsolicited goods as an unconditional gift to him if they are not collected by the sender (at the sender's expense) within six months, or thirty days if the consumer has given written notice 'however expressed' that the goods were unsolicited. ('Unsolicited' means that the goods were sent 'without any prior request' made by the consumer.) In the period before the goods pass into the ownership of the consumer, the consumer must not unreasonably refuse to permit the sender to collect them. Criminal law sanctions also have a role to play here, in preventing exploitation of consumer ignorance of civil law rights. Demands or threats for payment made by a trader who does not have reasonable cause to believe that there is a right to payment and who knows that the goods were unsolicited, constitute a criminal offence, triable summarily. On conviction of the trader, a consumer who has paid for the unsolicited goods in response to the demands or threats made might be able to obtain a compensation order at the discretion of the criminal court (*see* Chap. 24).

Confusion sometimes arises here with book and record clubs. If the 'editor's choice' has not been declined it is likely to be delivered, and should be paid for. This is, of course, because here we are discussing the performance of a contract – the consumer agreed at the outset to deal this way – whereas with unsolicited goods we are dealing with the formation (or not) of a contract. Naturally if the 'editor's choice' has been declined in the agreed manner and it is still sent, then it will be unsolicited.

## 10. Generic goods

By s. 18, Rule 5, in a contract for the sale of unascertained or future goods identifiable by description, property passes when goods of that description in a deliverable state are unconditionally appropriated to the contract by one party with the consent of the other. Such consent may be express or implied, and may be given either before or after the appropriation is made. On a self-service garage forecourt petrol is pumped by the customer (the buyer) with the consent of the proprietor (the seller). Where the forecourt is attended the unconditional appropriation will be made by the seller with the consent of the buyer.

Another example of the operation of Rule 5 would be where a consumer orders a new freezer from a dealer, who in turn orders the model the consumer has chosen from the manufacturer. The goods will be future goods at the date of the contract. Probably the freezer would not be regarded as unconditionally appropriated to the contract until actually delivered to the consumer. By Rule 5(2) delivery to an independent carrier without the reservation of the right of disposal amounts to an unconditional appropriation of the goods to the contract.

> *Philip Head & Sons Ltd* v. *Showfronts Ltd* (1970): a buyer ordered carpeting which was to be laid by the house furnishers selling it. The carpets were delivered but were stolen before they could be laid. HELD: The house furnishers must bear the loss because property had not passed to the buyer. The carpeting was not in a 'deliverable state' until it had been laid, and so goods in a deliverable state had not been unconditionally appropriated to the contract.

# PERISHING OF THE GOODS

## 11. Meaning of 'perish'

Although the Sale of Goods Act uses this term, as will be seen, it does not define it. It clearly covers goods which are physically destroyed. The meaning also includes goods which disappear through theft (*Barrow, Lane & Ballard Ltd* v. *Phillip Phillips & Co. Ltd* (1929), and goods which cease to exist in a commercial sense (*Asfar & Co. Ltd* v. *Blundell* (1896) CA: contaminated dates had 'perished'). Perished goods are those which are unavailable – for one reason or another!

## 12. When the consumer bears the cost of perished goods

The rules as to the passing of property and risk have been reviewed in the preceding paragraphs. The position may be summarized thus:

**(a)** *Specific goods.* If they perish after property, and therefore risk, have passed, the consumer bears the loss. (But remember the three provisos to s. 20: *see* 3). The contract is at an end.

**(b)** *Unascertained goods.* If they perish after unconditional appropriation to the contract, the consumer again bears the loss (subject to the s. 20 provisos). The contract is at an end. The retailer does not have to supply further goods conforming to the contractual description.

## 13. Effects of mistake and frustration

Where the rules so work that the retailer bears the cost of perished goods, there may nevertheless still be outstanding obligations to take into account in unscrambling the legal position. The nature of these obligations will depend upon whether the goods are specific or unascertained.

(a) *Specific goods.* Where there is a contract for the sale of specific goods which, without the knowledge of the seller, have perished at the time when the contract is made, the contract is void for mistake (s. 6) and no further obligations arise, except that the consumer is entitled to recover any money paid as there has been a total failure of consideration. On the other hand, if specific goods perish after the contract has been made but before risk passes (so that the retailer still bears the loss) the contract is frustrated (s. 7) and no further obligations arise, except that again the consumer is entitled to recover any money paid.

> *Note*: The Law Reform (Frustrated Contracts) Act 1943 does not apply to any contract to which s. 7 of the SGA applies, i.e. no apportionment of loss can be made between retailer and consumer: s. 2(5) of the 1943 Act (as amended).

(b) *Unascertained goods.* If they are purely generic (*see* 4), the contract is not affected merely because the retailer's intended source of supply is or becomes unavailable. Since ownership (and therefore risk) cannot be transferred in unascertained goods (s. 16) the retailer must bear the entire loss. He will, moreover, still have to supply goods conforming to the contractual description, for which the consumer for his part will have to pay if he has not already done so. On the other hand, if the retailer's source of supply is specified in the contract but is or becomes unavailable, then common law rules analogous to ss. 6 and 7 of the SGA will apply and the contract will be void for mistake or discharged through frustration according to the facts of the case. Consequently, in this eventuality the retailer will not have to supply other goods conforming to the contractual description, though he will (subject to the following note) have to return any money received from the consumer.

> *Note*: Where the contract is frustrated under common law rules, as above, the 1943 Act will apply, e.g. adjustment is possible, out of any advance payment, for any expense incurred by the retailer.

## Progress test 2

1.  What is the general rule governing the passing of risk? What are the exceptions to the rule?

2.  What is the meaning of 'unascertained goods'?

3.  Define 'specific goods'.

4.  Decide whether the goods in each of the following cases are unascertained or specific: (*a*) 'a tape recorder'; (*b*) 'that tape recorder'; (*c*) 'one of those tape recorders'.

5. What is the fundamental rule governing the passing of property in goods?

6. A agrees to buy 'this antique table' from B, an antique dealer, 'payment and delivery to be made next week'. When does property pass? If the table is destroyed by fire (a) during the week; or (b) ten days later while the table is still in B's possession; or (c) in transit to A, who bears the loss?

7. When does property pass in goods which are sold at an auction?

8. C agrees to buy a second-hand car from D, a dealer. D agrees to put new tyres on all the wheels before C takes delivery of the car. When does property in the car pass?

9. Every month E receives stamps on approval from a firm of stamp dealers. E keeps one batch of stamps for three months without either paying for them or returning them. Has property passed?

10. The F Mail Order Co. send a quartz watch to G at G's request. Who bears the risk of the watch being damaged in the post?

11. Although J has not requested it, he is sent a set of encyclopaedias by the K Co. The K Co. demands payment. What are J's rights? Has the K Co. committed any criminal offence? Suppose J had agreed to take the set at one volume each month, but decided, after three months, that he did not want any more of the books. Does this affect your answer?

12. L orders an oven from electrical showrooms. The retailers place an order with the manufacturers. The oven duly arrives at the retailer's stock-rooms and L is informed that delivery will be made the next week. Heavy rain floods the stock-room before delivery is due and the oven is damaged. Who bears the loss?

13. What is meant when the Sale of Goods Act speaks of goods having 'perished'?

14. M inspects a second-hand car at N's premises. Next day M telephones the salesman to confirm that he will buy the car. He puts a deposit in the post. Unknown to either M or the salesman, the car had been stolen overnight from N's yard where it was kept. What are M's rights? (Dival case)

15. O contracts to buy eight dozen bottles of a named vintage wine from what are described as 'the renowned cellars' of P, a wine merchant. After the contract is made but before the wine can be selected from stock and despatched to O, P's cellars are devastated by fire and the contents ruined. Consider (a) whether O has to pay for the wine; and (b) whether P has to supply O with wine of the vintage ordered.

# 3

# SALE BY NON-OWNER

## *NEMO DAT*: THE BASIC RULE

### 1. *Nemo dat quod non habet*

This maxim may be roughly translated as meaning that no one can transfer ownership when he is not the owner. The *nemo dat* rule, as it may be abbreviated, means in practical terms that a consumer who has bought goods may find himself faced with a claim to ownership by a third party, who turns out to have a better right to possession than the seller from whom he acquired the goods. If this is the case, the consumer will still have a personal right of action against the seller, who will be in breach of the implied condition of good right to sell: s. 12 SGA (*see* Chap. 5). This condition cannot be excluded (s. 6. Unfair Contract Terms Act); nevertheless it may be rather cold comfort to the consumer faced with the trouble of finding the seller and the expense of enforcing the right. But whatever the implications for the consumer, the Sale of Goods Act enshrines the *nemo dat* principle in s. 21(1): 'Subject to this Act, where goods are sold by a person who is not their owner, and who does not sell them under the authority or with the consent of the owner, the buyer acquires no better title to the goods than the seller had . . .' Obviously where this principle applies it favours the original owner, and where any exception applies it will benefit third parties.

## PRINCIPAL EXCEPTIONS

### 2. The exceptions

The exceptions to the *nemo dat* rule of primary concern to the consumer may be listed as follows:

**(a)** estoppel

**(b)** sale in market overt (repealed with effect from 1995)

**(c)** disposition by a mercantile agent

**(d)** sale under a voidable title

**(e)** second sale by a seller in possession

**(f)** sale by a buyer in possession

**(g)** sale under various common law and statutory powers

**(h)** disposition of a motor vehicle under Part III of the Hire-Purchase Act 1964.

## 3. Estoppel

This exception is expressly preserved by s. 21(1) of the SGA which, having stated that the buyer acquires no better title to goods than the seller had, continues: '. . . unless the owner of the goods is by his conduct precluded from denying the seller's authority to sell.' This is the essence of estoppel, namely that a person will be prevented (estopped) from denying the truth of a fact previously represented, expressly or impliedly, by him. In practice, however, it will be very difficult for a consumer to succeed in having an owner estopped from asserting his ownership. As Lord Fraser said in *Moorgate Mercantile Co. Ltd* v. *Twitchings* (1976) HL: 'The owner of property is entitled to be careless with it if he likes, and even extreme carelessness with his own property will not preclude him from recovering it from a person who has bought if from someone who dishonestly purported to sell it'.

> *Central Newbury Car Auctions Ltd* v. *Unity Finance Ltd* (1957): a rogue was allowed by a car dealer to take away a car and its registration book on filling up a proposal form for a hire-purchase agreement with a finance company. The rogue sold the car to a third party. The finance company were dissatisfied with the completed hire-purchase proposal form and declined the proposal. Ownership of the car therefore remained at all times with the dealer. The question arose whether the dealer was estopped by his negligence from denying the rogue's authority to sell. HELD: by the Court of Appeal (Lord Denning dissenting): The dealer was not precluded by his conduct from setting up his title against the third party and subsequent purchasers. Delivery of goods of itself did not give rise to an estoppel, even if the owner was careless. The handing over of the registration book (not a document of title) did not without more invest the rogue with the indicia of property. (But cf. *Eastern Distributors* v. *Goldring* (1957).)

## 4. Repeal of market overt

This was a notable (but capricious) exception to the *nemo dat* rule in relation to contracts for the sale of goods made before 3 January 1995. For contracts made thereafter the rule is repealed by the Sale of Goods (Amendment) Act 1994. In order to appreciate the significance of the 1994 Act, a brief review of the former law is necessary.

Market overt went back some 800 years. As formulated in s. 22(1) of the Sale of Goods Act 1979, the rule formerly provided that 'where goods are sold in market overt, according to the usage of the market, the buyer acquires a good title to the goods, provided he buys them in good faith and without notice of any defect or want of title on the part of the seller'. Market overt meant an open, public and legally constituted market, or the public areas of shops in the City of

London. To come within the rule the sale had to be public and open, according to the custom of the market (see *Bishopsgate Motor Finance Corpn* v. *Transport Brakes Ltd* (1949) CA); the goods had to be those of a kind usually sold in the market or shop; and the sale had to take place between sunrise and sunset (see *Reid* v. *Metropolitan Police Commissioner* (1973) CA). Naturally, the buyer had to have acted in good faith. Market overt applied to markets in England but not Wales (or Scotland). Bermondsey market, a traditional street market, was a typical example of an ancient market to which the rule applied.

As long ago as 1966 the Law Reform Committee Report on Transfer of Title, Cmnd 2958, had recommended that market overt should be extended to all retail sales; Lord Donovan, in a minority note of reservation, however, recommended that the market overt rule should be abolished, because the majority proposals would make the disposal of stolen goods easier. Either proposal would at least have been less capricious than the existing rule (why, for instance, must the sale take place during the daylight in these days of electric lighting and late night shopping?). The DTI Consultation Document on *Transfer of Title: Sections 21 to 26 of the Sale of Goods Act 1979*, published in January 1994, sought views on the proposed abolition of the rule. But meanwhile patience with the 'thieves' charter' (as the rule was dubbed) finally broke and, as mentioned above, the Sale of Goods (Amendment) Act 1994 *repealed* market overt. Thus Lord Donovan's view finally prevailed well over a quarter of a century later.

## 5. Disposition by a mercantile agent

Under the common law rules of agency, an agent who sells goods will bind his principal to the transaction and give the consumer good title to the goods if the agent has express or implied authority to sell. Note that just as possession of goods (e.g. a car and its registration document) does not of itself give rise to an estoppel (*see* 3), neither does it amount to ostensible authority binding the principal if the agent wrongfully sells the goods. But special statutory rules apply to dispositions by 'a mercantile agent', defined by the Factors Act 1889 as a person having in the customary course of his business authority either to sell or buy or raise money on goods. By s. 2 of the Factors Act, any sale or other disposition in the ordinary course of his business by a mercantile agent in possession of goods or document of title with the owner's consent confers the owner's title on a buyer who takes in good faith without notice of the agent's lack of authority.

The Factors Act thus affords considerable protection to the consumer. But note that the mercantile agent must have possession of the goods for the purpose of the disposition and not for some other purpose such as repairs. The owner's consent to possession is valid even if it was obtained by fraud. The owner's consent is presumed in the absence of evidence to the contrary: s. 2(4) of the Factors Act. Termination of consent does not affect a subsequent sale unless the buyer has notice: s. 2(2). So far as second-hand cars are concerned, the owner's consent must extend to possession of the registration document and ignition key, otherwise the sale will not be in the ordinary course of business of a mercantile agent.

*Stadium Finance Ltd* v. *Robbins* (1962): the owner of a Jaguar car left it with a car dealer with a view to a purchaser being found. The owner intended to control the sale of the car himself and he took the ignition key away with him but accidentally left the registration book in the locked glove compartment of the dashboard. Without the owner's consent, the dealer opened the glove compartment, obtained possession of the registration book and sold the car. HELD: Title did not pass to the purchaser under s. 2 of the Factors Act because although the dealer was a mercantile agent within the meaning of the Act and the purchaser had taken in good faith, the sale was not in the ordinary course of business as the dealer did not possess the ignition key and had obtained possession of the registration book unlawfully (Court of Appeal).

## 6. Sale under a voidable title

'Where the seller of goods has a voidable title to them, but his title has not been avoided at the time of the sale, the buyer acquires a good title to the goods, provided he buys them in good faith and without notice of the seller's defect of title': s. 23 SGA.

*Car & Universal Finance Co.* v. *Caldwell* (1965): the owner of a car sold it to a rogue, who took the car away, paying for it by cheque. When the cheque was dishonoured the owner notified the police and the Automobile Association. Thereafter the car was sold by the rogue to X, who took in bad faith, who in turn resold to the plaintiff, who took in good faith. HELD: The rogue's title was voidable and had been avoided by the owner notifying the police, even though communication of rescission of the contract (which is normally required) had not been possible. Rescission had been effected before the plaintiff purchased the car, and so the plaintiff did not acquire title under s. 23 of the SGA (Court of Appeal).

*Note*: (1) If X in the above case had bought in *good* faith, then under s. 25 of the SGA the plaintiff would have acquired good title (*see* 9). (2) The Law Reform Committee Report on Transfer of Title (Cmnd 2958, 1966) recommended that an innocent purchaser should obtain a good title until notice of rescission is actually communicated to the other party.

## 7. Torts (Interference with Goods) Act 1977, s. 6

Where the activities of a rogue are involved, either the innocent original owner, or the innocent third party consumer, will suffer loss. In *Ingram* v. *Little* (1961) CA, Devlin LJ suggested that in such circumstances the loss should be borne equally between the innocent parties. Yet the law does not normally apportion loss, Lord Devlin's suggestion having been rejected by the Law Reform Committee (*ibid.*) as impracticable. An exception occurs where an innocent third party improves goods which he has bought, only to be deprived of them by the true owner when he duly asserts his rights to the goods. Section 6 of the Torts (Interference with Goods) Act 1977 provides that in proceedings for wrongful interference against a person who has improved goods in the mistaken but honest belief that he had a good title to them, or against a subsequent purchaser in good faith, an allowance shall be made for the value of the goods attributable to the improvement.

## Example

(Adapted from that given in s. 6): T steals a car from O and sells it to I, who buys in good faith and improves it by putting in a new engine. I then sells to X, who buys in good faith. O traces the car and sues X in conversion. The damages may be reduced to reflect the improvement. Further, under s. 6(3) if X then sues I for failure of consideration, there will be a comparable reduction in the damages which X will recover from I.

## 8. Second sale by a seller in possession

If a seller having sold goods remains in possession of them, any *delivery* of the goods under a second sale or other disposition, to a person taking in good faith and without notice of the previous sale, confers title on that person: s. 24 SGA (s. 8 of the Factors Act 1889 provides similarly).

## 9. Sale by a buyer in possession

If a buyer who has bought or agreed to buy goods obtains possession of them with the seller's consent, any *delivery* by the buyer under a subsequent sale or other disposition, to a person taking in good faith and without notice of the seller's rights, confers title on that person: s. 25(1) SGA (s. 9 of the Factors Act 1889 provides similarly).

> *Note*: Section 25 does not apply to hire-purchase – indeed it has been suggested that the notion of hire-purchase was developed to avoid s. 25: *Helby* v. *Matthews* (1895) HL (*see* 1:**13**); nor does s. 25 apply to conditional sale (*see* 13:**15**) if a consumer credit agreement (*see* 13:**4**): s. 25(2) SGA.

> *Newtons of Wembley Ltd* v. *Williams* (1965): the plaintiffs sold a car to a rogue who paid by cheque. The cheque was dishonoured and the plaintiffs re-scinded the agreement by taking all reasonable steps to trace the rogue and the car by informing the police. The rogue's title to the car was in the circumstances a voidable one, and title reverted to the plaintiffs on rescission of the contract. The rogue subsequently sold the car to a third party in Warren Street market, an established street market for second-hand cars (but not market overt). HELD: Because of the way in which s. 25 is actually worded, the provision only operates if the disposition made by the buyer was in the ordinary course of business of a mercantile agent, i.e. was made in a way in which a mercantile agent could normally be expected to act. By selling in Warren Street market the rogue had acted in such a way. The third party had taken in good faith, and he therefore acquired good title to the car as against the plaintiffs, whose claim accordingly failed (Court of Appeal).

## 10. Sale under various common law and statutory powers

Certain sales will operate so as to transfer good title to the buyer despite its lack in the seller. These include sales by pawnbrokers, innkeepers, repairers and so on, and sales under court powers, e.g. to enforce judgment debts. All these are subject to procedures and limitations, but nevertheless they are examples of where the buyer obtains more than the seller had to sell.

# MOTOR VEHICLES

## 11. The problem

There remains a final exception to the *nemo dat* rule which must be considered. It will not have escaped the reader's notice in the preceding paragraphs that fraud concerning motor vehicles (by definition, as it were, a highly mobile form of wealth) features frequently. A particular problem arises when a motor vehicle is subject to a hire-purchase (or conditional sale) agreement and is wrongfully sold, possibly through a dealer, to an innocent consumer. It should be understood that the typical hire-purchase transaction comprises negotiations between dealer and consumer, followed by a sale of the agreed vehicle by the dealer to a finance company, who lets the vehicle on hire to the consumer with an option to purchase it after payment of the agreed instalments. Unless and until all the instalments under the agreements are paid, title to the vehicle remains with the finance company. The consumer cannot therefore sell the vehicle in the interim. If he wrongfully purports to do so, title will not in principle pass to the purchaser, however innocent he may be. Section 25 will not avail: see note in **9** above. The third party buying a vehicle subject to a hire-purchase agreement can only acquire title where:

**(a)** title is 'fed' to him by the outstanding instalments being paid to the finance company (*Butterworth* v. *Kingsway Motors* (1954)); *or*

**(b)** Part III of the Hire-Purchase Act 1964 applies.

## 12. Part III of the Hire-Purchase Act 1964

The relevant provisions will be found in Schedule 4 to the Consumer Credit Act 1974, para. 22. The provisions are complicated but their effect is to give good title to the innocent purchaser who acquires a motor vehicle which is still subject to a hire-purchase or conditional sale agreement. To be protected, the purchaser must take the vehicle in good faith and without notice of the relevant agreement.

## 13. The scope of the Part III protection

It is essential to appreciate that the protection afforded to the consumer by Part III applies only in respect of motor-vehicles and not other goods which are subject to a hire-purchase or conditional sale agreement. The following points are also important:

**(a)** Only a 'private purchaser' is protected, defined by s. 29(2) of the HPA 1964 as a purchaser who, at the time of the sale to him, does not carry on the business of a trade or finance purchaser. A 'trade or finance purchaser' is defined as one who, at the time of the sale to him, carries on a business which consists, wholly or partly

(*i*) of purchasing motor vehicles for the purpose of offering or exposing them for sale; *or*

(*ii*) of providing finance by purchasing motor vehicles for the purpose of bailing them under hire-purchase agreements or agreeing to sell them under conditional sale agreements.

**(b)** The purchaser is protected whether he buys from the original party to the hire-purchase or conditional sale agreement, or from a dealer or finance company to whom the vehicle has been sold. The purchaser is protected even if he himself takes the vehicle on hire-purchase or conditional sale terms. The essential point is that the *first* private purchaser must take in good faith and without notice of the relevant agreement. Then (and only then) do all subsequent purchasers acquire title whether or not they are trade or finance purchasers and irrespective of their knowledge about the original transaction.

*Stevenson* v. *Beverley Bentinck Ltd* (1976): X, a tool inspector, bought and sold motor vehicles in his spare time. On one particular occasion he bought a second-hand Jaguar car for his own use. Unknown to him it was subject to a hire-purchase agreement and the finance company seized it two months later. HELD: X was not protected by Part III as he had the *status* of a trade purchaser. It was irrelevant that he had bought the vehicle in a private capacity (Court of Appeal).

*Note*: Trade or finance purchasers can protect themselves by becoming members of Hire Purchase Information Ltd ('HPI'). They can then have a search made of the records of HPI to see if a particular vehicle is registered as being the subject of a hire-purchase agreement (about 98 per cent of all hire-purchase agreements relating to cars are registered with HPI). Consumers can search HPI records by applying through one of the motoring organizations or the Citizens' Advice Bureaux, but Part III of the HPA 1964 renders this unnecessary and, indeed, it seems that (apart from Part III) there is no protection for an inquirer if an agreement has not in fact been registered with HPI or is not reported by HPI as having been so registered (*Moorgate Mercantile & Co. Ltd* v. *Twitchings* (1976) HL).

## 14. Proposals for reform

In January 1994 the DTI published a Consultation Document on *Transfer of Title: Sections 21 to 26 of the Sale of Goods Act 1979*. This sought views on three propositions put forward for discussion, viz:

**(a)** 'The law should be simplified, and protection for innocent purchasers extended, by replacing the present detailed provisions of [the Sale of Goods Act] with a broad principle [as recommended by Professor Diamond in his *Review of Security Interests in Property* (HMSO 1989)], that where the owner of goods has entrusted those goods, or acquiesced in their possession by, another person, then an innocent purchaser of those goods should acquire good title'.

**(b)** 'The rule of market overt should be abolished' – something which has already come to pass, as recorded in para. 4 above.

**(c)** 'The principle already embodied in Part III [of the Hire-Purchase Act 1964] should be extended to all goods subject to a hire-purchase or conditional sale agreement, and also to goods held on lease or covered by a bill of sale'.

Let us hope that the outcome of this consultation process will see the legislative light of day before another quarter-century passes.

## Progress test 3

1. What does the maxim *nemo dat quod non habet* mean? What are the principal exceptions to the rule?

2. Will the careless delivery of goods by an owner to another party give rise to an estoppel against the owner if that other party wrongfully sells the goods to a third-party consumer?

3. What was unsatisfactory and capricious about the market overt rule? How have these problems been resolved?

4. A takes his car to B, a used car dealer and repairer, for repairs to be carried out. A carelessly leaves the car's registration document lying on the front passenger's seat. B, without A's authority, sells the car to C, who buys in good faith. B absconds with the proceeds. Will C obtain title to the car?

5. D sells his car to E, who pays by cheque. E drives the car away and sells it to F in Warren Street market. After that transaction has occurred, D learns from his bankers that E's cheque has been dishonoured. D informs the police and the Royal Automobile Club, and the car is traced into F's possession. Does F acquire title to the car? Would it make any difference to the legal result if the facts were that D discovered the fraud and notified the police *before* E sold the car to F?

6. 'For the doing of justice, the relevant question in this sort of case is . . . which of two innocent parties shall suffer for the fraud of a third. The plain answer is that the loss should be divided between them in such proportion as is just in all the circumstances' (per Devlin LJ in *Ingram* v. *Little* (1961) CA). To what extent has the law adopted this suggestion?

7. G, an antique dealer, sells some furniture to H, who pays for it immediately but who desires to have it delivered after his return from holiday in ten days' time. In the interim G inadvertently sells the

furniture to J, who takes delivery directly. G is prepared to refund H's money to him, but cannot supply similar furniture, which being antique is irreplaceable. This does not satisfy H. Can H claim the actual furniture from J?

8. The K Finance Co. allows L to take a colour television set on hire-purchase terms. L sells the television set to M. Who owns the television?

9. Would it make any difference to the question of ownership in question 8 if L had taken a car (and not a television) from the finance company?

10. Is it worthwhile for a consumer to request one of the motoring organizations to have a search made of Hire Purchase Information Ltd's records in respect of a vehicle which the consumer is contemplating purchasing? Would the value of a search be any greater if the consumer were a part-time dealer in used cars who was seeking a car for his own private use?

11. Assume that you are responding today to the DTI's Consultation Document of January 1994 on *Transfer of Title: Sections 21 to 26 of the Sale of Goods Act 1979*, and explain how you would like to see the law relating to *nemo dat* reformed.

# 4

# PRE-CONTRACTUAL STATEMENTS AND CONTRACTUAL TERMS

## 1. Introductory

The legal implications of statements made by a trader to the consumer during negotiations differ according to the circumstances in which the statements are made and the parties' intention. Pre-contractual statements may be classified as falling into one or more of the following categories:

**(a)** trader's 'puff'

**(b)** representation

**(c)** collateral warranty

**(d)** express contractual term.

## TRADER'S PUFF

## 2. Contractual intention

Certain statements made by a trader are regarded as mere 'puffs' not intended to have any legal consequences. A typical example is the estate agent's 'puff'. But the courts will generally seek to give legal effects to statements which might otherwise be regarded as puffs whenever they can reasonably find, on an objective assessment of the whole circumstances, an intention to create legal consequences.

> *Carlill* v. *Carbolic Smoke Ball Co.* (1893): an advertisement offered to pay £100 to any purchaser of the company's smoke balls who caught influenza after using the product in the prescribed way. HELD by the Court of Appeal: This was not a mere 'puff'. The advertisers intended the statement to be legally binding since they had stated in the advertisement that £1,000 had been deposited with their bankers 'to show their sincerity'.

> *Wood* v. *Lectrik Ltd* (1932): the manufacturers of an electric comb advertised thus: 'What is your trouble? Is it grey hair? In ten days not a grey hair left.

£500 guarantee'. The plaintiff's hair was still grey after ten days' use of the comb, which had, however, scratched his scalp. HELD: The advertisement had a contractual effect so that the plaintiff succeeded in his claim for £500, even though no money had been deposited with bankers.

*Lambert* v. *Lewis* (1980): The manufacturers of a towing hitch claimed in promotional literature that it was 'foolproof' and 'required no maintenance'. One hitch was supplied through intermediaries to dealers, who in turn sold it to a customer. The hitch proved to have a design defect, causing a serious road accident. One issue in the litigation arising from this incident was whether the manufacturers' claim gave rise to a contract between themselves and the dealers. HELD by the Court of Appeal: The claims in the promotional literature were not intended to be, nor were they in fact, acted on as being express warranties. Therefore they were not binding on the manufacturers. *Note*: The decision of the Court of Appeal in respect of the proceedings against the manufacturers was affirmed by the House of Lords (1981), but without reference to this particular point.)

# REPRESENTATIONS

### 3. Misrepresentation defined

A representation becomes legally significant if it turns out to be false, i.e. a misrepresentation. A misrepresentation may be defined as a false statement of fact which induces the other party to enter into the contract. Apropos this definition, note that:

**(a)** The statement must purport to be one of fact, not of law, or opinion, or future intention. A statement of opinion, or of future intention, may be held to be one of fact if the maker of the statement at the time of the contract did not hold the opinion or have the intention in question. ('The state of a man's mind is as much a fact as the state of his digestion' – Bowne LJ in *Edgington* v. *Fitzmaurice* (1885).) A half-truth may be a misrepresentation. Silence, where a duty to disclose existed, can be misrepresentation, e.g. on insurance proposal forms.

**(b)** The statement must *induce* the consumer to contract, though it need not be the sole inducement. If the consumer does not believe the statement or knows it to be false, it clearly cannot induce him to contract, even if he does in fact go ahead with the contract for some reason. There is no duty on the consumer to verify the truth of a representation, however; it is enough if the statement is believed and the fact that it could easily have been verified by the consumer is irrelevant (*Redgrave* v. *Hurd* (1881) CA).

### 4. Categories of misrepresentation

A misrepresentation may be either fraudulent, or negligent, or innocent.

**(a)** *Fraudulent misrepresentation*. A misstatement is made fraudulently if it is made knowingly, or without belief in its truth, or recklessly, careless whether it be true of false (*Derry* v. *Peek* (1889) HL). Fraud is very difficult to prove in practice. A fraudulent misstatement is actionable, in the tort of deceit, whether or not it led to the conclusion of a contract, provided that the consumer suffered loss.

**(b)** *Negligent misrepresentation*. A false statement of fact will be deemed to have been made negligently unless the party making the statement 'proves that he had reasonable ground to believe and did believe up to the time the contract was made that the facts represented were true': s. 2(1) Misrepresentation Act 1967. Note from s. 2(1) that the burden of proof will be on the trader to disprove negligence, so this course of action is much more attractive for the consumer than an attempt to prove fraud.

**(c)** *Innocent misrepresentation*, i.e. a false statement honestly made, where the maker of the statement is able to disprove negligence.

## 5. Remedies for misrepresentation

The consumer's remedies depend upon the kind of misrepresentation involved although the basic remedy of rescission ('a giving and taking back on both sides') is available, at least at the outset, for any kind of misrepresentation. After all, the least that can be expected if you have been misled into a contract is to be allowed out of it. The problem is that rescission is an equitable remedy and is therefore only available at the discretion of the court. The usual bars to equitable remedies will thus apply, e.g. there must be no undue delay (laches) prejudicial to the defendant; there must be no undue hardship caused to the defendant; there must be no prejudice to innocent third parties; and the consumer must not have affirmed the contract. Restitution must be possible.

**(a)** *Innocent misrepresentation*. For innocent (non-negligent) misrepresentation, damages will not normally be available to the consumer, but an indemnity for expenses may be available in appropriate cases. Further, by s. 2(2) of the Misrepresentation Act 1967, the court 'if of opinion that it would be equitable to do so, having regard to the nature of the misrepresentation and the loss that would be caused by it if the contract were upheld, as well as the loss that rescission would cause to the other party' may award damages in lieu of rescission. It is essential to understand that damages can only be awarded under s. 2(2) if rescission is available and has not been lost for one of the reasons indicated above. If damages are awarded under s. 2(2), it is in place of, and not as well as, rescission.

**(b)** *Negligent misrepresentation*. The remedies available here to the consumer are rescission and/or damages: s. 2(1). While rescission is a discretionary remedy, damages are available as of right.

After some doubt it is now clear that damages under s. 2(1) will be assessed in tort on the basis of restoring the consumer to the position he would have been in had neither the misrepresentation nor the ensuing contract been made, rather than in contract on the basis of putting the consumer in the position he would have been in had the facts misrepresented been true. Accordingly no damages for loss of bargain will be available. On the other hand, the *remoteness* rule in the tort of deceit applies (the 'fiction of fraud'), so that the victim is entitled to recover any loss which flowed from the misrepresentation, even if the loss could not have been foreseen (*Royscot Trust Ltd* v. *Rogerson* (1991) CA).

**(c)** *Fraudulent misrepresentation.* Again, the consumer's possible remedies are rescission and/or damages.

## 6. Exclusion of liability for misrepresentation

By s. 3 of the Misrepresentation Act, as substituted by s. 8 of the Unfair Contract Terms Act 1977, any purported exclusion of liability for misrepresentation is of no effect except in so far as it satisfies a reasonableness test. The onus is on the trader to show that the purported exclusion is fair and reasonable having regard to the circumstances which were, or ought reasonably to have been, known to or in the contemplation of the parties when the contract was made.

> *Note*: Section 3 of the 1967 Act does not prevent a principal from publicly limiting his agent's authority (*Overbrooke Estates Ltd* v. *Glencombe Properties Ltd* (1974); on the other hand a person who makes a representation of fact cannot negative the representation by asserting that the statement is not to be treated as a statement of fact and is not to be relied upon (cf. *Cremdean Properties Ltd* v. *Nash* (1977) CA; *Walker* v. *Boyle* (1982)).

## 7. *Caveat emptor*

Section 3 of the Misrepresentation Act 1967 (above), together with s. 2(1) (*see* **4(b)**), means that the maxim *caveat emptor* (let the buyer beware) has been effectively reversed; it is now the trader who must beware if he commits himself to any statement. The trader can of course always keep silent, for there is no general duty of disclosure (except that a statement true when made but subsequently rendered untrue by changed circumstances before the contract is actually made, must be corrected: *With* v. *O'Flanagan* (1936)).

> *Note*: Sections 56 and 75 of the Consumer Credit Act 1974 provide a means whereby an action based upon misrepresentation can be brought against a creditor for the wrongdoing of a supplier (*see* 16:3, 5).

## 8. Trade Descriptions Acts

A misrepresentation may also give rise to criminal liability on the part of the trader under the Trade Descriptions Acts (*see* Chap. 19). On the trader's conviction the consumer may, at the criminal court's discretion, obtain a compensation order (*see* Chap. 22).

## 9. Damages under the rule in Hedley Byrne v. Heller

In *Esso Petroleum Co. Ltd* v. *Mardon* (1976) CA, it was held that a negligent misstatement can give rise to damages in tort under the rule laid down by the House of Lords in *Hedley Byrne & Co. Ltd* v. *Heller & Partners Ltd* (1964), even though the statement is a pre-contractual statement amounting to a misrepresentation.

In *Mardon*, Lord Denning MR explained the *Hedley Byrne* rule as it operates in this context as follows:

'It seems to me that *Hedley Byrne*, properly understood, covers this particular proposition: if a man, who has or professes to have special knowledge or skill, makes a representation by virtue thereof to another – be it advice, information or opinion – with the intention of inducing him to enter into a contract with him, he is under a duty to use reasonable care to see that the representation is correct, and that the advice, information or opinion is reliable. If he negligently gives unsound advice or misleading information or expresses an erroneous opinion, and thereby induces the other side into a contract, he is liable in damages.'

*Mardon* involved a contract which was formed before the coming into force of the 1967 Act. Generally the consumer would now rely simply on s. 2(1) because *Hedley Byrne* requires the consumer to prove negligence, the reverse of the s. 2(1) position. In *Mardon* Lord Denning said that damages would be the same whether the plaintiff sued in contract or in tort.

# COLLATERAL WARRANTIES

## 10. Collateral warranty

It is not always easy to ascertain whether a pre-contractual statement is a mere representation (or misrepresentation, if inaccurate) or whether it is important enough to amount to a binding contractual promise. Such a binding promise or stipulation may be part of the main contract or it may, strictly speaking, be collateral to it, i.e. binding as a separate contract. In the former instance the statement is called a 'warranty' and in the latter it is called a 'collateral warranty', though in practice the expressions are often loosely used inter-changeably.

*Note*: This use of the word 'warranty' meaning binding promise must be carefully distinguished both from the use of the word 'warranty' meaning a guarantee and from the use of the word in a technical sense meaning a subsidiary contractual term as opposed to a major term called a 'condition' (*see* **13, 14**). 'Warranty' is a slippery word. Its meaning is usually derived from its context.

When will a pre-contractual statement amount to more than a mere represen-tation and have the status of a binding contractual stipulation? The answer is that it is a question of intention – not what the parties actually intended, but what the intelligent bystander would infer as to the parties' intention from their words or conduct. The court will readily infer such an intention where the trader states a fact which is or should be within his own knowledge, and of which the consumer is ignorant, or where the trader makes a promise about something which is or should be within his own control. Obviously the courts will normally construe a statement which has been reduced into writing and incorporated into a written contract as a contractual stipulation.

*Oscar Chess Ltd* v. *Williams* (1957): the consumer acquired a new car on hire-purchase terms through dealers. The consumer traded in his used car in part exchange, describing it in accordance with the registration book as a 1948 Morris. Eight months later the dealers discovered that the true date was 1939 (car models did not then change so frequently in appearance as they do today). It was far too late for the contract to be rescinded for innocent misrepresentation. The dealers claimed damages for breach of warranty. HELD by the Court of Appeal: The consumer had no personal knowledge of the date of manufacture. The dealers on the other hand, as experts, were in a position to check the point. There was accordingly no inference from the facts that a warranty was intended, and the dealers' claim failed.

*Dick Bentley Productions Ltd* v. *Harold Smith (Motors) Ltd* (1965): the consumer asked a car dealer to find him a 'well-vetted' Bentley car. The dealer found a car which he told the consumer had done only 20,000 miles since it had been fitted with a replacement engine and gearbox; unknown to either party the car had done 100,000 miles since then. HELD by the Court of Appeal: In contrast to the *Oscar Chess* case, the maker of the statement (the dealer) was in a position to find out the history of the car. The inference had not been rebutted that the representation was intended to be a warranty, i.e. a binding promise. Lord Denning MR explained: 'Looking at the cases once more, as we have done so often, it seems to me that if a representation is made in the course of dealings for a contract for the very purpose of inducing the other to act on it, and it actually induces him to act on it by entering into the contract, that is prima facie ground for inferring that the representation was intended as a warranty.'

*Note*: These two cases show the general policy considerations which are often (not always) applied in circumstances of inequality of bargaining power and expertise. In short, the traders here ought to have known better!

## 11. Significance of collateral warranty

The significance of the distinction between representation and (collateral) warranty lies in the remedies available to the consumer (damages will be available for breach of warranty). In many circumstances it will not indeed matter into which classification a statement falls, particularly in view of the Misrepresentation Act 1967 which introduced the remedy of damages for negligent misrepresentation. But the distinction could in certain circumstances still have practical consequences. For example, where the trader can prove that he believed on reasonable grounds that his statement was true, he will not be liable in damages under s. 2(1) of the 1967 Act for a misstatement. But if the statement is also a collateral warranty, the trader's honest and reasonably held belief will be no defence to an action for damages for breach of warranty.

# CONTRACTUAL TERMS

## 12. Conditions, warranties, intermediate stipulations

Once it has been determined that a statement has the status of a contractual term, i.e. a binding contractual stipulation, and is not a mere representation, the final analysis which may be required is identification of the kind of term involved. It might be either a condition, or a warranty, or an intermediate stipulation. The point may be important on account of the remedies available on breach of the term, as will be seen. The analysis in the following paragraphs applies to all contractual terms, whether or not they are reduced into writing, and whether express or implied.

## 13. Conditions

A condition is a vital or major term, breach of which entitles the innocent party to treat the contract as at an end. Additionally, or as an alternative to termination of the contract, the innocent party can claim damages for breach of condition. But in sale of goods cases, the consumer's right to reject the goods and recover his money is subject to s. 11(4) of the SGA, which provides that 'where a contract of sale is not severable and the buyer has accepted the goods or part of them', the buyer can only claim damages for breach of condition by the seller and he cannot reject the goods. (This severe limitation on the consumer's rights will be examined in detail later. *see* 8:**6–14**.)

> *Note*: In *Schuler A.G.* v. *Wickman Machine Tool Sales Ltd* (1974), the House of Lords held that though the use of the word 'condition' in a written contract gave rise to a presumption that the term was in fact technically a condition entitling the innocent party to repudiate the contract, nevertheless if construction of the term as a condition in this sense produced so unreasonable a result that the parties could not have intended it, then the court was free to construe the word 'condition' as an obligation not carrying that technical meaning. In this event, breach of the obligation would not give rise to a right to repudiation of the contract.

## 14. Warranties

As opposed to a condition, a warranty is a subsidiary or minor term, breach of which entitles the innocent party to damages only. In the context of sale of goods, s. 61 of the SGA defines a warranty as being 'collateral to the main purpose' of the contract.

## 15. Intermediate stipulations

'An innominate or intermediate term is one the effect of non-performance of which the parties expressly or (as is more usual) impliedly agree will depend on the nature and consequences of breach' (Lord Scarman in *Bunge* v. *Tradax* (1981)).

It used to be thought that contractual terms could only be conditions or warranties. But the House of Lords in *Bunge* v. *Tradax* confirmed a development first affirmed in modern times by the Court of Appeal in the *Hong Kong Fir* case

(1961), and it is now clear that a term may, on its true construction, be neither a condition nor a warranty, but an 'intermediate stipulation' or 'innominate term', allowing the innocent party to claim damages on breach, and also to terminate the contract if the consequences of the breach are sufficiently serious (i.e. such as to deprive him of substantially the whole benefit of the contract) – a 'wait and see' approach.

In *Cehave* v. *Bremer* (1975) the Court of Appeal extended this development to contracts for the sale of goods, and held that an express term that goods were to be shipped 'in good condition' was (in effect) an intermediate stipulation, breach of which in the circumstances of the case was not sufficiently serious as to justify rejection of the goods.

A term is likely to be construed as an intermediate stipulation, in the absence of some express provision or necessary implication to the contrary, where breach of the term might equally well incur either trivial or serious consequences.

## 16. Significance of contractual terms

Two points may be specially singled out:

**(a)** Unlike an action for damages under s. 2(1) of the Misrepresentation Act 1967, the trader's honest and reasonably held belief will be no defence to an action for damages for breach of condition or warranty (*see* **11**).

**(b)** Where breach of condition can be shown, the consumer can repudiate the contract (subject to s. 11(4) of the SGA in sale of goods cases) even though there is no actionable misrepresentation involved.

## Progress test 4

1.  What is a trader's 'puff'? Are the following statements puffs: (*a*) 'whiter than white'; and (*b*) 'money refunded if not absolutely delighted'?

2.  Define misrepresentation.

3.  During negotiations for the sale of a second-hand car, A, the dealer, tells B, the consumer, that the car 'goes like a bomb'. B buys the car. The engine's big end breaks while B is still driving the car home.
    (*a*) Is A's statement a mere 'puff'?
    (*b*) If not, is it an actionable misrepresentation?
    (*c*) If it is, what kind of misrepresentation is it, and what remedy or remedies are available to B in respect thereof?

4.  Can any of the following statements amount to a misrepresentation: (*a*) a statement of law; (*b*) a statement of intention; (*c*) a statement of opinion; and (*d*) a statement by the trader which the consumer does not believe?

5.  In respect of a misrepresentation, who has the burden of proving (or disproving) (a) fraud; and (b) negligence?

6.  When will the equitable remedy of rescission be unavailable to the consumer in respect of a misrepresentation?

7.  When may the consumer obtain damages as a remedy for a misrepresentation which is (a) fraudulent; (b) negligent; and (c) innocent?

8.  What does the maxim *caveat emptor* mean? How true is it today so far as misrepresentation is concerned?

9.  Does the criminal law have any role to play in the sphere of misrepresentation, and if so, is it of any direct help to the consumer?

10. Is it worthwhile for the consumer to plead the rule in *Hedley Byrne* v. *Heller* in respect of a misrepresentation?

11. What is a collateral warranty? In what circumstances will the courts construe such a warranty?

12. Is the dealer's statement in question 3 above a collateral warranty? If so, does that fact add to the consumer's remedies in any real way?

13. Distinguish between (a) condition; (b) warranty; and (c) intermediate stipulation, explaining how the different categories of contractual term affect the remedies available to the consumer.

14. Does the fact that a written contract describes a term as a 'condition' necessarily mean that the courts will allow the contract to be repudiated by the innocent party, however trivial breach of the term may be in its consequences?

15. Give an example of circumstances in which it will be of value to the consumer to show that a false statement is a contractual condition which a trader has broken, rather than a mere misrepresentation.

# 5

# IMPLIED TERMS

## TERMS IMPLIED BY STATUTE IN CONTRACTS FOR THE SALE OF GOODS

### 1. The statutory rights

The Sale of Goods Act 1893, ss. 12–15, imposed a series of implied terms which greatly strengthened the position of the consumer. The precise formulation of these terms was revised to the consumer's advantage by the Supply of Goods (Implied Terms) Act 1973 and more recently by the Sale and Supply of Goods Act 1994. When in this chapter reference is made to any or all of ss. 12–15, it means the Sale of Goods Act 1979 (as amended).

For the present it may briefly be noted that the provisions of s. 12 of the SGA cannot be excluded from any contract to which the Act applies, nor can the provisions of ss. 13–15 be excluded as against a person dealing as consumer (*see* s. 6 of the Unfair Contract Terms Act 1977, considered in the next chapter). The 'statutory' or 'inalienable' rights contained in ss. 12–15 of the SGA are therefore central planks in the platform of private law rights erected in support of the consumer.

### 2. Title

In every contract of sale there is 'an implied term on the part of the seller that in the case of a sale he has a right to sell the goods, and in the case of an agreement to sell he will have such a right at the time when the property is to pass': s. 12(1). This term is technically a condition: s. 12(5A).

The Act further implies warranties of freedom from undisclosed encumbrances (e.g. a lien) and of the right to quiet possession of the goods: s. 12(2). Normally the condition of right to sell will be all that will concern the consumer, since if there turns out to be an undisclosed encumbrance, or if the consumer's quiet possession of the goods is in the event disturbed, this will generally mean that the seller had no right to sell at the time of the sale.

The condition of right to sell does not apply where it can be inferred from the circumstances of the contract that the seller is only transferring such title as he or a third party may have: s. 12(3). In such cases limited warranties only as to freedom from undisclosed encumbrances and of right to quiet possession will apply: s. 12(4).

*Rowland* v. *Divall* (1923): the plaintiff bought a car from the defendant and used it for some four months before discovering that the defendant was not the true owner. The plaintiff, who had to return the car to the true owner, claimed for recovery of the full purchase price, as there had been a total failure of consideration. HELD: The plaintiff was entitled to recovery of the full price. There being nothing to accept, no 'acceptance' had taken place limiting the plaintiff to a claim for damages for breach of warranty. Neither was there need for any allowance to be made for the use the plaintiff had enjoyed of the car, because he had paid for ownership and not just the right to use, and he had been exposed, moreover, to an action for conversion of the car.

*Mason* v. *Burningham* (1949): the buyer of a typewriter had it repaired before learning that it had been stolen. HELD: The buyer could recover the cost of repairs in addition to the purchase price, for breach of the warranty of quiet possession.

## 3. Description

In a contract for the sale of goods by description, there is implied a condition that the goods shall correspond with the description; and in a contract for the sale of goods by sample as well as description, a condition that the goods must correspond with both: s. 13(1).

The following points should be noted:

**(a)** Like s. 12, s. 13 applies to all contracts including purely private sales and not just sales by trader to consumer.

**(b)** Section 13(3) accords recognition to modern marketing methods: a sale of goods is not to be prevented from being a sale by description by reason only that, being exposed for sale or hire, they are selected by the consumer (as, for instance, in a supermarket).

**(c)** Crucial to s. 13 is the question of what is covered by the phrase, 'sale by description'. A sale of future or unascertained goods will necessarily be a sale by description, as where goods are ordered from a mail order company. But there may still be a sale by description where the consumer selects goods himself (cf. s. 13(3)) or even carefully examines them himself, so long as there is some measure of reliance on the description. Specific goods may be sold by description 'so long as it is sold not merely as the specific thing, but as a thing corresponding to a description, e.g. woollen undergarments, a hot-water bottle . . .' (Lord Wright in *Grant* v. *Australian Knitting Mills Ltd* (1936)).

> *Note*: In *Harlingdon and Leinster Enterprises Ltd* v. *Christopher Hull Fine Art Ltd* (1990) a painting was wrongly attributed to a German artist when sold between dealers. It was held by the Court of Appeal not to have been a sale by description – because the description was not sufficiently influential in the sale.

**(d)** Assuming that there is a *sale by description*, which matters are capable of forming part of the *contract description* itself? The 'description' with which the goods must correspond may not necessarily include everything that has been said about the goods. But it will include matters of quantity, packaging and components. It can also include matters of quality, at least in cases where the description characterizes the goods and allows them to be identified (cf. Lord Wilberforce in *Reardon Smith Line Ltd* v. *Hansen-Tangen* (1976) HL): e.g. if a 'waterproof' watch leaks it has been misdescribed in breach of s. 13. This last point could be especially important in a private sale, where s. 14 (*see* **4** and **7**) is not available to the buyer.

> *Beale* v. *Taylor* (1967): a private motorist advertised his car as a 'Herald Convertible, white, 1961, twin carbs'. The rear of the car carried the figures '1200' as an indication of the engine's cubic capacity. The car was bought by another private motorist, who later discovered that the vehicle was an amalgam of two vehicles; the back half was a 1200cc model of 1961, whereas the front half was from an earlier model with an inferior engine, welded on to the back. These facts were unknown to the seller. The composite vehicle was unroadworthy. HELD: Although the buyer had examined the vehicle, he had relied (in part) on the description, so that it was a sale by description, and the seller was in breach of s. 13 and the car was not a '1961 Herald' (Court of Appeal).

> *Note*: Misdescription under s. 13 will often overlap with misrepresentation (and also with the Trade Descriptions Act 1968: *see* Chap 22). If so, an action for breach of s. 13 is likely to prove more fruitful than one for misrepresentation, because the measure of damages under s. 13 will be on the contractual basis, allowing damages for loss of bargain; moreover, the seller's honest and reasonably held belief will be no defence to an action under s. 13 (cf. 4:5(*b*) and **16**(*a*)).

## 4. Substandard goods

The Sale of Goods Act, as the cornerstone of English civil consumer law, had always imposed 'merchantable quality' as the required standard for goods, statutorily defined since 1973 thus:

> 'Goods of any kind are of merchantable quality . . . if they are as fit for the purpose or purposes for which goods of that kind are commonly bought as it is reasonable to expect having regard to any description applied to them, the price (if relevant) and all other relevant circumstances': s. 14(6) SGA 1979.

This definition had long been seen as problematic because not only did it perpetuate the outmoded expression 'merchantable' but also because it was tied too closely to the concept of *usability* rather than *acceptability* to the fully informed buyer acting reasonably. That opened up all sorts of uncertainties, including whether minor or cosmetic defects were caught by the definition, and whether it extended to issues concerning the durability of goods.

The passing years saw repeated proposals for law reform, most notably by the Law Commission in their Reports, *Implied Terms in Contracts for the Supply of Goods 1979 (LAW COM.95)* and *Sale and Supply of Goods 1987 (LAW COM.160)*. After various parliamentary vicissitudes the main thrust of the latter Report was eventually enacted in the Sale and Supply of Goods Act 1994 (hereafter SSGA). This Act applies to contracts made on or after 3 January 1995.

## 5. Implied term about quality

Section 1 of the SSGA *substitutes* the following provision for section 14(2) SGA. (Note that point: the statutory authority for the implied term is accordingly still to be cited as s. 14(2) SGA.) It will be seen that the new provision turns on the requirement that goods be of '**satisfactory quality**'.

'Where the seller sells goods in the course of a business, there is an implied term that the goods supplied under the contract are of satisfactory quality': s. 14(2) SGA, as substituted.

The SSGA next clarifies the basic principle by inserting this subsection into the SGA:

'For the purposes of this Act, the goods are of satisfactory quality if they meet the standard that a reasonable person would regard as satisfactory, taking account of any description of the goods, the price (if relevant) and all the other relevant circumstances': s. 14(2A) SGA; cf. the old s. 14(6), quoted above.

The key test is therefore *satisfactoriness to the reasonable buyer* (n.b. this is not a standard of perfection).

The SSGA gives further guidance in the form of a list of aspects of quality inserted into the SGA:

'For the purposes of this Act, the quality of goods includes their state and condition and the following (among others) are in appropriate cases aspects of the quality of goods –
(a) fitness for all the purposes for which goods of the kind in question are commonly supplied,
(b) appearance and finish,
(c) freedom from minor defects,
(d) safety, and
(e) durability': s. 14(2B) SGA.

The redefined requirement of quality does *not* extend to:

'. . . any matter making the quality of goods unsatisfactory –
(a) which is specifically drawn to the buyer's attention before the contract is made,
(b) where the buyer examines the goods before the contract is made, which that examination ought to reveal, or
(c) in the case of a contract for sale by sample, which would have been apparent on a reasonable examination of the sample': s. 14(2C) SGA.

This provision largely corresponds to the previous rules about merchantable quality. Finally, the substituted provisions confirm the legal status of the re-defined requirement of quality:

'. . . the terms implied by subsections (2) [satisfactory quality] and (3) [fitness for purpose] above are conditions': s. 14(6) SGA, as substituted.

The status of *condition* – as distinct from warranty – has implications for the customer's remedies, considered below.

## 6. Application of the requirement of satisfactory quality

The wording of the statutory requirement needs noting with particularity. The old cases, where the law has not been changed by its new formulation, may give guidance. The following points should be noted:

**(a)** *'in the course of a business'* [s. 14(2)]: the requirement of satisfactory quality applies only to sales in the course of a business. The sale need not be in the usual course of business but, reflecting decisions on the same phrase in the Unfair Contract Terms Act 1977 and the Trade Descriptions Act 1968, it seems that the sale must be *integral* to the business: *see R & B Customs Brokers Co Ltd* v. *UDT Ltd* (1988) CA and *Davies* v. *Sumner* (1984) HL, in relation to UCTA and TDA respectively.

**(b)** *'the goods supplied under the contract'* [s. 14(2)]: these include packaging, instructions for use (cf. *Wormell* v. *RHM Agricultural (East) Ltd* (1986) CA) and even goods supplied unintentionally.

> *Geddling* v. *Marsh* (1920): bottles of mineral water were sold, the bottles remaining the property of the seller and to be returned to him after use. A bottle burst, causing injury. HELD: the 'goods' were unmerchantable.

> *Wilson* v. *Rickett Cockerell & Co Ltd* (1954) CA: a lady ordered 'coalite' fuel. A detonator was accidentally included amongst the coalite delivered and it exploded causing damage. HELD: the goods supplied were not merchantable because coalite accompanied by a detonator was not fit for burning.

**(c)** *'are of satisfactory quality'* [s. 14(2)]: 'are', not 'can be made to be'; so ease of **repairs** is not relevant. 'Yet the fact that a defect is reparable does not prevent it from making the *res venditur* unmerchantable if it is of sufficient degree' (per Mustill LJ in *Rogers* v. *Parish* (1987) CA).

> *Jackson* v. *Rotax Motor Cycle Co* (1910): a high proportion of motor horns delivered under a contract for the sale of goods was dented and scratched. HELD: the horns were unmerchantable notwithstanding that they could easily have been repaired at small expense.

**(d)** *'taking account of any description of the goods'* [s. 14(2A)]: one would reasonably expect rather less of goods described as 'seconds', 'shop soiled', or 'job lot'; nevertheless, such goods must still give value for money (*see* **(e)** immediately below).

**(e)** *'the price (if relevant)'* [s. 14(2A)]: in general the customer is entitled to value for money (higher price may sometimes imply higher quality [cf. *Brown* v. *Craiks* (1970) HL]); but where the goods are of a standard type price will not be relevant and a customer who does not 'shop around' cannot demand a higher standard by reason only of paying a higher price than charged elsewhere for the same goods. Nor, for that matter, can the customer be fobbed off with a lower standard simply because the goods were sold cheap. 'Sale' goods must meet normal standards (subject to any description [*see* **(d)**, above], and to the circumstances envisaged by s. 14(2C), below).

**(f)** *'all the other relevant circumstances'* [s. 14(2A)]: these might include the adequacy of any instructions or warnings. But the existence of a manufacturer's guarantee 'is an addition to the buyer's rights, not a subtraction from them' (Mustill LJ in *Rogers* v. *Parish* (1987) CA) and is unlikely to be seen as diminishing the buyer's reasonable expectations of the seller.

**(g)** *'fitness for all the purposes for which goods of that kind are commonly supplied'* [s. 14(2B)(a)]: multi-purpose goods must therefore be fit for all their normal purposes. If an unusual purpose is intended for the goods, the applicable standard is a matter for consideration under s. 14(3) [fitness for purpose].

> In *Rogers* v. *Parish* (1987) CA, Mustill LJ observed, apropos a new motor car, 'Starting with the purpose for which "goods of that kind" are commonly bought, one would include in respect of any passenger vehicle not merely the buyer's purpose of driving the car from one place to another but of doing so with the appropriate degree of comfort, ease of handling and reliability and, one may add, of pride in the vehicle's outward and interior appearance.' This case thus anticipates the 'appearance and finish' and 'freedom from minor defects' criteria of the new s. 14 (2B)(b) and (c) of the SGA. Secondhand goods would also have to meet the buyer's reasonable expectations as to value for money: cf. *Shine* v. *General Guarantee Corp Ltd* (1988) CA.
>
> *Note*: even under the old law, the cumulative effect of a series of relatively minor defects could amount in toto to a breach of the condition of merchantable quality: cf. Rougier J in *Bernstein* v. *Pamson Motors Ltd* (1987).

**(h)** *'safety'* [s. 14(2B)(d)]: dangerous goods have always been a breach of s. 14 SGA. For example:

> *Grant* v. *Australian Knitting Mills* (1936) PC: underpants containing excessive sulphite, HELD to be unmerchantable.
>
> *Godley* v. *Perry* (1960): a catapult which broke after three days' use blinded in one eye the boy who had purchased it, HELD to be unmerchantable.

**(i)** *'durability'* [s. 14(2B)(e)]: this aspect of quality was anticipated by the House of Lords in *Lambert* v. *Lewis* (1981), where Lord Diplock observed: 'I do not doubt that [fitness] is a continuing warranty that the goods will be fit for [their] purpose for a reasonable time after delivery, so long as they remain in the same apparent state as that in which they were delivered, apart from normal wear and tear. What is a reasonable time will depend upon the nature of the goods ...'

**(j)** *Specified defects* [s. 14(2C)(a)]: other than for minor blemishes covered by a phrase such as 'shop-soiled' or 'seconds', a general disclaimer (e.g. 'damaged') will not do; if the seller wishes to escape liability the defect must be *specifically* drawn to the customer's attention.

**(k)** *Examination of the goods* [s. 14(2C)(b)]: there is no obligation on the buyer to examine goods before the purchase (though it may be prudent to do so). If the goods are examined, however, it seems from the wording of s. 14(2C)(b) ('that examination') that the test of what ought to be revealed is subjective, i.e. what the *actual* examination should have revealed, and not objective in the sense of what a reasonable examination would reveal. So a buyer would not be required to discover as much on a cursory examination of the goods as on a full examination of them (*Bristol Tramways* v. *Fiat Motors* (1910) CA; for an apparently contrary view, cf. *Thornett & Fehr* v. *Beers & Sons* (1919)). If *Bristol Tramways* is correct, then the buyer of a used motor car who had not test driven it before purchase could still validly complain of mechanical defects which only a test drive would have revealed.

## 7. Remedies

Obviously, the value of the customer's rights is closely connected with the efficacy of the remedy available for breach. It was mentioned above that the requirement of satisfactory quality [as well as the implied term of fitness for purpose in s. 14(3)] was a contractual condition and not a warranty. Contractual performance and remedies are discrete topics, but some consideration of the question of remedies will be pertinent at this juncture, not least because, in addition to redefining quality, the Sale and Supply of Goods Act 1994 also resolves certain hitherto unsatisfactory points.

In practical terms, breach of condition (e.g. as to quality) in a contract for the sale of goods allows the innocent consumer to **reject** the goods for a cash refund, and/or claim damages for loss of bargain and any expenses incurred. But this right to reject goods, as distinct from keeping them and merely claiming damages, is subject to s. 11(4) of the SGA, which in effect disallows rejection where the buyer has '**accepted**' the goods or part of them.

The buyer on request must be given 'a reasonable opportunity of examining the goods for the purpose of ascertaining whether they are in conformity with the contract' (s. 34 SGA), but is otherwise **deemed to have accepted the goods**,

> '(a) when he intimates to the seller that he has accepted them, or (b) when the goods have been delivered to him and he does any act in relation to them which is inconsistent with the ownership of the seller': s. 35(1) SGA, as substituted by s. 2 of the SSGA.

However, under the SGA as redrafted by the SSGA, *in the absence of a reasonable opportunity of examining the goods*, there can be **no deemed acceptance** either where the buyer does an act inconsistent with the seller's ownership or where the buyer has intimated acceptance (e.g. by signing an 'acceptance note'): s. 35(2) SGA. The latter part of this rule is new. By s. 35(3) the buyer who deals as consumer cannot lose the right to rely on s. 35(2).

Furthermore, the buyer is also **deemed to have accepted** the goods 'when after the lapse of a reasonable time he retains the goods without intimating to the seller that he has rejected them': s. 35(4) SGA, as substituted. What is new here by virtue of the SSGA is that it is now clear that any decision whether a reasonable time has elapsed so as to amount to acceptance must take into account whether the buyer has been given a reasonable opportunity of examining the goods: s. 35(5) SGA, as substituted.

Another important clarification (or, perhaps more strictly, innovation) by the SSGA is that the buyer is **not to be deemed** to have accepted the goods *merely* because '(a) he asks for, or agrees to, their repair by or under an arrangement with the seller, or (b) the goods are delivered to another under a sub-sale or other disposition' [e.g. gift]: s. 35(6) SGA, as substituted.

Finally, s. 3 of the SSGA inserts a new section, s. 35A, into the SGA to allow for the first time a right of **partial rejection** where some of the goods are in conformity with the contract and some not. (*See*, further, 8:**12**.)

## 8. Fitness for purpose

Where the seller sells goods in the course of a business and the buyer, expressly or by implication, makes known to the seller (or, where the purchase price or part of it is payable by instalments and the goods were previously sold by a credit-broker to the seller, to that credit-broker) any particular purpose for which the goods are being bought, there is an implied term (i.e. condition) that the goods supplied under the contract are reasonably fit for that purpose, whether or not that is a purpose for which such goods are commonly supplied, except where the circumstances show that the buyer does not rely, or that it is unreasonable for him to rely, on the skill or judgment of the seller (or credit-broker): s. 14(3) SGA. (A credit-broker is a person acting in the course of a business of effecting introductions of individuals desiring to obtain credit to other persons providing such credit: s. 61(1).)

The following are points to note.

**(a)** Overlap with s. 14(2): in many cases the consumer will have a cause of action under both s. 14(2) and (3) (and possibly under s. 13 too). Nevertheless there will be occasions when only s. 14(3) will assist the consumer, namely where the consumer has made known to the seller a particular purpose demanding a higher standard of the goods than the standard required of the goods for fitness for normal purposes.

**(b)** As with the implied condition of satisfactory quality, the fitness for purpose condition applies only where the sale is 'in the course of a business' (*see* **6(a)**).

**(c)** Where the purpose is obvious, it is made known by implication (*Priest* v. *Last* (1903) CA, where a hot-water bottle which burst was held to be unfit for its purpose). But if the purchaser requires the goods for an abnormal purpose, that purpose must expressly be made known to the seller (*Griffiths* v. *Peter Conway Ltd* (1939) CA, where the purchaser of a Harris Tweed coat did not disclose the fact of her abnormally sensitive skin to the seller; HELD: that there was no breach of what is now s. 14(3) when the coat caused the purchaser to contract dermatitis).

**(d)** The onus of proof is on the seller to show that the consumer did not rely, or that it was unreasonable for him to rely, on the seller's skill or judgment. In the case of a purchase from a retailer, 'the reliance will be in general inferred from the fact that a buyer goes to the shop in the confidence that the tradesman has selected his stock with skill and judgment' (Lord Wright in *Grant* v. *Australian Knitting Mills Ltd*).

**(e)** The goods need only be 'reasonably' fit for their purpose. Thus the underpants

41

in *Grant* v. *Australian Knitting Mills Ltd* were not fit because it is not reasonably to be expected that the consumer will wash such garments before wearing them for the first time.

*Bartlett* v. *Sidney Marcus Ltd* (1965): the consumer was informed that the clutch of a car he was contemplating purchasing was defective. Offered the choice of having the dealers put the clutch right, or a price reduction instead, he accepted a £25 price reduction. In the event, after 300 miles of motoring the necessary repair to the clutch cost him £45 more than anticipated. HELD by the Court of Appeal: The car was fit for its purpose. It was not unfit merely because the defect proved more serious than anticipated. The car was usable even though not perfect. 'A buyer should realize that, when he buys a second-hand car, defects may appear sooner or later; and in the absence of express warranty, he has no redress' (Lord Denning MR).

*Crowther* v. *Shannon Motor Co.* (1975): the consumer bought a second-hand Jaguar car from dealers. The car had done over 82,000 miles ('hardly run in' for a Jaguar, said the dealers). Three weeks and 2,300 miles later the engine seized up completely. The previous owner gave evidence that the car was 'clapped out'. HELD by the Court of Appeal: While the buyer of a second-hand car might expect minor repairs to be necessary sooner or later, replacing the engine was not a minor repair. The car was not reasonably fit for its purpose at the time of sale.

*Aswan Engineering* v. *Lupdine Ltd* (1987) CA: this case shows that goods need only be reasonably fit for their purpose. Liquid waterproofing compound was packed in heavy duty plastic pails which collapsed under the intense heat on a quayside in Kuwait. The pails were nevertheless HELD reasonably fit for their purpose (export) despite the fact that, as stacked, they collapsed in these extreme conditions.

*Note*: 'the [provisions as to quality and fitness] apply to a sale by a person who in the course of a business is acting as an agent [e.g. an auctioneer] for another as they apply to a sale by a principal in the course of a business, except where that other is not selling in the course of a business and either the buyer knows that fact or reasonable steps are taken to bring it to the notice of the buyer before the contract is made': s. 14(5) SGA. In *Boyter* v. *Thomson* (1995) HL it was HELD that this provision was applicable to any sale by an agent on behalf of a principal, *whether disclosed or undisclosed*, so that under the normal common law rules of agency a private seller selling through an agent could be liable for breach of the implied terms as to quality and fitness.

## 9. The Consumer Guarantees Bill 1990 (a close-run thing)

In February 1992 the DTI published their Consultation Document on *Consumer Guarantees*, inviting views on the following proposals:

(1)  The manufacturer should be civilly liable under statute for the performance of his guarantee to the consumer. In cases where the manufacturer is outside the UK, the manufacturer's guarantee would be enforceable against the importer.

(2)  The retailer should be jointly and severally liable with the manufacturer for the manufacturer's guarantee to a consumer.

(3)  Manufacturers or, in the case of imported goods, importers should be liable with the seller for the satisfactory quality of goods under the Sale of Goods Act.

Subsequently, debate has centred on the *European Commission's Green Paper on Guarantees and After-Sales Services* (COM(93) 509), published for consultation in November 1993. The Green Paper deals with legal [consumer] guarantees, commercial guarantees and also after-sales services. The issues are complex, whether the solution lies in the adaptation of the relevant rules of private international law or in the harmonisation of national laws, and national legislation will presumably have to await the outcome of the debate.

## 10. Spare parts and facilities for servicing goods

Although many businesses do provide spare parts and servicing facilities, unless otherwise agreed there is no legal duty requiring them to do so. Instead, voluntary Codes of Practice approved by the Office of Fair Trading are seen as being of increasing value to consumers, e.g. the Codes produced respectively by the Association of Manufacturers of Domestic Electrical Appliances (AMDEA), by the Radio, Electrical and Television Retailers' Association (RETRA), and by the Electricity Boards (*see* 20:4–6).

## 11. Sale by sample

In a contract for sale by sample there is implied term (i.e. condition) that the bulk shall correspond with the sample in quality; and that the goods shall be free from any defect, making their quality unsatisfactory which would not be apparent on reasonable examination of the sample: s. 15 SGA, as amended by the SSGA.

This rule in effect requires the buyer in a sale by sample to examine the goods before making the contract, and it reverses the normal rule applicable to s. 14(2) SGA that there is no need to examine the goods before purchase: cf. s. 14(2C)(c) SGA, as amended by the SGSA.

> *Godley* v. *Perry* (1960): the retailer who was liable under what is now s. 14(2) and (3) of the SGA to the boy injured by the defective catapult which the boy had purchased from him (*see* 6(*h*)) in turn sued the wholesaler. HELD: The latent defect in the catapult was a breach of s. 15.

## 12. Strict liability

Once breach of an implied term is proved, liability is strict, i.e. the trader has no defence even if he can prove that all reasonable care had been taken. The trader cannot, for instance, escape liability to his customer simply by blaming the manufacturer. This is an important aspect of civil consumer law based in contract rather than tort. In contract the liability is strict, in tort it is based on fault. That is, somebody must be to blame.

> *Frost* v. *Aylesbury Dairy Co. Ltd* (1905): typhoid germs were found in milk. The dairy as seller was held liable under what is now s. 14(3) of the SGA, even though the exercise of all reasonable skill by the dairy could not have detected the defect which caused the germs.

## TERMS IMPLIED BY STATUTE IN HIRE-PURCHASE AGREEMENTS

### 13. Hire-purchase

In relation to hire-purchase agreements, the statutory rights in ss. 12–15 of the SGA are repeated in substance in ss. 8–11 of the Supply of Goods (Implied Terms) Act 1973 (as amended). This is why this piece of legislation is entitled the Supply [rather than Sale] of Goods (Implied Terms) Act. The consumer is in exactly the same position so far as the substantive conditions as to title, description, quality, fitness and samples are concerned (and as regards the prohibition on exclusion clauses), whether he buys outright or with the assistance of some form of financial accommodation. In the latter case, however, the consumer's remedies for breach of implied condition may be superior, as in hire-purchase transactions the right to reject goods is not lost on acceptance (*see* 8:**15**). Furthermore, the redefinition of 'merchantable' to 'satisfactory' quality within the SGA as noted above (*see* **5**) extends to contracts of hire-purchase within the 1973 Act.

## TERMS IMPLIED UNDER PART I OF THE SUPPLY OF GOODS AND SERVICES ACT 1982

### 14. Contracts for the transfer of goods

These contracts were defined in Chapter 1 (*see* 1:**5, 6**). They include contracts for the supply of work and materials and contracts of exchange or barter. Part I of the SGSA, as amended by the SSGA, clarifies what was the common law position and provides that implied in all contracts for the transfer of goods are obligations as to title (s. 2), correspondence with description (s. 3) and sample (s. 5), satisfactory quality and fitness for purpose (s. 4).

Sections 2–5 above, including the definition of satisfactory quality, are modelled exactly on the corresponding provisions in the Sale of Goods Act. However, unlike the SGA, the SGSA does not define the words 'condition' and 'warranty'. (Nor, for that matter, does the Supply of Goods (Implied Terms) Act 1973 define them.) Arguably this could give the courts greater flexibility concerning the appropriate remedies for breach of the terms, though it is probable that the courts will not avail themselves of this opportunity but will treat the words as implying the normal consequences for breach of condition or warranty as the case may be (*see* 4:**13, 14**).

It may be added that the 1982 Act, like the 1973 Act, does not contain any equivalent to the restrictive s. 11(4) SGA, and accordingly the right to reject goods will only be lost on affirmation of the contract under common law rules (*see* 8:**15**). The question of remedies apart, the technical classification of the contract whereby goods are acquired can now make no difference to the customer's legal position as regards description and quality etc., and in practice this will be true too with regard to exclusion clauses (*see* 6:**20**).

## 15. Hire

Part I of the SGSA similarly implies terms modelled on the Sale of Goods Act in all contracts for the hire of goods (*see* 1:**11**), i.e. implied conditions as to correspondence with description (s. 8) and sample (s. 10), satisfactory quality and fitness for purpose (s. 9). The nature of hire means that the Sale of Goods Act model for the implied terms about *title* cannot be exactly followed. Instead, the SGSA imposes an implied condition as to the right of the bailor to transfer possession of the goods for the period of the hire, and an implied warranty as to the right of the hirer to quiet possession of the goods for this period (s. 7). These implied terms do not affect any contractual right of the bailor to repossess the goods.

> *Note*: The effect of ss. 7–10 is basically to clarify what was the common law position. For control over exclusion clauses, *see* 6:**20**.

# TERMS IMPLIED IN CONTRACTS FOR THE SUPPLY OF SERVICES UNDER PART II OF THE SUPPLY OF GOODS AND SERVICES ACT 1982

## 16. Services

A contract for the supply of a service was defined in Chapter 1 (*see* 1:**14**). Part II of the SGSA was based upon a report from the National Consumer Council and arguably did nothing more than put existing common law obligations into statutory form in relation to such contracts.

## 17. Care and skill

There is an 'implied term' in a contract for the supply of a service that the supplier acting in the course of a business will carry out the service with 'reasonable care and skill': s. 13. 'Business' includes a profession and the activities of any government department or local or public authority: s. 18.

The use of the words 'implied terms' here and elsewhere in Part II of the Act leaves the door open for the courts to interpret the terms as intermediate stipulations or innominate terms, with the customer's remedies dependent upon the nature and consequences of the breach (*see* 4:**15**).

*Note*: When things go wrong with a contract for the supply of work and materials, the consumer may need to ascertain whether the fault lies in the work or the materials. The reason for this is that liability for breach of the statutory obligations as to the description, fitness or quality of the goods is strict (cf. **12**), whereas if the fault lies in the performance of the services part of the contract, then under s. 13 lack of reasonable care and skill must be proved.

The professional or skilled person – architect, engineer, accountant, solicitor, doctor, etc. – has to exercise the ordinary skill of an ordinary competent person exercising that particular profession or art: cf. *Bolam* v. *Friern Hospital Management Committee* (1957). There is no implied warranty that the professional person will achieve the desired result, however. 'The surgeon does not warrant that he will save the patient. Nor does the solicitor warrant that he will win the case' (Lord Denning MR in *Greaves & Co. (Contractors) Ltd* v. *Baynham Meikle & Partners* (1975) CA).

## 18. Time

There is an 'implied term' in a contract for the supply of a service that the supplier acting in the course of a business will carry out the service within a reasonable time (a question of fact), unless the contract itself fixes the time or leaves it to be fixed in an agreed manner or determined by a previous course of dealing: s. 14.

## 19. Price

Where the price in a contract for the supply of a service has not been fixed or left to be determined in an agreed manner or previous course of dealing, then there is an 'implied term' that a reasonable charge is payable for the service: s. 15.

## 20. Exclusion clauses

Exclusion of obligations arising under Part II of the SGSA will normally be covered by the reasonableness test under the Unfair Contract Terms Act 1977. This is an extraordinary mixture of consumer protection. In a contract for work and materials no exclusion is possible in a consumer sale for liability arising from breach of the implied terms relating to the materials (SGSA Part I), whereas for the work element exclusion is possible but limited by the test of reasonableness. This situation is the result of a political compromise. It has not, as yet, produced bizarre effects in court. However, the business supplier cannot in any circumstances exclude or restrict liability for death or personal injury resulting from negligence (cf. s. 2 of the Unfair Contract Terms Act: *see* 6: **12**).

## 21. Exclusion orders

The Secretary of State has power under s. 12(4) to provide by order that one or more of ss. 13–15 of the Act shall not apply to services of a description specified in the order. Under this power orders have been made excluding from s. 13 the services of (*inter alia*):

(a) an advocate in court or before any tribunal, inquiry or arbitrator (this exclusion extends to the carrying out of preliminary work directly affecting the conduct of the hearing); *and*

(b) services rendered by an arbitrator in his capacity as such.

Obligations (if any) owed by such persons will accordingly be governed by the common law.

*Rondel* v. *Worsley* (1969): a client sued the barrister who had conducted his case, for alleged negligence. HELD: On public policy grounds a barrister owes no legal duty of care to the client in the conduct and management of litigation. Were it otherwise the barrister could not properly fulfil his duty to the court and to the administration of justice (House of Lords).

*Saif Ali* v. *Sydney Mitchell & Co.* (1978): the House of Lords reviewed *Rondel* and held by a majority that a barrister's immunity in respect of pre-trial work existed only where the particular work was so intimately connected with the conduct of the cause in court that it could fairly be said to be a preliminary decision affecting the way that the cause was to be conducted at the hearing. (Lords Wilberforce, Diplock and Salmon thought that the same immunity attaches to a solicitor acting as an advocate in court as attaches to a barrister.)

## 22. Dual liability

Where the consumer has a complaint, particularly a complaint in respect of unsatisfactory services, he may have a cause of action against the supplier sounding in both contract and tort. For example, the supplier of services whose negligence causes loss or injury may be liable both in contract for breach of the implied term to exercise reasonable care and skill, and in tort for the tort of negligence. The Court of Appeal have made it clear that there is no reason why judgment should not be entered on both heads, contract and tort (*Batty* v. *Metropolitan Property Realisations Ltd* (1978)). The extent of the duty will be regulated by the express and implied terms of the contract (*Lancashire and Cheshire Association of Baptist Churches* v. *Howard and Seddon* (1993)).

*Midland Bank Trust Co. Ltd* v. *Hett, Stubbs & Kemp* (1978): solicitors negligently omitted to register an option as an estate contract under the Land Charges Act 1925. HELD: The relationship of professional adviser and client imposed a duty of care irrespective of liability in contract (applying *Hedley Byrne & Co. Ltd* v. *Heller & Partners Ltd* (1964)). The solicitors were therefore liable in tort, and also in contract.

## Progress test 5

1. What implied terms as to title does the Sale of Goods Act impose? Are they conditions or warranties? Do they apply where it is clear that the seller is transferring only a limited title?

2. What is the meaning of 'satisfactory quality' as used in the Sale of Goods Act? Does it cover minor or cosmetic defects? How have recent modifications to the law improved the position of the consumer? Do you think the consumer's legal position would be any different on a purchase at a car boot sale?

3. B, a consumer, buys a car from A, a dealer. The contract describes the car as 'new'. After B has taken delivery of the car, he discovers that it has already done 5,000 miles, that it has a large dent in one wing, and that the gearbox is defective in that the car will not go into reverse. Consider whether A is in breach of:
   (a) s. 13 of the SGA (implied undertakings in sale by description);
   (b) s. 14(2) of the SGA (implied undertaking as to quality);
   (c) s. 14(3) of the SGA (implied undertaking as to fitness).

4. C, a consumer, buys a second-hand car from D, a dealer. The car is sold 'with all faults'. C gives the car a test drive and agrees to buy it for £1,500. Soon after C has taken delivery of the car, the back axle breaks. Consider whether D is in breach of s. 14(2) and/or s. 14(3) of the SGA.

5. How long do goods have to remain fit for their purpose?

6. E buys an expensive new bone china tea-set. The first time E uses the set, a cup is accidentally broken. When E tries to replace the broken cup, the retailer tells E that there are no more cups in stock and that the manufacturer does not make that pattern any longer. Does E have any rights in the matter?

7. F buys a new carpet from a sample examined by F at the retailers. The carpet is duly fitted at F's home, but already in the first month of use it shows clear signs of disintegration. F discovers that the carpet is made of a mixture of wool and synthetic substances, whereas the sample carpet was made of 100 per cent wool. Is the retailer in breach of contract? If so, would the retailer have any defence if he could prove that the fault lay entirely with the manufacturers of the carpet?

8. G is contemplating purchasing a new washing-machine. G has the money to pay cash for the machine, but is wondering whether his rights as a consumer as regards the quality of the machine will be greater in any way if he acquires it on hire-purchase terms. Advise G.

9. J, a garage proprietor, services and repairs cars. Consider the legal position of the respective consumers in the following situations:
   (a) J fits a new clutch on L's car. The clutch does not work.
   (b) J adjusts and relines the brakes on L's car. The brakes fail shortly thereafter and L is injured.

(c) J services M's car. M objects to the amount of the bill and to the fact that the servicing took over a week to complete.

10. N, an architect, prepares plans for an extension to O's house. The roof of the extension is unsatisfactory and leaks, partly for design reasons and partly because of the poor materials used by P, the builder. What is the legal position of O?

11. R hires a self-drive van to transport furniture. The van breaks down. What right does R have against the owner of the van?

12. S, a plumber, fixes a new washer to T's kitchen tap. S claims £65 for the job, saying that there is a call-out charge of £50. Does T have to pay the £65?

# 6

# LEGAL CONTROL OF EXEMPTION CLAUSES

## INTRODUCTORY NOTE

This chapter looks at the legal control of exclusion clauses, first under the common law and then under the Unfair Contract Terms Act 1977. Both common law and Act remain in force (the former modified in part by the latter, as will be seen). Nevertheless, anyone considering the validity of an exclusion clause must, as from 1995, also have regard to the Unfair Terms in Consumer Contracts Regulations 1994, which implement the EC Directive on Unfair Terms in Consumer Contracts (93/13/EEC). These important Regulations regulate unfair consumer contract terms generally and thus include exemption clauses within their ambit. But they do not repeal the Unfair Contract Terms Act, which thus co-exists with the 1994 Regulations as a separate but overlapping regime. In other words, both regimes may have to be considered in relation to an exemption clause which it is sought to impugn, because the outcome under one regime may not *necessarily* be as favourable to the consumer as under the other. Unfortunately, the new law on unfair consumer contract terms has not been introduced in an integrated form. There is no alternative but for the student to learn both regimes. This chapter deals with the Unfair Contract Terms Act (and the underlying common law); and the next chapter considers the 1994 Regulations and their significance both generally and in relation to exemption clauses.

## CONTROL UNDER THE COMMON LAW

### 1. Freedom of contract

In the nineteenth century the prevalent political and economic philosophy of *laissez-faire* found its legal expression in the doctrine of freedom of contract. According to this doctrine, the parties to a contract were free to make whatever bargain they liked, and, subject to certain requirements of public policy, the law would uphold the results of the parties' negotiations. The notion of *consensus ad idem* was at the conceptual heart of the law of contract. If the contracting parties had freely agreed the terms of the contract, then those terms, including any exemption clause, governed the contractual relationship.

## 2. Judicial intervention

While the courts have developed no comprehensive theory with which to protect consumer interests, they have developed a number of techniques for moderating the otherwise severe effects of the doctrine of freedom of contract as applied to exemption clauses. These techniques, still relevant (except as noted below) after the passing of the Unfair Contract Terms Act, may be summarized as falling under one of the following headings:

**(a)** incorporation

**(b)** misrepresentation

**(c)** the *contra proferentem* rule

**(d)** fundamental breach.

> *Note*: The doctrine of inequality of bargaining power has already been overshadowed by the Unfair Terms in Consumer Contracts Directive as well as by the Unfair Contract Terms Act – cf. Lord Scarman's judgment in the House of Lord's case of *National Westminster Bank plc* v. *Morgan* (1985).

## 3. Incorporation

Generally, where the consumer signs a contract, he will be bound by its terms, and he cannot argue that he did not read the contract or understand it (*L'Estrange* v. *Graucob* (1934) CA). The signed document merely has to be construed and applied. But where the contract is not signed, the question may arise whether printed conditions have been incorporated into the contract at all; if they have not, no application of them can be possible, for they are ineffective.

Where printed conditions are not regarded by the courts as constituting a contractual document, they are not incorporated into the contract and so are ineffective. Receipts and tickets are frequently not regarded as constituting contractual documents, and therefore conditions contained or referred to on them are not binding. It is true that in the nineteenth century there were a number of 'ticket cases' in which conditions contained or referred to on railway tickets were held to be of contractual effect and binding, providing either that the consumer knew that the ticket was issued subject to conditions, or that the other contracting party had taken reasonable steps to draw the consumer's attention to that fact (*Parker* v. *South Eastern Railway Co.* (1877) CA). But exclusion clauses in the context of public transport are now controlled by legislation, and the modern tendency in other contexts is to regard a ticket as a non-contractual document (cf. *Thornton* v. *Shoe Lane Parking Ltd* (1971) CA, below).

Further, even where a set of printed conditions is capable of constituting a contractual document, the document will not be incorporated into the contract, and so the conditions will be ineffective, if the document with its conditions is introduced after offer and acceptance have been concluded. The exception to this occurs where there has been a consistent previous course of dealing between the parties. Here the consumer may be bound by conditions contained in a document which would not otherwise have been incorporated into the contract.

*Note*: Of course even if an exclusion clause is incorporated into a contract it cannot, by reason of the doctrine of privity (*see* 11:2), benefit a person not a party to the contract. Thus a negligent employee or agent will not normally be protected by an exclusion clause incorporated into a contract between his employer and the consumer, even though the clause purports to cover employees (*Adler* v. *Dickson* (1955) CA).

*Chapelton* v. *Barry UDC* (1940): the consumer hired two deck-chairs at 2*d*. each. He was given two tickets on the back of which was printed a condition (which he did not read) purporting to exempt the defendant council from liability. The condition was not contained on the notice by the stack of chairs on the beach giving details of the rate of hire. The canvas on one of the chairs was defective and the consumer was injured. HELD: The printed condition was ineffective and the consumer was entitled to damages. The ticket was a mere voucher or receipt for payment. The notice constituted the offer, which the consumer accepted by taking the chairs. The ticket was not a contractual document (Court of Appeal).

*Thornton* v. *Shoe Lane Parking Ltd* (1971) CA: the consumer parked his car in the defendants' automatic car-park, which he had not previously used. A machine pushed out a ticket for customers to take as they drove into the car-park. The consumer did not read the words which he had seen printed on the ticket. They stated that the ticket was issued subject to the conditions displayed inside the premises. One condition thus displayed purported to exclude liability not only for damage to cars but also for injury to customers, howsoever caused. The consumer was injured, partly through the defendants' negligence. HELD: The exempting condition was ineffective. The defendants had not done what was reasonably sufficient to draw the customer's attention to the particular condition, which was framed in unusually wide terms. The wider the exempting condition, the more that would be necessary to draw attention to it. Lord Denning said: 'In order to give sufficient notice, it would need to be printed in red ink with a red hand pointing to it, or something equally startling'.

> *Note*: Lord Denning's exacting test was held applicable to particularly onerous or unusual contractual terms generally (and not just exemption clauses) in the commercial case of *Interfoto Picture Library Ltd* v. *Stiletto Visual Programmes Ltd* (1988) CA.

*Olley* v. *Marlborough Court Ltd* (1949): the consumer, a guest at an hotel, had her furs stolen from the hotel bedroom where she had left them having locked the bedroom door. On one of the walls of the bedroom was a notice stating: 'The proprietors will not hold themselves responsible for articles lost or stolen'. HELD: The contract was concluded before the consumer was shown to the bedroom and the notice was not therefore incorporated into the contract.

*Hollier* v. *Rambler Motors (AMC) Ltd* (1972): the consumer made an oral contract with the defendant garage proprietors for repairs to his car. A fire broke out in the garage through the defendant's negligence causing damage to the car. The defendants had carried out work for the consumer on some three of four occasions during the preceding five years and on at least two occasions the consumer had signed an invoice stating: 'The company is not responsible for damage caused by fire to customers' cars on the premises. Customers' cars are driven by staff at owner's risk'. The consumer sued in respect of the damage caused to his car. HELD: The consumer succeeded in his claim. Three of four dealings over a period of five years could not amount to a course of dealing such as to incorporate the exemption clause. Nor was the clause itself (even supposing it to have been incorporated) apt to exclude liability for negligence (Court of Appeal). (But cf. *Kendall* v. *Lillico* (1969) where a course of dealing involving 100 transactions over three years was sufficient to incorporate an exclusion clause, and consider incorporation by trade usage – whether or not the parties have dealt together before: *Cointat* v. *Myham* (1914).

## 4. Misrepresentation

If the effect of an exemption clause is misrepresented to the consumer, then the clause will be ineffective. Likewise, an oral warranty or assurance made to the consumer may bind the trader and overrule any exemption clause contained in the written contract.

*Curtis* v. *Chemical Cleaning and Dyeing Co.* (1951): the consumer took a wedding dress to the cleaners. When asked to sign a document the consumer was told that it excluded liability for damage to beads and sequins only. In fact the document, which the consumer did not read, excluded liability for 'any damage howsoever arising'. The dress was stained through the negligence of the cleaners. HELD: The cleaners were liable for the damage and could not rely on the exemption clause as the extent of it had been misrepresented to the consumer (Court of Appeal).

*J. Evans & Son (Portsmouth) Ltd* v. *Andrea Merzario Ltd* (1976): an oral assurance was given that goods would be loaded under deck. In the event certain goods were loaded on deck and were lost overboard during the voyage. HELD: An exemption clause in the written contract excluding liability for loss and giving the carriers complete freedom as to the means of transportation was overridden by the oral assurance and was ineffective (Court of Appeal).

## 5. The *contra proferentem* rule

The courts do not like exemption clauses. An exemption clause will be construed against the person putting it forward (*contra proferentem*), i.e. against the person seeking to rely on it. If there is any ambiguity, the consumer is entitled to take advantage of it and to escape liability. Limitations on liability are more generously construed than claims which attempt to exclude liability entirely (*Ailsa Craig Fishing Co Ltd* v. *Malvern Fishing Co. Ltd* (1983) HL).

*Hollier* v. *Rambler Motors (AMC) Ltd* (*see* 3): the exemption clause, even if it had been incorporated into the contract, was held not widely enough drafted to exclude liability arising from negligence (Court of Appeal).

*Note*: As a matter of construction the words 'howsoever caused' added to an exclusion of all liability will be effective in excluding liability even where the cause of damage or loss is negligence (subject to the provisions of the Unfair Contract Terms Act).

*Levison* v. *Patent Steam Carpet Cleaning Co. Ltd* (1977): a valuable Chinese carpet disappeared at the cleaners' in unexplained circumstances. The printed contract stated that 'All merchandise is expressly accepted at the owner's risk;. The consumers sued in respect of the missing carpet. HELD: They were entitled to succeed. The exemption clause was not sufficiently clear to exempt liability for loss due to the cleaners' fundamental breach of contract (Court of Appeal).

## 6. Fundamental breach

The doctrine of fundamental breach asserts that breaches of contract which are so fundamental as to defeat the central purpose of the contract cannot normally be excluded. The House of Lords have held this doctrine to be a rule of construction only (the *Suisse Atlantique case* (1967), reaffirmed in *Photo Production Ltd* v. *Securicor Transport Ltd* (1980) HL), i.e. exemption clauses are presumed not to be intended to cover a fundamental breach of contract. The significance of the doctrine in consumer contracts was substantially diminished by the advent of the Unfair Contract Terms Act in 1977, as it is unlikely that an exemption clause which is construed so as to survive fundamental breach will be held to satisfy the reasonableness test (*see* 14). Indeed it could be argued that the doctrine has been so adversely affected by the *Photo Production* case and UCTA that it no longer exists for any practical purpose.

## 7. The common law after the Unfair Contract Terms Act

The above-mentioned judicial techniques for moderating the effects of exemption clauses remain of value to the consumer after the coming into force of the Unfair Contract Terms Act 1977. Where the Act makes an exemption clause totally void, the Act is all that the consumer need rely on; but where the Act subjects an exemption clause to the reasonableness test, the consumer might be better placed under the common law where the common law strikes down the clause altogether, for otherwise the trader might succeed in satisfying the reasonableness test. Better to find that a clause has not been incorporated into the contract, than to find it incorporated and to run the risk of it then being shown to be reasonable.

# CONTROL UNDER THE UNFAIR CONTRACT TERMS ACT 1977

## 8. Unfair Contract Terms Act: no new duties

It should be appreciated at the outset that the title of the Unfair Contract Terms Act (in this chapter referred to as 'the Act' or 'UCTA') is somewhat misleading. The Act does not deal with unfair contracts as such, but merely with one source of unfairness, namely exemption clauses. (On the other hand the Act controls certain non-contractual as well as contractual exemption clauses.) The original title given to the Bill – the Avoidance of Liability Bill – was perhaps more appropriate, for that is what the legislation actually controls. Let it be stressed that the Act does not create new duties: it only controls or prevents the exclusion of liability which would otherwise have arisen under existing rules.

## 9. Consumer protection

The UCTA is of primary significance as a measure of consumer protection. But its scope goes beyond this. Often both business and consumers are protected, though not always to an equal extent, as will become apparent.

## 10. Scope of the Unfair Contract Terms Act

Schedule 1 of the Act gives the exceptions where the Act does not apply. The list given includes:

**(a)** any contract of insurance

**(b)** any contract so far as it relates to the creation, transfer or termination of an interest in land.

(The other exceptions are not of primary concern to the consumer.)

## 11. Business liability

The control by the Act of exemption clauses applies (subject to the exceptions noted below: see **19, 22**) only to business liability. This is an important point to remember, and references to liability in the rest of this chapter mean (unless otherwise stated) liability arising in the course of a business. 'Business liability' is defined in s. 1(3) as 'liability for breach of obligations or duties arising:

**(a)** from things done or to be done by a person in the course of a business (whether his own business or another's); *or*

**(b)** from the occupation of premises used for business purposes of the occupier' (but liability of an occupier for breach of duty towards visitors using premises for recreational or educational purposes is not a business liability unless granting the access falls within the business purposes of the occupier: s. 1(3) UCTA as modified by s. 2 of the Occupiers' Liability Act 1984).

'Business' includes a profession and the activities of any government department or local or public authority: s. 14.

## 12. Avoidance of liability for negligence

'A person cannot by reference to any contract term or to a notice given to persons generally or to particular persons exclude or restrict his liability for death or personal injury resulting from negligence': s. 2(1).

But while liability for negligence causing personal injury or death cannot be excluded, the position is different in the case of financial loss or damage to property. In this case, continues the Act, 'a person cannot so exclude or restrict his liability for negligence except in so far as the term or notice satisfies the requirement of reasonableness': s. 2(2).

55

In making *void* the exclusion of liability for death or personal injury resulting from negligence, s. 2(1) UCTA goes beyond the regime introduced in accordance with the Unfair Terms in Consumer Contracts Directive, which merely makes such terms *not binding* on the consumer *if* (as is likely) they are found to be unfair (*see* next Chapter)

## 13. Meaning of 'negligence'

Here and elsewhere in the Act (*see* **17, 18**) 'negligence' means 'the breach:

**(a)** of any obligation, arising from the express or implied terms of a contract, to take reasonable care or exercise reasonable skill in the performance of the contract

**(b)** of any common law duty to take reasonable care or exercise reasonable skill (but not any stricter duty)

**(c)** of the common duty of care imposed by the Occupiers' Liability Act 1957 . . .': s. 1(1).

## 14. The reasonableness test

The requirement of reasonableness referred to in s. 2 and elsewhere in the Act is defined only broadly, in s. 11.

**(a)** In relation to a contract term, the requirement of reasonableness is that the term shall have been a 'fair and reasonable one to be included having regard to the circumstances which were, or ought reasonably to have been, known to or in the contemplation of the parties when the contract was made': s. 11(1).

**(b)** In relation to a non-contractual notice, the requirement of reasonableness is that it should be 'fair and reasonable to allow reliance on it, having regard to all the circumstances obtaining when the liability arose or (but for the notice) would have arisen': s. 11(3).

**(c)** Small businesses: with these in mind, s. 11(4) provides that where a contract term or notice seeks to restrict liability to a specified sum of money, and the question arises whether the term or notice satisfies the requirement of reasonableness, regard shall be had in particular to

(*i*) the resources of the defendant, *and*

(*ii*) how far it was open to him to cover himself by insurance.

**(d)** The burden of proving that the requirement of reasonableness has been satisfied is on the party seeking to rely on the exemption clause: s. 11(5).

*George Mitchell Ltd* v. *Finney Lock Seeds Ltd* (1983): seed merchants supplied farmers with cabbage seed of the wrong variety and inferior quality. There was an exemption clause limiting the merchants' liability to the contract price (some £200), whereas the loss suffered by the farmers on failure of the crop was nearly £62,000. HELD: On its true construction the clause was effective to limit the sellers' liability (applying the *Ailsa Craig* case (*see* 5)); but the clause failed to satisfy the reasonableness test (now in s. 11 UCTA) because (*a*) the normal practice of the merchants was to negotiate settlements of justified claims without relying on the clause; (*b*) the defective seed was supplied through the negligence of the merchants' associate company; (*c*) the merchants could have insured against claims without materially increasing prices (House of Lords); cf. *Green* v. *Cade* (1978) which involved the sale of seed potatoes on the standard terms of the trade association.

*Woodman* v. *Photo-Trade Processing Ltd* (1981): photographic processors lost the plaintiff's photographs which he had taken of a friend's wedding. A clause limited liability to replacement of the missing films with new ones. HELD: the clause was unreasonable because: (*a*) it excluded liability for negligence as well as accident; (*b*) the plaintiff had been given no choice but to accept the clause imposed by the processors in a monopoly situation – in particular a two-tier pricing system should have been available with a higher degree of liability being accepted if the consumer chose to pay the higher price; (*c*) no insurance facility was offered. Damages to include disappointment and distress were awarded in the sum of £75 (Exeter County Court).

*Smith* v. *Bush* (1989): it was held here that the valuers of the house for mortgage purposes owed a duty of care to the purchasers. This they had purported to exclude. This exclusion was subjected to the test of reasonableness. It failed – in the light of the imbalance of bargaining power between the parties, the unlikelihood of further and independent advice and the practical consequences of the inadequacy of the survey. Notice that in this case the House of Lords dealt with a typical draftsman's device, i.e. disclaiming any reliance or proximity so that (arguably) there could be no duty of care on the exclusion of which the Unfair Contract Terms Act could bite. The Court rejected this device. Lord Griffiths applied a 'but for' test to such disclaimers: but for the disclaimer of reliance would there be a duty of care? If so, the requirement of reasonableness was to be applied.

## 15. Meaning of exemption clause

The definition of exemption clause may be usefully considered at this point, although the definition is applicable not only to s. 2, already considered, but generally to the various controls in the Act. The meaning of exemption clause is extremely wide, because to the extent that the Act prevents the exclusion or restriction of any liability it also prevents:

**(a)** making a liability or its enforcement subject to restrictive or onerous conditions (e.g. by limiting liability to a specified sum or specifying a time limit within which the liability must arise)

**(b)** excluding or restricting any right or remedy (e.g. by disallowing rescission of a contract and allowing only damages as a remedy), or subjecting a person to any prejudice in consequence of his pursuing any such right or remedy (e.g. by requiring him to indemnify a third party as the 'price' of the remedy)

(c) excluding or restricting rules of evidence or procedure (e.g. by using clauses like 'the customer's signature on this form shall be conclusive evidence that . . .'): s. 13.

> *Note*: For the purposes of ss. 2 and 5–7 (*see* **18–20**), terms and notices which prevent a 'relevant obligation of duty' from arising will also be treated as exemption clauses: s. 13(1). (A 'relevant obligation or duty' is one which but for the term or notice in question would otherwise have arisen: cf. *Smith* v. *Bush* (1989), above.) On the other hand note that a written agreement to submit disputes to arbitration is not to be treated under the Act as an exemption clause: s. 13(2) (but *see* the Consumer Arbitration Agreements Act 1988 which preserves the right of consumers to use the small claims procedure in the County Court notwithstanding any contractual requirement to submit certain disputes for arbitration).

## 16. Liability arising in contract

Section 3 of the Act restricts the exclusion of liability arising in contract. Where one party to a contract deals as consumer *or* on the other's written standard terms of business, then, as against that party, the other cannot, unless the reasonableness test is satisfied, rely on a contract term which:

**(a)** excludes or restricts any liability in respect of breach of contract; *or*

**(b)** purports to entitle him to render a contractual performance substantially different from that which was reasonably expected of him, or to render no performance at all: s. 3.

> *Note*: The reasonableness test was considered above (*see* **14**); the meaning of the phrase 'deals as consumer' is more conveniently considered later (*see* **21**).

## 17. Unreasonable indemnity clauses

A person dealing as consumer cannot, unless the requirement of reasonableness is satisfied, be required by any contract term to indemnify another person in respect of liability for negligence or breach of contract: s. 4.

The example of a case governed by s. 4 given during the progress of the Bill through Parliament was of indemnity clauses found on the back of cross-Channel car ferry tickets. These clauses often required passengers to indemnify the shipowner against damage to third parties caused by negligent handling of the car by the ship's crew. Such clauses must satisfy the reasonableness test.

## 18. Manufacturers' guarantees

'In the case of goods of a type ordinarily supplied for private use or consumption, where loss or damage:

**(a)** arises from the goods providing defective while in consumer use; *and*

**(b)** results from the negligence of a person concerned in the manufacture or distribution of the goods,

liability for the loss or damage cannot be excluded or restricted by any contract term or notice contained in or operating by reference to a guarantee of the goods':

s. 5(1). Goods 'are to be regarded as "in consumer use" when a person is using them, or has them in his possession for use, otherwise than exclusively for the purposes of a business': s. 5(2)(*a*).

Section 5 applies to manufacturers' guarantees, and not guarantees 'as between the parties to a contract under or in pursuance of which possession or ownership of the goods passed': s. 5(3). So retailers' guarantees are not covered by s. 5. In such cases the consumer must look to s. 2 (*see* **12**) or s. 6 (*see* **19**) for protection. Note that where s. 5 does apply, it makes the exemption clause void; there is no question of applying a reasonableness test.

## 19. Sale and hire-purchase

The UCTA 1977 replaces with minor modifications the controls first contained in the Supply of Goods (Implied Terms) Act 1973. By s. 6(1) of the UCTA, liability for breach of s. 12 of the SGA 1979 (implied undertakings as to title) or s. 8 of the 1973 Act (the corresponding provisions for hire-purchase), cannot be excluded or restricted by reference to any contract term. Further, as against a person dealing as consumer, liability for breach of ss. 13, 14 or 15 of the SGA 1979 (implied undertakings as to conformity of goods with description or sample, or as to their quality or fitness for a particular purpose), or ss. 9, 10 or 11 of the 1973 Act (the corresponding provisions for hire-purchase), likewise cannot be excluded or restricted by reference to any contract term: s. 6(2) UCTA.

> *Note*: (1) As against a person dealing otherwise than as consumer, a clause excluding liability under ss. 13, 14 or 15 of the SGA or the corresponding hire-purchase provisions, may be allowed in so far as it satisfies the reasonableness test: s. 6(3). Guidelines as to the application of the reasonableness test in these non-consumer cases are given in Schedule 2 to the UCTA. Factors to be taken into account include the relative bargaining position of the parties. (The reader should note that strictly speaking the Schedule 2 guidelines only apply to the attempted exclusion of the statutory rights.)
> (2) The controls in s. 6 of the UCTA extend not only to business liability, but to liability arising under any contract of sale of goods or hire-purchase: s. 6(4) (contrast s. 7, *see* **20**).
> (3) Section 6(2) of UCTA is stronger than the regime introduced in accordance with the Unfair Terms in Consumer Contracts Directive, for the same reason as given in the *Note* to **12** above, in relation to s. 2(1) UCTA.

## 20. Contracts for the transfer of goods and contracts of hire

Section 7 of the UCTA applies to contracts, other than sale or hire-purchase, for the passing of possession or ownership of goods. In other words s. 7 relates to contracts which are regulated by Part I of the Supply of Goods and Service Act 1982. Section 7 (as amended by the 1982 Act) applies only to the business supplier, but otherwise reflects the s. 6 controls (*see* **19**). Thus the implied terms as to title cannot be excluded; and the implied terms as to conformity of goods with description or sample, or as to their quality or fitness for a particular purpose, cannot be excluded against a person dealing as consumer (and as against others cannot be excluded except in so far as is reasonable).

*Note*: The exclusion of business liability for breach of the implied terms about the right to transfer possession etc. in contracts of *hire* (*see* 5:**15**) is subject to the reasonableness test irrespective of the status of the hirer: s. 7(4) UCTA (as amended).

## 21. Dealing as consumer

It is now necessary to examine the exact meaning of the phrase 'deals as consumer' (*see* **16, 17, 19, 20**). Section 12(1) gives the definition: 'A party to a contract "deals as consumer" in relation to another party if:

**(a)** he neither makes the contract in the course of a business nor holds himself out as doing so; *and*

**(b)** the other party does make the contract in the course of a business; *and*

**(c)** in the case of a contract governed by the law of sale of goods or hire-purchase, or by section 7 of this Act, the goods passing under or in pursuance of the contract are of a type ordinarily supplied for private use or consumption'.

Note that:

(*i*) the buyer on a sale by auction is not in any circumstances to be regarded as dealing as consumer: s. 12(2);

(*ii*) 'it is for those claiming that a party does not deal as consumer to show that he does not': s. 12(3), i.e. the burden of proof is on the trader.

*R&B Customs Brokers Co. Ltd* v. *United Dominions Trust Ltd* (1988): here a shipping company (shipping brokers) bought a car for its directors to use. The company was only five years old, but it had bought two or three cars before. Nevertheless, it was held for the purposes of invalidating an exemption clause covering quality that the purchase had been made other than 'in the course of business'. That is, the company had 'dealt as a consumer' within s. 12 of UCTA. (*See* also *Rasbora Ltd* v. *J.C.L. Marine Ltd* (1977) for a similar decision taken on earlier legislation.)

## 22. Misrepresentation

Section 8 of the UCTA modifies s. 3 of the Misrepresentation Act 1967. Section 3, as modified, subjects to the reasonableness test contained in s. 11(1) of the UCTA (*see* **14**) any contract term which would 'exclude or restrict:

**(a)** any liability to which a party to a contract may be subject by reason of any misrepresentation made by him before the contract was made; *or*

**(b)** any remedy available to another party to the contract by reason of such misrepresentation'.

Note that:

(*i*) the burden of proof that the exemption clause satisfies the reasonableness test is on the party seeking to rely on the clause;

(*ii*) s. 3 of the Misrepresentation Act is *not* confined to the exclusion of business liability for misrepresentation. Section 3 is of general application to all contracts.

# CONTROL BY THE CRIMINAL LAW

## 23. Use of void exemption clauses

While the consumer's statutory rights under the SGA and the Supply of Goods (Implied Terms) Act are made inalienable by s. 6 of the UCTA, there is nothing in these Acts to prevent a trader purporting to exclude liability for breach of the statutory rights in the expectation that some at least of his customers will be taken in by the clause and on that account fail to assert their rights (e.g. by using phrases such as 'bought as seen'). Accordingly, an Order (*see* **24**) under the Fair Trading Act 1973 has been made, invoking the sanctions of the criminal law (*see* 20:**7–14**).

## 24. Consumer Transactions (Restrictions on Statements) Order 1976

This Order, as amended by the Consumer Transactions (Restrictions on Statements) (Amendment) Order 1978, makes it a criminal offence for persons who, in the course of a business, sell goods to consumers or supply them under hire-purchase or trading stamp agreements:

**(a)** to purport by notices (Art. 3(*a*)), advertisements (Art. 3(*b*)), or statements on or with goods (Art. 3(*c*) and (*d*)), to apply terms which are void by virtue of s. 6 of the UCTA or inconsistent with a warranty implied by the Trading Stamps Act 1964; *or*

**(b)** to supply statements about the consumer's rights against the supplier or about the obligations accepted by the supplier in respect of goods which are defective or not fit for a purpose or do not correspond with a description, unless there is in close proximity to any such statement a clear and conspicuous statement to the effect that the statutory rights of the consumer are not affected (Art. 4).

> *Note*: Rules similar to those contained in Art. 4 are applied to manufacturers and wholesalers (Art. 5), *see* 11:**5**.

By way of illustrating the effect of the Order, consider the once common practice of displaying a notice at a sales counter stating something like: 'No cash refunds'. This practice would constitute a criminal offence under Art. 3(*a*). because it purports to restrict the consumer's statutory rights. If the goods were (say) unmerchantable, the consumer would be entitled to have his money back on rejection of the goods for breach of condition. The consumer cannot be obliged to accept less than this entitlement (assuming always that the right of rejection has not been lost through 'acceptance' of the goods). He does not have to accept a credit note, or repairs or replacements, and any notice etc. which asserts the contrary will constitute an offence.

> *Hughes* v. *Hall* (1981): second-hand cars were sold 'as seen and inspected'.

HELD: This phrase prima facie purported to exclude the implied term of correspondence with description under s. 13 SGA (because the words meant that the sale would not be a sale by description) and therefore was capable of contravening the Order (Divisional Court).

*Cavendish-Woodhouse Ltd* v. *Manley* (1984): a suite of furniture was sold in a sale. The words 'bought as seen' were written on the cash sale invoice. HELD: The Order was not thereby contravened. The sale (it was common ground) was not a sale by description anyway, since the purchaser had chosen specific goods which he had inspected. The words merely confirmed that the purchaser had seen beforehand the goods which he had purchased. The words were not intended to exclude liability for hidden defects or other breach of s. 14 SGA (Divisional Court) (and *see Cavendish Woodhouse Ltd* v. *Wright* (1985)).

*Note*: Somewhat anomalously, the Order does not prohibit exemption clauses void by virtue of s. 7 UCTA (*see* **20**). The use of all sorts of void exemption clauses (e.g. void under s. 2 UCTA (*see* **12**)) is a widespread practice and is not generally prohibited by the criminal law.

## Progress test 6

1. In what circumstances would conditions printed on a receipt or ticket be binding on a consumer under the common law?

2. If the consumer in *Olley* v. *Marlborough Court Ltd* had been an habitual visitor to the hotel, would the exempting condition have been binding on her?

3. Summarize the techniques which the courts have developed for dealing with objectionable exemption clauses. Do these techniques continue to be relevant in consumer protection in view of the provisions of the UCTA?

4. A notice prominently displayed at the counter of a firm of dry cleaners states: 'Customers are advised that curtaining materials may shrink during cleaning. No responsibility can be accepted for any shrinkage which does occur.' Would the condition bind the consumer in either of the following alternative situations?
   (a) The consumer asked the counter assistant whether particular curtains would be likely to shrink, and was told: 'Definitely not.'
   (b) The shrinkage occurred solely through the negligence of the cleaners. Would it make any difference to your answer in this second situation if the facts were that the words 'howsoever caused' had been added at the end of the printed condition?

5. Give the meaning of 'business liability' as defined in the UCTA, and indicate the provisions of the Act which may also be applicable to the purported exclusion of liability other than business liability.

6. In what circumstances can liability for negligence be excluded? What does 'negligence' mean in the context of the UCTA?

7. (a) What is the requirement of reasonableness for the purposes of the UCTA (i) in relation to a contract term, and (ii) in relation to a non-contractual notice? Is it for the consumer to prove that the requirement of reasonableness has not been satisfied?
   (b) How does the requirement of reasonableness take special account of the needs of small businesses?

8. Consider whether the following printed condition would be an exemption clause within the meaning of the UCTA: 'This film will be accepted by the Company for processing and printing only on the basis that its value does not exceed that of the film itself. In any event the Company's liability is limited to replacement of the film itself'.

9. How does the UCTA seek to protect the consumer against the attempted exclusion of liability for misfeasance or nonfeasance of a contract? Is this same protection available in any circumstances when one business contracts with another business?

10. How does the UCTA afford the consumer protection in respect of (a) manufacturers' guarantees; (b) retailers' guarantees?

11. Are the rights contained in ss. 12–15 of the SGA (and the corresponding provisions for hire-purchase) 'inalienable'? Can the same be said of the similar terms implied in contracts of hire or contracts for work and materials?

12. (a) What does the UCTA mean by the expression 'deals as consumer'? Does the private buyer at an auction sale 'deal as consumer'? Does the seller, via the auctioneer, deal in the course of a business?
    (b) G, a secretary, buys a word processor for use at home in a purely private capacity. Does G 'deal as consumer'? On whom is the burden of proving (or disproving) the point?

13. To what extent is it possible for a party to a contract to exclude liability for misrepresentation?

14. Comment on the legality of a notice displayed by a cash desk in a shop and stating: 'Money cannot be refunded on sale goods'. Would it make any difference if the notice read instead: 'Sale goods cannot be exchanged'?

15 List the exemption clauses and non-contractual notices which are (a) totally void by virtue of the UCTA; and (b) valid only in so far as they satisfy the reasonableness test.

# 7

# UNFAIR TERMS IN CONSUMER CONTRACTS

## REGULATION OF UNFAIR CONSUMER CONTRACT TERMS

### 1. Introductory

At first sight the EC Directive on Unfair Terms in Consumer Contracts (93/13/EEC) introduces a general unifying concept of fairness into consumer law. Basically the Directive provides that

> *a contractual term which has not been individually negotiated shall be regarded as unfair and not binding on the consumer if, contrary to the requirement of good faith, it causes significant imbalance in the parties' contractual rights and obligations, to the detriment of the consumer.*

This requirement of fairness is not confined to exclusion clauses. However, on closer inspection this apparently comprehensive provision turns out to be considerably restricted in scope, not least because the Directive does not directly regulate either the price or the main subject-matter of the contract, as we shall see (para. 7 below).

The regulations which are designed to implement the Directive in the UK do not replace but co-exist with the Unfair Contract Terms Act 1977 as a separate but overlapping regime. The ambit of the Directive is at once broader and more circumscribed than the 1977 Act. As indicated above, the Directive is not confined to exemption clauses. But unlike the Act the Directive applies only to contracts involving consumers, who in this context are a narrowly defined category; moreover, unlike the Act, the Directive applies only to terms which have not been individually negotiated. Again, as interpreted by the UK Government at any rate, the Directive governs only contracts for the supply of goods or services. And the Unfair Contract Terms Act is broader than the Directive in so far as it also regulates exclusion clauses in business contracts, individually negotiated contracts, and non-contractual notices. The test of reasonableness in the Act, however, is not the same as the test of fairness in the Directive.

The Directive is implemented in the United Kingdom by the **Unfair Terms in Consumer Contracts Regulations 1994** (hereafter referred to simply as 'the Regulations'). The Regulations came into force on 1 July 1995, although the Directive itself stipulated that its provisions should apply to all contracts concluded after 31 December 1994. We will now unpack the Regulations in more detail.

## 2. Scope of the Regulations

Subject to certain core contractual terms (*see* **6** below), the Regulations apply to any term in a contract concluded between a seller or supplier and a consumer where the term has not been individually negotiated: reg. 3(1). A term is to be treated as not having been individually negotiated where it has been drafted in advance and the consumer has not been able to influence the substance of the term: reg. 3(3). Even if a specific term has been individually negotiated, the Regulations apply to the rest of the contract if on an overall assessment the contract is a pre-formulated standard form contract: reg. 3(4). The onus of proof is on the seller or supplier to show that a term was individually negotiated: reg. 3(5).

Schedule 1 excludes from the ambit of the Regulations:

**(a)** contracts of employment

**(b)** contracts relating to succession rights

**(c)** contracts relating to rights under family law

**(d)** contracts relating to the incorporation and organisation of companies or partnerships

**(e)** terms which are mandatory, statutory or regulatory provisions of the United Kingdom, or which reflect the provisions or principles of applicable inter-national conventions.

## 3. Definitions

Regulation 2 includes these definitions:

- 'Business' includes a trade or profession and the activities of any govern-ment department or local or public authority.
- 'Consumer' means a natural person who, in making a contract to which the Regulations apply, is acting for purposes which are outside his business [a definition which therefore excludes not only bodies corporate but also partnerships and other unincorporated bodies].
- 'Seller' means a person who sells goods and who, in making a contract to which the Regulations apply, is acting for purposes relating to his business.
- 'Supplier' means a person who supplies goods or services and who, in making a contract to which the Regulations apply, is acting for purposes relating to his business.

## 4. Meaning of 'unfair term'

This is the key concept (and *see* further below, **7**). 'Unfair term' means any term which contrary to the requirement of good faith causes a significant imbalance in the parties' rights and obligations under the contract to the detriment of the consumer: reg. 4(1). Assessment of unfairness must be made taking into account the nature of the goods or services for which the contract was concluded and referring, as at the time of the conclusion of the contract, to all the circumstances attending the conclusion of the contract and to all the other terms of the contract or of another contract on which it is dependent: reg. 4(2).

The chief conceptual elements of unfairness are thus (*i*) lack of good faith (*ii*) causing significant imbalance (*iii*) to the detriment of the consumer. Schedule 2 specifies matters to which particular regard shall be had in determining the element of good faith or lack of it:

- The strength of the bargaining position of the parties
- Whether the consumer had an inducement to agree to the term
- Whether the goods or services were sold or supplied to the special order of the consumer
- The extent to which the seller or supplier has dealt fairly and equitably with the consumer.

Note that the requirement for good faith is not the same as the test of reasonableness in the Unfair Contract Terms Act. No doubt the result of applying the respective tests to identical circumstances would usually be the same, but the possibility exists that a different outcome might ensue.

Schedule 3 gives an indicative and non-exhaustive (if exhausting!) list of terms which *may* be regarded as unfair – in effect a 'greylist'. This useful list is taken from the Annex to the Directive and is reproduced in substance below at the end of the present survey (*see* **10** below).

## 5. Plain language

A seller or supplier must ensure that any written term of a contract is expressed in plain, intelligible language; any doubt about the meaning is to be interpreted in favour of the consumer: reg. 6. This may be seen as a formulation of the well-known *contra proferentem* rule of construction.

## 6. Core provisions

It is important to appreciate that the generality of the concept of unfairness is significantly restricted by the exclusion of core contractual provisions from the scope of the Directive (and hence Regulations). Thus – provided it is in plain, intelligible language – no assessment can be made of the fairness of any term which either (i) *defines the main subject-matter of the contract* or (ii) *concerns the adequacy of the price or remuneration of the goods or services sold or supplied*: reg. 3(2). Of course, the price or subject-matter of goods or services could be relevant to the fairness of other terms in the contract.

## 7. Effect of unfairness

If an unfair term is included in a consumer contract by a seller or supplier that term is *not binding on the consumer*; but the contract continues to bind the parties if it is capable of continuing in existence without the unfair term: reg. 5. This rule amounts to a type of 'blue-pencil' test. Interestingly, whilst certain terms are subject to the test of fairness in the Regulations (and hence are voidable) they will actually be void independently under other UK laws, e.g. the purported exclusion of liability under section 2(1) of the Unfair Contract Terms Act for death or personal injury resulting from negligence. This discrepancy reflects the Directive, which, not unusually, permits member States to adopt or (as in this case) retain the most stringent provisions compatible with the Directive, to ensure a maximum degree of protection for the consumer: Art. 8.

## 8. Choice of law clauses

If a contract has a close connection with a member State of the European Economic Area, then a consumer cannot lose the protection of the Directive – or Regulations – by the choice of the law of a non-member State as the law applicable to the contract: reg. 7. This of course is a standard anti-avoidance provision.

## 9. Prevention of continued use of unfair terms

The Directive requires member States to ensure that adequate and effective means exist to prevent the continued use of unfair terms in consumer contracts: Art. 7(1). This envisages the possible use of representative actions, by 'persons or organizations having a legitimate interest under national law in protecting consumers'. Through such a mechanism the courts or competent administrative authorities may determine the fairness of contractual terms drawn up for general use by individual or sectoral sellers or suppliers or their trade associations: Art. 7(2), (3). After some initial reluctance the Department of Trade and Industry decided that the Regulations would impose on the Director General of Fair Trading a statutory duty to consider any complaint made to him that any contract drawn up for general use is unfair, save in cases where the complaint appears to the Director to be frivolous or vexatious: reg. 8(1). This recourse to the Director General of Fair Trading is comparable with the 'last resort' provisions under the Control of Misleading Advertisements Regulations 1988 – themselves made pursuant to a Council Directive (84/450/EEC). The Director may bring court proceedings for an injunction against the trader(s) or trade association concerned (reg. 8(2)) or may accept an undertaking instead (reg. 8(3)), to procure discontinuance in the use of the term (or of similar objectionable terms: reg. 8(6)). The Director is empowered to disseminate information and advice on the operation of the Regulations to traders and the public: reg. 8(7). Unlike the statutory rights secured by section 6 of the Unfair Contract Terms Act, no criminal sanctions are incurred solely by use of an unfair term, although obviously disregard of an injunction will amount to contempt of court and is likely to be viewed as a serious matter. Somewhat controversially the Department of Trade and Industry declined the invitation in the Directive to establish a general right of representative action by consumer organisations (e.g. Consumers' Association) in the law of the UK, a decision likely to be challenged before the European Court of Justice.

# INDICATIVE LIST OF UNFAIR TERMS

## 10. List of terms which *may* be regarded as unfair

The 'indicative and non-exhaustive' list in the *Annex* to the Directive, reproduced in Schedule 3 to the Regulations, reads substantially as follows:

TERMS WHICH HAVE THE OBJECT OR EFFECT OF:

**(a)** excluding or limiting the legal liability of a seller or supplier in the event of the death of a consumer or personal injury to the latter resulting from an act or omission of that seller or supplier

**(b)** inappropriately excluding or limiting the legal rights of the consumer *vis-à-vis* the seller or supplier or another party in the event of total or partial non-performance or inadequate performance by the seller or supplier of any of the contractual obligations, including the option of offsetting a debt owed by the seller or supplier against any claim which the consumer may have against him

**(c)** making an agreement binding on the consumer whereas provision of services by the seller or supplier is subject to a condition whose realisation depends on his own will alone

**(d)** permitting the seller or supplier to retain sums paid by the consumer where the latter decides not to conclude or perform the contract, without providing for the consumer to receive compensation of an equivalent amount from the seller or supplier where the latter is the party cancelling the contract

**(e)** requiring any consumer who fails to fulfil his obligations to pay a disproportionately high sum in compensation

**(f)** authorising the seller or supplier to dissolve the contract on a discretionary basis where the same facility is not granted to the consumer, or permitting the seller or supplier to retain sums paid for services not yet supplied by him where it is the seller or supplier himself who dissolves the contract

**(g)** enabling the seller or supplier to terminate a contract of indeterminate duration without reasonable notice except where there are serious grounds for doing so [Subparagraph (g) is without hindrance to terms by which a supplier of financial services reserves the right to terminate unilaterally a contract of indeterminate duration without notice where there is a valid reason, provided that the supplier is required to inform the other contracting party or parties thereof immediately]

**(h)** automatically extending a contract of fixed duration where the consumer does not indicate otherwise, when the deadline fixed for the consumer to express this desire not to extend the contract is unreasonably early

**(i)** irrevocably binding the consumer to terms with which he had no real opportunity of becoming acquainted before the conclusion of the contract

**(j)** enabling the seller or supplier to alter the terms of the contract unilaterally without a valid reason which is specified in the contract [Subparagraph (j) is without hindrance to terms under which a supplier of financial services reserves the right to alter a rate of interest payable by the consumer or due to the latter, or the amount of other charges for financial services without notice where there is a valid reason, provided that the supplier is required to inform the other contracting party or parties thereof at the earliest opportunity and that the latter are free to dissolve the contract immediately]

**(k)** enabling the seller or supplier to alter unilaterally without a valid reason any characteristics of the product or service to be provided

**(l)** providing for the price of goods to be determined at the time of delivery or allowing a seller of goods or supplier of services to increase their price without in both cases giving the consumer the corresponding right to cancel the contract if the final price is too high in relation to the price agreed when the contract was concluded [Subparagraph (l) is without hindrance to price indexation clauses, where lawful, provided that the method by which prices vary is explicitly described]

**(m)** giving the seller or supplier the right to determine whether the goods or services supplied are in conformity with the contract, or giving him the exclusive right to interpret any term of the contract

**(n)** limiting the seller's or supplier's obligation to respect commitments undertaken by his agents or making his commitments subject to compliance with a particular formality

**(o)** obliging the consumer to fulfil all his obligations where the seller or supplier does not perform his

**(p)** giving the seller or supplier the possibility of transferring his rights and obligations under the contract, where this may serve to reduce the guarantees for the consumer, without the latter's agreement

**(q)** excluding or hindering the consumer's right to take legal action or exercise any other legal remedy, particularly by requiring the consumer to take disputes exclusively to arbitration not covered by legal provisions, unduly restricting the evidence available to him or imposing on him a burden of proof which, according to the applicable law, should lie with another party to the contract.

*Scope:* Subparagraphs (g), (j) and (l) do not apply to:

- transactions in transferable securities, financial instruments and other products or services where the price is linked to fluctuations in a stock exchange quotation or index or a financial market rate that the seller or supplier does not control
- contracts for the purchase or sale of foreign currency, traveller's cheques or international money orders denominated in a foreign currency.

## Progress test 7

1. What is the basic objective of the EC Directive on Unfair Terms in Consumer Contracts?

2. The Unfair Terms in Consumer Contracts Regulations 1994 co-exist with the Unfair Contract Terms Act 1977 as a separate but overlapping regime. Identify some points of difference between the ambit of the respective regimes.

3. When are contract terms said not to be individually negotiated for the purposes of the 1994 Regulations? What types of contract are excluded from the scope of the Regulations?

4. For the purposes of the 1994 Regulations, define:
   (*i*) 'consumer'
   (*ii*) 'unfair term'.
   Specify the matters to which particular regard must be had in determining the element of good faith or lack of it.

5. How do the 1994 Regulations ensure that consumer contracts are expressed in plain language?

6. What are the so-called 'core' provisions of a consumer contract and why are they important?

7. What effect on a (consumer) contract does the incorporation of an unfair term have?

8. Consider the validity of the following clause in a consumer contract:
   'This agreement shall be governed by Swiss law and the customer consents to the exclusive jurisdiction of the Swiss courts in all matters regarding it save to the extent that the dealer invokes the jurisdiction of the courts of any other country.'

9. Article 7 of the EC Directive on Unfair Terms in Consumer Contracts provides:
   '1. Member States shall ensure that, in the interests of consumers and of competitors, adequate and effective means exist to prevent the continued use of unfair terms in contracts concluded with consumers by sellers or suppliers.
   2. The means referred to in paragraph 1 shall include provisions whereby persons or organizations, having a legitimate interest under national law in protecting consumers, may take action according to the national law concerned before the courts . . . for a decision as to whether contractual terms drawn up for general use are unfair, so

that they can apply appropriate and effective means to prevent the continued use of such terms.
3. . . . . the legal remedies referred to in paragraph 2 may be directed separately or jointly against a number of sellers or suppliers from the same economic sector or their associations which use or which recommend the use of the same general contractual terms or similar terms.'

How has the UK implemented these requirements?

10. Consider the validity of the following standard terms which feature in different consumer contracts:

(*i*) 'On signing this agreement the customer shall pay to the dealer a non-returnable deposit of 10%. The delivery period quoted overleaf is an estimate and not a term of the agreement and the dealer shall not be liable for any loss due to delayed delivery.'

(*ii*) 'The dealer shall have the right at any time before delivery of the goods the subject of this agreement to raise his prices for any increase in the prices of materials or parts or any other costs of any kind arising for any reason.'

(*iii*) 'If any money payable by the customer to the dealer under this agreement is not paid on the due date, the customer shall pay to the dealer interest on it at the rate of 20% from the due date until it is paid in full.'

(*iv*) 'Any complaint that the goods the subject of this agreement do not comply with their description or are otherwise defective shall be notified in writing by the customer to the dealer within seven days of their delivery (subject to the customer's statutory rights).'

(*v*) 'The dealer shall not be liable for any failure in the performance of any of his obligations under this agreement caused by factors outside his control.'

# 8

# PERFORMANCE OF CONSUMER CONTRACTS FOR THE SALE OF GOODS

## DELIVERY

### 1. What constitutes delivery

Delivery (the 'voluntary transfer of possession from one person to another': s. 61 SGA) is usually effected by a simple physical transfer of the goods to the consumer. A common alternative is the transfer of the means of control, as where a car's ignition key is handed over to the buyer. Other methods of delivery are possible, but unlikely to arise in consumer transactions. The possibility of constructive delivery is worth noting, however. For example, the consumer may be in possession before the contract of sale is made, as where goods are sent on approval. Here, when the consumer adopts the transaction (cf. SGA s. 18, Rule 4), he thereupon possesses the goods as owner rather than as bailee; constructive delivery has been effected. Finally, it may be noted that where the seller is by the contract authorized to send the goods to the consumer by carrier, delivery to the carrier is prima facie delivery to the consumer: s. 32(1). In this case the seller must make such contract with the carrier on behalf of the consumer as is reasonable having regard to the nature of the goods and all the other circumstances: s. 32(2)

### 2. Delivery dates

The time of delivery will not generally be of the essence (i.e. condition) in a consumer contract, unless a contrary intention can be derived from the terms of the contract (cf. s. 10 SGA). If the delivery date is not met, or, in the absence of any specified delivery date, if delivery is not made within a reasonable time, the consumer can make time of the essence by giving reasonable notice to that effect to the trader. (The consumer can do this even if he had previously waived a delivery date in the hope of receiving the goods eventually.) If time is of the essence, or has by reasonable notice been made of the essence, failure by the trader to meet the delivery date is a breach of condition and entitles the consumer to repudiate the contract.

*Note*: Similar rules as to making time of the essence apply to contracts for the supply of services. Cf. too s. 14 SGSA (*see* 5:**18**).

*Charles Rickards Ltd* v. *Oppenheim* (1950): the plaintiffs contracted to build a car body on to a Rolls-Royce chassis, the work to be completed by 20th March. The car was not ready by that date. The defendant did not then repudiate the contract, but pressed for delivery. At the end of June the defendant gave four weeks' notice for delivery, failing which he would regard the contract as repudiated. Delivery was tendered in October. The defendant rejected the car, and was sued by the plaintiffs. HELD: The defendant was entitled to reject the car. Although he had waived the original delivery date, by giving reasonable notice he had made the new delivery date of the essence (Court of Appeal).

### 3. Place of delivery

Most retailers will deliver goods to the consumer's home when the goods are such that the consumer cannot reasonably be expected to take them away with him. Sometimes a charge is made for delivery. Nevertheless, the strict legal position is that unless otherwise agreed (expressly or impliedly), the place of delivery is the retailer's premises: s. 29(2). But where it is agreed that the goods are to be delivered to the consumer's home, this must be done within a reasonable time: s. 29(3), and the retailer and his servants or agents must exercise reasonable care. Delivery at the consumer's home may be made to anyone who appears to be authorized to receive the goods (*Galbraith & Grant Ltd* v. *Block* (1922)). Delivery must be made at a reasonable hour: s. 29(5).

### 4. Expenses

The seller must bear the expenses of putting goods into a deliverable state, unless otherwise agreed: s. 29(6).

### 5. Delivery by instalments

The consumer is under no obligation to accept part only of the goods: s. 30(1). Further, unless otherwise agreed, the consumer is under no obligation to accept delivery by instalments: s. 31(1).

## ACCEPTANCE

### 6. What constitutes acceptance?

Acceptance and delivery are correlative concepts, yet delivery by the seller by no means necessarily involves acceptance by the consumer. We had a preliminary look at this topic in Chapter 5 on *Implied Terms* in the context of the remedies available for breach of the statutory rights. We saw that the Sale and Supply of Goods Act 1994 (SSGA) modified the acceptance rule at the same time as it redefined the meaning of quality. Here we will review the same general area of law but from a different perspective. The SGA will be cited as amended by the SSGA, which effected various clarifications and improvements in the law.

*Note*: for the legal effect of acceptance, *see* **14** below.

Subject as follows (*see* **8** below), acceptance is deemed to take place when:

**(a)** the buyer intimates to the seller that he has accepted the goods *or*

**(b)** when the goods have been delivered to the buyer and he does any act in relation to them which is inconsistent to the seller's ownership: s. 35(1).

## 7. Buyer's right of examining the goods

Unless otherwise agreed, when the seller tenders delivery of the goods he is bound on request to afford the buyer a reasonable opportunity of examining the goods for the purpose of ascertaining whether they are in conformity with the contract (and in the case of a sale by sample, of comparing the bulk with the sample): s. 34.

## 8. Legal implications of examining the goods

Where goods are delivered to the buyer and he has not previously examined them, deemed acceptance under s. 35(1) (*see* **6** above) cannot take place until the buyer has had a reasonable opportunity of examining the goods for the purpose

**(a)** of ascertaining whether they are in conformity with the contract *and*

**(b)** in the case of a sale by sample, of comparing the bulk with the sample: s. 35(2).

*Where the buyer deals as consumer*, the right to examine the goods cannot be lost by agreement, waiver or otherwise: s. 35(3). This is an improvement in the consumer's legal position brought about by the SSGA, and it means that the consumer cannot be prejudiced by (say) signing a so-called 'acceptance' note. (For the possible application of s. 35(2) to latent defects, *see* **9** below.)

## 9. Lapse of time

Apart from s. 35(2) (*see* **8** above), the buyer is also deemed to have accepted the goods when *after the lapse of a reasonable time* he retains the goods without intimating to the seller that he has rejected them: s. 35(4). Thanks to the SSGA, any decision whether a reasonable time has elapsed must take into account (though the point is not conclusive) whether the buyer has had the reasonable opportunity to examine the goods envisaged by s. 35(2): s. 35(5) SGA.

This *possible* annulment, whenever there is absence of reasonable opportunity to examine the goods, of the normal effect of lapse of time, *may* go some way to preserve the consumer's rights to reject substandard goods when time reasonably passes before they are examined because (say) the goods were purchased as a gift in advance of the due date (e.g. birthday or Christmas); or were purchased in a 'Sale' for use at a later season (e.g. winter clothes purchased in a Spring Sale).

It remains to be seen what effect (if any) s. 35(5) together with s. 35(2) will have on acceptance of goods having a **latent defect**. The argument could be advanced that use of the product over a reasonable period of time is the only method of enjoying a reasonable opportunity of examining the goods to see if they are in conformity with the contract with no hidden defects; such testing of the product should not therefore be caught either by the rule of acceptance through lapse of time or by the rule that an act inconsistent with the seller's ownership (i.e. use) amounts to acceptance. Doubtless, in each case an answer to the vexed question of latent defects will in practice turn on the particular facts involved. Certainly one would hope for some relaxation of the strict interpretation of the law in the notorious case of *Bernstein* v. *Pamson Motors (Golders Green) Ltd* (1987), where driving a new car for about 140 miles over a period of some three weeks was held to be unreasonably long. In *Bernstein*, Rougier J failed to draw any distinction between commercial and consumer cases, and held that, in the context of the sale of a motor car, reasonable time meant 'a reasonable time to inspect and try out the car *generally* rather than with an eye to any specific defect'. *Bernstein* has been the subject of considerable criticism, but for the present it stands as a precedent of sorts (an appeal in the case was dropped after the plaintiff's claim was eventually conceded).

## 10. Effect of repairs etc. on 'acceptance'

By virtue of the SSGA it is clear that the buyer is not to be deemed to have accepted goods *merely* because

**(a)** he asks for, or agrees to, their repair by or under arrangement with the seller *or*

**(b)** the goods are delivered to another under a sub-sale or other disposition: s. 35(6) SGA.

So the consumer will not be prejudiced because the goods are given as a gift to a friend or family member (though technically, under the rule of privity of contract, it is still the purchaser who must pursue the complaint about substandard goods, unless of course the trader waives this rule in the interests of goodwill).

As regards repairs, however, agreeing to repairs *under a manufacturer's guarantee* (without going through the retailer) will presumably still amount to acceptance as an act inconsistent with the seller's ownership under s. 35(1)(b) (*see* **6** above).

## 11. Replacements, credit notes

Another difficulty arises where a consumer complains about a defect and accepts a replacement article from the retailer for the defective one. If the replacement itself proves defective, is the consumer nevertheless deemed to have 'accepted' it? Probably not, if the replacement rescinds the original contract and substitutes a new one. Indeed, the replacement article is presumably obtained under a contract for the transfer of goods (contract of exchange: *see* 1:8) and is accordingly governed by Part I of the Supply of Goods and Services Act 1982. Part I contains no provision corresponding with s. 11(4) SGA (*see* **14** below) and so the more generous common law rule that the right to reject is only lost on affirmation of the contract would apply: *see* **15**. Of course, if the consumer takes replacement goods under a manufacturer's guarantee without reference back to the retailer, that must amount to acceptance as an act inconsistent with the seller's ownership.

Where the consumer accepts a credit note in exchange for defective goods, that again would seem to rescind the original contract and to substitute a new one, presumably governed by the SGSA as a contract of barter, though the point is not free from doubt.

> *Note*: If the consumer can justifiably reject goods, he cannot be obliged to take a credit note, or repairs, or a replacement instead. Likewise, neither can the consumer insist upon repairs or a replacement (unless under a guarantee). Naturally the parties may always agree to the contrary at the time the complaint is made.

## 12. Right of partial rejection

Where the contract is for the sale of goods making one or more *commercial units*, a buyer accepting any goods included in a unit is deemed to have accepted all the goods making the unit: s. 35(7) SGA. 'Commercial unit' means a unit which if divided would materially impair the value of the goods or the character of the unit. Thus the consumer could not, for instance, reject one of a pair of gloves. Section 35(7) relates to the new s. 35A, inserted in the SGA by the SSGA. Subject to s. 35(7), s. 35A gives a buyer the right of *partial rejection* in certain circumstances. These arise when the buyer has the right to reject the goods by reason of a breach by the seller that affects some or all of the goods which are not in conformity with the contract. Under the new rule, the buyer does not by accepting *all* the conforming goods thereby lose the right to reject the nonconforming goods or some of them. The new facility of partial rejection is subject to any contrary intention in the contract. In any event the new rule is modified in non-consumer cases. By s. 15A of the SGA as inserted by the SSGA, the buyer who does *not* deal as consumer cannot exercise the right to reject substandard goods where 'the breach is so slight that it would be unreasonable for him to reject them': s. 15A(1). Damages may be claimed instead.

> *Note*: this limitation in non-consumer cases on the right to reject for breach of sections 13, 14 or 15 of the SGA is a corollary of having cosmetic and minor defects brought within the scope of the redefined implied term as to quality (s. 14(2B)(b) and (c) SGA); commercial buyers are not to be able to use a technical breach of condition as an excuse unreasonably to reject the whole consignment.

The SSGA also modifies s. 30 SGA to impose a similar restriction on unreasonable rejection in non-consumer where the wrong quantity has been delivered: s. 30(2A) SGA (cf. **5** above).

## 13. Rejected goods

If the consumer refuses to accept the goods, having the right to do so, he does not have to return them to the seller but need only tell him that he refuses to accept them: s. 36. If the seller then fails to collect the goods and the consumer is put to expense in respect of them, that expense may be recovered by the consumer (*Kolfor Plant Ltd* v. *Tilbury Plant Ltd* (1977)).

## 14. Legal effect of acceptance

Once goods have been accepted in a non-severable contract, the consumer can no longer reject them: s. 11(4). This is so even if the grounds for rejection are breach of the Sale of Goods Act 'statutory rights'. The consumer's right to reject defective goods is thus severely restricted by s. 11(4), which when it applies *leaves the consumer with a claim for damages only*. Section 11(4) reads:

> Subject to [the right of partial rejection], where a contract of sale is not severable, and the buyer has accepted the goods or part of them the breach of any condition to be fulfilled by the seller can only be treated as a breach of warranty, and not as a ground for rejecting the goods and treating the contract as repudiated, unless there is an express or implied term of the contract to that effect.

> *Note*: a contract is severable where it can be regarded as a series of 'mini-contracts' (e.g. a contract for delivery of goods by instalments will be severable if each instalment is to be paid for separately, but not where payment is to be by one lump sum: s. 31(2)).

## 15. Conditional sale and hire-purchase agreements

The consumer is better placed under these agreements so far as the right to reject goods and treat the contract as repudiated is concerned.

**(a)** *Conditional sale agreements.* Section 11(4) of the SGA does not apply to a conditional sale agreement where the buyer deals as consumer within the UCTA: s. 14(1) of the Supply of Goods (Implied Terms) Act 1973 (as amended).

**(b)** *Hire-purchase agreements.* These are not controlled by the Sale of Goods Act (*Helby* v. *Matthews* (1895) HL), and the common law rule about rejection in these cases is much less restrictive. In hire-purchase (and conditional sale) agreements the right to reject is lost on affirmation of the contract. But since hire-purchase involves continuing obligations, breach of contract for defective goods will be a continuing breach so long as the defects remain unremedied, and the right to treat the contract as repudiated will continue also (*Yeoman Credit Ltd* v. *Apps* (1962) CA).

> *Farnworth Finance Facilities Ltd* v. *Attryde* (1970): the consumer took a motor cycle on hire-purchase terms. Many things were defective and the machine was repeatedly returned for repairs. After more than four months and some 4,000 miles, the rear chain broke, whereupon the consumer repudiated the contract. HELD: The consumer was entitled to do so. He had not affirmed the contract, but had indicated by his conduct that he would not accept the motor

cycle unless the defects were remedied. The consumer therefore recovered all payments he had made, no deduction for use being imposed by the court as the consumer had been subject to a great deal of inconvenience (Court of Appeal).

## Progress test 8

1. In April A ordered a new colour television set from B Ltd. No delivery date was specified. By July the set had still not been delivered. Advise A. Would it make any difference to your advice if the agreement had said: 'Delivery to be made in time for Wimbledon fortnight'?

2. C buys a three piece suite of furniture from D Ltd. C pays the full purchase price. C is then told to collect the furniture himself. Advise C. If the facts were that D Ltd agreed to deliver the suite, but tendered only one piece on the day fixed for delivery with the promise to deliver the remaining pieces the next week, would C be entitled to (a) reject the part tendered; and (b) repudiate the whole contract?

3. E buys a carpet from F & Co., who are to deliver it to E's home. When they do so E is out, so they leave it outside E's front door. Rain damages the carpet. Consider whether E can reject the carpet. If E can reject it, does E have to transport it back to F & Co.?

4. Explain when 'acceptance' of goods takes place. How is this affected by the consumer's right to examine the goods? What are the legal consequences of acceptance?

5. L buys a refrigerator. The motor break down after three months' use. Can L reject the refrigerator and recover the purchase price? Would it make any difference if L had taken the refrigerator on either (a) conditional sale terms; or (b) hire-purchase terms?

6. M buys a watch from N & Co. The watch does not work so M has it repaired by N. It still does not work. N then replaces the watch with an identical one. The replacement works but cannot be made to keep good time despite N's attempts at regulating it when M repeatedly returns the watch to N for attention. Tired of the whole business, some four months after the initial purchase M returns the replacement watch to N and demands the return of the purchase price. N offers M a credit note. Advise M

7. Is the new right of partial rejection likely to be of any practical use to consumers?

# 9

## REMEDIES

### 1. The measure of damages

Contract law thinks almost exclusively in terms of damages – monetary compensation for lost expectations – as the remedy for breach of contract. The victim of a breach of contract is to be put in the same position, so far as money can do this, as if the contract had been properly carried out. Accordingly the victim can recover *expectation damages*: damages for loss of bargain (where the consumer is at fault) or for loss of profit (where the trader is at fault). The damages will include any consequential loss sustained. Sometimes, instead of compensation for loss of bargain the victim may be awarded *reliance losses*, typically compensation for wasted expenditure. This would be appropriate where the consumer cannot establish the value of a loss of bargain. Exceptionally the aggrieved party can succeed in a claim to protect *restitutionary interests*, which means that the guilty party is deprived of an unjust benefit. An example of this would be a cash refund where the consumer has justifiably rejected faulty goods and terminated the contract.

### 2. Remoteness of damage

As a matter of policy the law imposes a limit on the amount of damages recoverable in pursuit of the aim of monetary compensation. Certain kinds of loss will be held to be too remote to attract compensation. In contract the test for remoteness was laid down by the Court of Exchequer in *Hadley* v. *Baxendale* (1854):

> 'Where two parties have made a contract which one of them has broken, the damages which the other party ought to receive in respect of such breach of contract should be such as may fairly and reasonably be considered as either arising naturally, i.e. according to the usual course of things, from such breach of contract itself, or such as may reasonably be supposed to have been in the contemplation of both parties, at the time they made the contract, as the probable result of the breach of it.' (*per* Alderson B).

Explaining *Hadley* v. *Baxendale* in *Victoria Laundry (Windsor) Ltd* v. *Newman Industries Ltd* (1949), the Court of Appeal, *per* Asquith LJ, identified two limbs to the rule, that is two types of recoverable loss arising from breach of contract:

**(a)** loss arising naturally (knowledge of the serious possibility of the occurrence of such loss being imputed to the contract-breaker); *and*

**(b)** loss arising in special circumstances where the contract-breaker had actual knowledge that breach of contract in those circumstances would be liable to result in special loss being suffered.

In *The Heron II, Koufos* v. *Czarnikow* (1969), the House of Lords stressed that the test for remoteness in contract was that the loss should be reasonably contemplated loss, which required a much higher degree of probability for its occurrence than that the loss should merely be 'reasonably foreseeable' – the test for remoteness in tort (*see* 11:**13**). The substantive validity of this distinction between the tests for remoteness of damage in contract and tort was doubted, however, by members of the Court of Appeal in *Parsons (Livestock) Ltd* v. *Uttley Ingham & Co. Ltd* (1978). What the Court of Appeal did affirm in *Parsons* was that so long as the serious possibility of the occurrence of the kind of damage which did in fact occur was within the reasonable contemplation of the parties when they made their contract, then there is liability for all the loss of that kind, even if such loss was more extensive than was foreseeable. The facts of *Parsons* will illustrate the point.

> *Parsons (Livestock) Ltd* v. *Uttley Ingham & Co. Ltd* (1978): the ventilator on a food hopper was not opened on installation, with the consequence that the food deteriorated, poisoning the pigs fed by the hopper and killing many of them. HELD: Some illness in the pigs was reasonably to be contemplated as probable in the circumstances, and so the party in breach of contract was liable for all the damage (i.e. death of the pigs) caused by the illness turning out to be much more severe than might have been contemplated. (But damages for loss of profits from future sales of pigs were too remote.)

> *Note*: In *Parsons* Lord Denning MR, in a minority on this point, thought that a different test for remoteness (i.e. the 'foreseeability' test) was applicable in cases of physical loss (as distinct from loss of profit) arising from breach of contract.

## 3. Damages for disappointment

It used to be thought from *Addis* v. *Gramophone Co. Ltd* (1909) HL, that damages for breach of contract were confined to compensation for financial loss, that is loss quantifiable in monetary terms, but a series of cases, commencing with *Jarvis* v. *Swans Tours Ltd* (1973) CA, has allowed moderate damages in compensation for disappointment and distress suffered by the innocent party. (Of course, for such damages to be recoverable, the disappointment etc. must have been within the reasonable contemplation of the parties.)

> *Jarvis* v. *Swans Tours Ltd* (1973): the consumer, a solicitor, booked a skiing cum houseparty holiday in Switzerland for £63, in response to what was described by Edmund Davies LJ as the 'ecstatic text' of a brochure. The holiday was a disaster. Among other shortcomings, there were only thirteen guests in the first week and none at all in the second; no English was spoken by the owner; no full-length skis were available; there was no welcoming party on arrival, no Swiss cakes, and no proper yodeller – all of which had been promised. HELD: The plaintiff was entitled to damages for loss of enjoyment, assessed by the court at £125 (Court of Appeal).

*Jackson* v. *Horizon Holidays Ltd* (1975): this was another case involving a disappointing holiday (in Sri Lanka) which failed to match the description given by the defendants. The price including air fares was £1,200. HELD: The plaintiff could recover damages for diminution in the value of the holiday and for disappointment, not only his own disappointment but also that of his wife and children (the damages once recovered being money had and received to their use). On this basis, the total sum awarded as damages amounted to £1,100 (say £600 for diminution in value and £500 for mental distress) (Court of Appeal).

*Note: Jackson* does not abrogate the doctrine of privity of contract (*see* 11:2), but 'may be supported either as a broad decision on the measure of damages . . . or possibly as an example of a type of contract, examples of which are persons contracting for family holidays, ordering meals in restaurants for a party, hiring a taxi for a group, calling for special treatment' (Lord Wilberforce in *Woodar Investment* v. *Wimpey Ltd* (1980) HL).

*Watts* v. *Morrow* (1991): a surveyor negligently reported a house to be in sound condition whereas urgent and expensive repairs were in fact necessary. On the issue of damages for mental distress, the Court of Appeal HELD (following previous decisions) that such damages were only recoverable where the object of the contract was to provide pleasure, relaxation, peace of mind or freedom from distress; a contract to survey a house was not such a contract, though 'modest' damages (£750) were awarded for physical discomfort endured while the undisclosed defects were repaired. [On the measure of damages in respect of the defects – whether repairs or diminution in value – *see Note* under **5(e)** below.]

*Heywood* v. *Wellers* (1976): the plaintiff instructed solicitors to apply for an injunction to restrain a man from molesting her. The solicitors were negligently slow in obtaining and enforcing the injunction, so that the plaintiff suffered mental distress and was molested on three or four occasions. HELD: The mental distress suffered was within the solicitor's contemplation, and damages for the molestation and distress were assessed in total at £150, less the £25 the plaintiff would have paid had the solicitors done their duty (Court of Appeal).

*Woodman* v. *Photo-Trade Processing* (1981) (*see* 6:**14**): here a film processing laboratory lost a film containing wedding photographs. £75 was added to the award for the predictable disappointment.

## 4. Mitigation of damages

The plaintiff claiming damages for breach of contract (whether as consumer or trader) must take reasonable steps to mitigate the loss, otherwise damages will be reduced. For example, where the consumer justifiably rejects defective goods, or where the trader fails to deliver the goods in the first place, the consumer must whenever possible buy similar goods elsewhere at the lowest price reasonably obtainable. On the other hand, if the consumer has accepted defective goods, or chooses to accept them, and by reason of s. 11(4) SGA can no longer reject them (*see* 8:**14**), then the consumer must avail himself of any reasonable offers of repairs or replacement by the trader (cf. *Payzu Ltd* v. *Saunders* (1919) – a commercial case) – or alternatively the consumer should avail himself of any manufacturer's guarantee. The consumer need not have the goods repaired by the trader, however, where he has reasonably lost confidence in the trader's ability to effect the repairs satisfactorily. Nor need the consumer take a replacement where he has reasonably lost confidence in the product itself. Similar rules as to mitigation of loss by submitting to repairs apply to contracts for the supply of a service. Where the plaintiff does act reasonably in an attempt to mitigate loss, the cost of the attempt will be recoverable even if the effect of the attempt is to increase the total damages incurred (*Hoffberger* v. *Ascot International Bloodstock Bureau Ltd* (1976)).

> *Note*: Nothing in the above rules prevents a consumer who has not 'accepted' goods from rejecting them if they are defective in breach of the statutory rights and from claiming the return of the price (*see* **5(c)** and **(d)**). But once the consumer claims *damages* (e.g. for consequential loss) he must mitigate that loss where reasonable along the lines indicated above.

## 5. Contracts for the sale of goods

The principles considered in the foregoing paragraphs are applicable to all types of contract. But it will be useful to summarize the various remedies available to the consumer in sale of goods cases.

**(a)** *Damages for non-delivery*. The Sale of Goods Act in effect codifies *Hadley* v. *Baxendale*. Thus, 'the measure of damages is the estimated loss directly and naturally resulting, in the ordinary course of events, from the seller's breach of contract': s. 51(2), which corresponds to the first limb of *Hadley* v. *Baxendale*. Spelling the matter out further, the Act continues: 'Where there is an available market for the goods in question the measure of damages is prima facie to be ascertained by the difference between the contract price and the market or current price of the goods at the time or times when they ought to have been delivered, or (if no time was fixed) then at the time of the refusal to deliver': s. 51(3), which envisages that the buyer will mitigate his loss by purchasing elsewhere. The meaning of 'available market' is considered below (*see* **8**).

Section 51(3) is only a prima facie rule. If the serious possibility of special loss was within the reasonable contemplation of the contract-breaker, damages for such loss will be recoverable in accordance with the second limb of *Hadley* v. *Baxendale*, for the s. 54 of the SGA, nothing in the Act is to affect the consumer's (or trader's) right to recover special damages. Nevertheless, the normal outcome of breach of contract by the seller will be that the consumer will be able to buy the goods elsewhere and recover any additional expenditure incurred.

> *Note*: Non-delivery for the purpose of the above-mentioned rules includes cases where the consumer justifiably rejects the goods.

**(b)** *Specific performance*. This is an equitable remedy and accordingly will be available subject to the usual rules. In particular, damages must be an inadequate remedy. The consequence of this requirement is that the trader would only be directed to perform the contract specifically where the goods were in some way unique (e.g. an antique) and not otherwise available – an unusual thing in run-of-the-mill consumer contracts. Other bars to obtaining a decree of specific performance include undue delay prejudicial to the defendant; undue hardship caused to the defendant; prejudice to an innocent third party. Where specific performance is obtained, this does not necessarily preclude an award of damages as well: s. 52.

**(c)** *Action for return of the price* if the consideration has wholly failed: s. 54.

**(d)** *Rejection of goods* for breach of condition (subject to s. 11(4) of the SGA: *see* 8:**14**). To be effective, the rejection must be unequivocal (*Lee* v. *York Coach and Marine* (1977) CA). Damages will be available in appropriate cases as well as the remedy of rejection of the goods and consequent return of the price under s. 54. Where the buyer justifiably rejects goods he need not return them to the seller, unless otherwise agreed, but may simply tell the seller he rejects them: s. 36. Nevertheless it would normally be advisable for the consumer to return goods which are portable and to claim any incidental expenses incurred.

**(e)** *Damages for breach of warranty.* In the case of breach of warranty of quality, the damages will prima facie be the difference in value of the goods at the time of delivery to the consumer and the value they would have had if they had fulfilled the warranty: s. 53(3). If the price has not yet been paid, damages on this basis can be deducted from the amount payable: s. 53(1).

> *Note*: Section 53(3) is only a *prima facie* rule, so that in a consumer contract the actual cost of repairs may be recoverable where defective goods are reasonably repairable. In *Keeley* v. *Guy McDonald Ltd* (1984), the cost of repairs for an unmerchantable second-hand Rolls Royce were recoverable under s. 53(3) as the difference between the actual unrepaired value of the car and the value it would have possessed if the implied condition had not been broken. Yet *Ruxley Electronics and Construction Ltd* v. *Forsyth* (1995) HL (a building contract case) in effect affirms that no remedy will be available – sale of goods cases included – based on reinstatement or repairs [i.e. the 'cost of cure'] where the expenditure is out of all proportion to the benefit to be obtained; this is so even if on the alternative basis, diminution in value, the loss is purely nominal. Cf. *Watts* v. *Morrow* (1991) – not a sale of goods case – where substantial repairs to property were necessary following reliance by the purchaser on a negligent surveyor's report which failed to disclose the defects; the Court of Appeal awarded the purchaser damages based not on the cost of repairs but on the lesser sum representing the diminution in value of the property in its true as compared with its reported condition.

## 6. Entire contracts

An entire contract is one where the consideration is indivisible (e.g. payment by one lump sum) and is not intended by the parties to pass until the other party has completely performed his side of the contract. This is known as the rule in *Cutter* v. *Powell* (1795). It means that complete performance of the contract will be a condition precedent to payment, and it is therefore an important common law doctrine which the consumer can take advantage of in cases of partial or defective performance by the supplier of goods or services. Take a lump sum building contract, for example. If the builder fails to complete the job after time has been made of the essence (*see* 7:2), then the consumer will not have to pay anything at all – at least not unless the contract has before expiry of the deadline been *substantially performed*. Consider the following two cases by way of illustration of the doctrine:

> *Hoenig* v. *Isaacs* (1952): the plaintiff agreed to redecorate and furnish a flat for £750. The work was defective in certain minor respects and cost the flat owner £55 to put right. HELD: The contract had been substantially performed and the decorator was entitled to the contract price less the cost of making good the defects (Court of Appeal).

> *Bolton* v. *Mahadeva* (1972): a central heating system at an agreed price of £560 was installed by a contractor. There were serious defects which the contractor refused to remedy. The deficiencies were assessed at £174. HELD: The contract had not been substantially performed and the contractor was not entitled to the contract price or any part of it (Court of Appeal).

# THE CONSUMER AT FAULT

## 7. General principles

The rules as to measure of damages, remoteness and mitigation of loss, considered above, will be equally applicable in cases where it is the consumer who is in breach of contract, whether the contract is for the sale of goods or the supply of services.

## 8. Contracts for the sale of goods

The consumer at fault may find himself faced with one of the following personal actions brought by the trader.

**(a)** *Action for the price*. This action is open to the trader where property in the goods has passed to the consumer: s. 49 SGA. The consumer will not of course be liable to pay the price if there is an unexpired credit period, or if the consumer can validly reject the goods. Further, the trader can sue for the price only if he is ready and willing to deliver the goods.

> *Note*: Cf. s. 49 with the common law rule that where the supplier of a service can perform his side of the contract without the co-operation of his customer, then the supplier can ignore a wrongful cancellation by the customer and go ahead and perform the service and claim the *full contract price* – though not if the customer can show that the supplier had 'no legitimate interest, financial or otherwise' in performing the contract rather than in merely claiming damages: *see White & Carter (Councils) Ltd* v. *McGregor* (1961) HL and *Clea Shipping* v. *Bulk Oil* (1984).

**(b)** *Action for damages for non-acceptance*, where the consumer wrongfully refuses to accept and pay for the goods: s. 50(1). Damages may include a reasonable charge for the care and custody of the goods: s. 37. The measure of damages for non-acceptance is the estimated loss directly and naturally resulting, in the ordinary course of events, from the consumer's breach of contract: s. 50(2).

Further, s. 50(3) provides: 'Where there is an available market for the goods in question the measure of damages is *prima facie* to be ascertained by the difference between the contract price and the market or current price at the time or times when the goods ought to have been accepted, or (if no time was fixed for acceptance) then at the time of the refusal to accept.' The correspondence of these provisions with those contained in s. 51 (*see* 5) will not escape the reader. As for the meaning of 'available market', this expression has been discussed by the courts without final conclusions being reached. Probably the expression means no more than that the goods may be freely sold in a situation in which the price is fixed by supply and demand.

*W. L. Thompson Ltd* v. *Robinson (Gunmakers) Ltd* (1955): the defendants ordered a Vanguard car from the plaintiffs, but refused to accept delivery of it. The plaintiffs claimed damages for loss of profit. There was then a fixed retail price for the car, and the contract price and the market price at the date of breach were the same. The defendants therefore claimed that they were liable only for nominal damages. HELD: Section 50(3) of the SGA did not apply, because there could be no 'available market' in a situation (which then existed) where supply exceeded demand. The plaintiffs' damages were not merely nominal; they had lost their bargain and were entitled to recover their loss of profit.

*Charter* v. *Sullivan* (1957): here it was a Hillman car which the buyer ordered but later refused to accept. The facts were different from *Thompson* v. *Robinson* in that demand exceeded supply, there being a shortage of Hillman cars. HELD: The plaintiff dealer could obtain only nominal damages. Even if there was an 'available market' (which the court doubted in view of the then fixed retail price), the *prima facie* rule as to damages in s. 50(3) of the SGA was to be rejected where demand exceeded supply. This was because the dealer could mitigate his loss by a resale. The dealer lost no profit on any abortive sale, for he simply sold to the next customer. Further, applying s. 50(2) of the SGA the plaintiff had suffered no 'loss directly and naturally resulting, in the ordinary course of events, from the buyer's breach of contract' (Court of Appeal).

*Lazenby Garages Ltd* v. *Wright* (1976): the defendant consumer agreed to buy a used BMW car from dealers for £1,670. The defendant then repudiated the contract. The dealers had bought the BMW for £1,325, and they claimed £345 loss of profit, although two months after the defendant's repudiation of the contract they had sold the car for £1,770. HELD: There could be no 'available market' for unique goods such as second-hand cars. Section 50(3) of the SGA was therefore inapplicable. Applying s. 50(2), the most that the buyer would have contemplated was that he would be liable for the difference if the car was resold at a loss on breach of contract. Loss of profit was not recoverable as no loss had been suffered on the particular transaction (Court of Appeal).

*Shearson Lehman Hutton Inc.* v. *Maclaine Watson & Co. Ltd* (1989): this was a commercial case about the sale of 7,755 tonnes of tin. The court held that the test for determining the market or current price (s. 50(3)) is objective and should not be coloured by any lack of negotiating skill on the part of the seller.

## 9. Remedies against the goods

The two actions considered in the preceding paragraph are personal actions against the consumer. An unpaid seller also has certain 'real' remedies, i.e. remedies against the goods themselves. A seller is 'unpaid' if either the whole of the price has not been paid or tendered, or a negotiable instrument taken as conditional payment has not been honoured: s. 38 of the SGA. Included among the unpaid seller's 'real' remedies are the following remedies of interest to the consumer:

**(a)** *Lien*, i.e. the right to retain goods until the price has been paid. Lien arises if:

(*i*)  there is no provision as to credit; *or*
(*ii*)  the credit term has expired; *or*
(*iii*)  the buyer becomes insolvent: s. 41.

The right of lien reflects the rule that delivery of goods and payment are concurrent conditions, which means that the consumer must pay for the goods on delivery, unless credit is given: s. 28. The lien is lost if the seller delivers the goods or waives the lien: s. 43.

> *Note*: Lien presupposes that property in the goods remains with the seller. Where property in the goods has passed to the consumer, however, the unpaid seller has a right of retention co-extensive to the right of lien: s. 39(2).

**(b)** *Right of resale*. The unpaid seller who has exercised the right of lien or retention can give notice to the consumer of his intention to resell. If the consumer does not pay within a reasonable time, the seller can sell and in addition recover from the consumer any loss occasioned by the breach of contract: s. 48(3). The effect of a resale is to give the second buyer a good title as against the original consumer: s. 48(2). This is so even if the original consumer was not given reasonable notice of the resale.

## 10. Deposits

Once the consumer enters into the contract (whether for the sale of goods or the supply of services), any deposit paid or payable by him will, subject to contrary agreement, be forfeited if he wrongly repudiates the contract. Similarly, goods given in part-exchange in lieu of a deposit would be forfeited. Where the seller exercises his right of resale of goods under s. 48(3) (*see* **9(b)**), the first consumer's deposit will be forfeited. In any of these cases, if the seller sues for damages the deposit will be taken into account in assessing the seller's loss. Of course, the seller will not necessarily make a loss. He may indeed succeed in selling the goods at a higher price to a third party. Even so, any deposit paid by the original consumer does not as a matter of law have to be returned.

> *Note*: A deposit (i.e. a guarantee of performance, say 10 per cent of the price) must be distinguished from a *part payment*, which will normally be recoverable on breach of contract by the payer, subject to any deduction for damages assessed under the ordinary principles.

## Progress test 9

1. What is the object of an award of damages as a remedy for breach of contract? On what basis or bases might this object be achieved?

2. What is the test for remoteness of damage in contract? How (if at all) does this test differ from the test for remoteness in tort?

3. A buys an oil-filled electric heater. It is faulty and starts an electrical fire, burning down A's house and destroying in the process some valuable pictures worth over £100,000. Will the damages to be awarded to A include (a) the value of the house (£50,000); and (b) the value of the pictures?

4. B, a builder, entered into a lump sum contract to build an extension to C's house, the work to be completed in three months. Time was expressly made of the essence. B took nine months over the work, and during the extra six months part of the inside of C's house was left exposed to the weather and was uninhabitable. C now wishes to deduct from B's final account £50 per month for six months as compensation for the vexation caused to C by the delay. Advise C. If the facts were that B had simply refused to complete the job, leaving the extension unroofed, what would C's legal position have been?

5. D engages a photographer to take photographs at his daughter's wedding. The photographer fails to turn up. Can D sue the photographer for damages for his own disappointment and that of his wife and daughter? If so, what kind of sum do you think a court might award? If the facts were that the wedding had been cancelled and that the photographer had turned up nevertheless, could he claim the full contract price?

6. E orders a new car from F, a dealer. The car is defective in many respects and E rejects it. E then buys the same model from another dealer who has it already in stock, but meanwhile there has been a price increase. Can E recover the difference from F?

7. G and H booked a holiday at a two-star hotel in a popular resort. Their room was to have a sea view but when they arrived at the hotel there was no such room available. G and H stayed at another hotel, which had the required accommodation, although they paid much more for their holiday as it was a luxury four-star hotel. There were numerous other hotels in the resort which appeared to afford a view of the sea, but G and H did not trouble to enquire whether these hotels had any vacancies. Can G and H recover the difference in tariff between the two-star and four-star hotel?

8. J agreed to buy an antique Sheraton parlour chair from K, a dealer. K later sold the chair to L because L offered K an extra £200 for the chair. The chair is still in K's possession. Is J likely to be able to obtain a decree of specific performance? If instead J sues for damages, on what basis would they be assessed?

9. M orders a new sofa. When it is delivered M discovers that part of the fabric is badly soiled. The trader refuses to do anything about the matter. Advise M whether he can bring an action for the return of the price which M has paid. If M decides to keep the sofa, can he recover the cost of repairing it?

10. In what circumstances can a trader bring an action for the price against a consumer?

11. N commissions his portrait from O, an artist, for £200. N unjustifiably refuses to accept the finished work. O is able to sell the picture to P for £30. What damages will N be liable to pay? Would it make any difference if instead of P it was Q, an eccentric collector, who bought the picture from O, and at a price of £300?

12. R orders a colour television set from S, a retailer, for £350. R pays a deposit of £50. Nothing is said about payment of the balance. When the set arrives at S's premises from the manufacturers, S informs R and requires payment of the balance. R refuses to pay until the set has been delivered and tested over a period of one week in R's house.
(a) Does S have to deliver the set?
(b) If R continues in his demands, can S sell the set to someone else? If so, will S have to return R's deposit?

# 10
# PACKAGE TRAVEL, HOLIDAYS AND TOURS

## COMMON LAW PRINCIPLES

### 1. Introductory

The main object of these pages is to outline the legal requirements and rules imposed by the Package Travel, Package Holidays and Package Tours Regulations 1992, which implement the EC Directive under that same heading (Council Directive 90/314/EEC). But first some preliminary observations as to the legal structure governing the travel industry may be helpful. As always in English law, the statutory (including European Union) material has to be seen against the underlying common law principles, which continue to apply except where superseded by the legislation.

### 2. Legal status of tour operators and travel agents

*Tour operators* put holiday packages together and sell them either directly to the public or (more often) through *travel agents*. Whether the latter are technically the agents of the tour operator or of the customer (or of both) is a point not entirely free from doubt (cf. *Kemp* v. *Intasun Holidays Limited* (1987) CA), but the better view seems to be that usually the travel agent will be the agent of the tour operator. Either way, the relationship of principal and agent arises under the common law. This means that normally the agent drops out of the picture – free of liability if the holiday goes wrong – and the customer's remedy lies against the tour operator. If acting as the tour operator's agent, the travel agent will have express or implied (ostensible) authority to bind the tour operator as principal, who will therefore be liable to the customer for any misrepresentations by the travel agent?

The contents of the legal relationship subsisting between tour operator and travel agent are outside the scope of this book, but it may be mentioned here that an agent owes the principal a duty to exercise reasonable professional care and skill, so that (quite apart from any express provisions) the agent will in turn be liable to indemnify the principal for the consequences of the former's negligence.

## 3. Liability of travel agent to customer at common law

Whilst the travel agent will normally drop out of the picture at common law – subject always to reg. 4 of the 1992 Regulations (see **10** below) – there are exceptions, the chief of which is the possibility of liability to the customer for negligent misstatement under the principle of *Hedley Byrne* v. *Heller* (1964) HL. Note that the travel agent (if the tour operator's agent) will *not* be liable to the customer for misrepresentation, because there exists no privity of contract between travel agent and customer. Of course, privity is not a requirement for liability founded under *Hedley Byrne*, because that is an action in tort and not contract. Another possibility for the customer is to seek to establish breach of collateral contract against the travel agent.

## 4. The ABTA Travel Agents' Code of Conduct

Perhaps of greater practical consequence than the foregoing common law rules, however, is the *Travel Agents' Code of Conduct* drawn up by the Association of British Travel Agents (ABTA) in consultation with the Office of Fair Trading. This is one of two ABTA Codes, the other being the Tour Operators' Code of Conduct. The Travel Agents' Code, although not applicable to non-members of ABTA, imposes high and comprehensive standards on travel agents. In the event of default, the customer may choose to have recourse to ABTA's scheme for inexpensive 'documents only' arbitration.

## 5. Liability of tour operator to customer at common law

Here again there is some uncertainty in the law. The customer's contract will be with the tour operator and not (say) the hotelier. So in the event of default by the hotelier, on what basis is the tour operator liable to the customer? Where the breach of contract is caused by the tour operator's own staff, liability is strict. But where the default is by a sub-contractor, e.g. hotel, transfer coach company or excursion company, etc., it seems that a lower level of liability applies, i.e. to take reasonable care in the choice and monitoring of sub-contractors and to alert customers to potential problems. Part II of the Supply of Goods and Services Act 1982 has a role to play here:

> 'In a contract for the supply of a service [e.g. to provide a holiday, whether or not through intermediaries] where the supplier is acting in the course of a business, there is an implied term that the supplier will carry out the service with reasonable care and skill': s. 13.

> *Wilson* v. *Best Travel Ltd* (1993): The plaintiff, while staying at a Greek hotel (in 1986) booked through Best Travel, was seriously injured after tripping and falling through glass doors at the hotel. The doors complied with Greek but not British safety standards. The plaintiff based his claim on breach of contract, either (i) breach of implied term that the hotel structure would be reasonably safe; or (ii) breach of the duty in s. 13 of the Supply of Goods and Services Act to exercise reasonable care and skill to see that the hotel was reasonably safe, i.e. to ensure that the hotel had been regularly and compe-

tently inspected for safety. HELD: the plaintiff's claim failed, because (i) under the 'officious bystander' test it would be neither necessary nor obvious nor reasonable to imply a term in a package holiday contract that the hotel be reasonably safe; and (ii) whilst in the circumstances there was a duty under s. 13 of the 1982 Act to exercise reasonable care in inspecting the hotel premises for safety, it was sufficient to check that there was compliance with local safety standards, unless the degree of danger was such that no reasonable holidaymaker would consent to stay at the hotel, which on the facts was not the case.

Contrast *Davey* v. *Cosmos Air Holidays* (1989), where it was HELD that Cosmos knew, or should have known, about a reported health risk at a Portuguese resort and should have taken precautions to minimise or eliminate the risk and have warned their customers accordingly; in default they were therefore liable for the resulting illness suffered by their customers.

## 6. The ABTA Tour Operators' Code of Conduct

The second ABTA Code referred to above, the *Tour Operator's Code of Conduct*, imposes duties on ABTA members as to booking conditions and minimum standards for brochures. Moreover, tour operators accept responsibility for the acts and omissions of their employees, agents, sub-contractors and suppliers. In addition, they accept responsibility (irrespective of fault) should the services agreed to be supplied prove deficient or not of reasonable standard (excluding, in the absence of negligence, claims for death, bodily injury or illness). Liability may be limited for air or sea travel in accordance with the international conventions – the Warsaw Convention of 1929 on International Carriage by Air, as amended by the Hague Protocol 1955; and the Athens Convention of 1974 on Carriage by Sea). There is provision for optional, inexpensive 'documents only' arbitration in the event of unresolved dispute. Altogether, the Tour Operators' Code of Conduct gives valuable protection to customers. Of course, tour operators' conditions of contract will be subject to both the Unfair Contract Terms Act 1977 and the Unfair Terms in Consumer Contracts Regulations 1994 – except in the latter case where the contract complies with the 1992 Regulations, which may well apply and to which we now turn.

# THE PACKAGE TRAVEL, PACKAGE HOLIDAYS AND PACKAGE TOURS REGULATIONS 1992

## 7. The EC Directive

The Package Travel, Package Holidays and Package Tours Regulations 1992 implement the Package Travel, Package Holidays and Package Tours Directive of 13 June 1990 (30/314/EEC). Hereafter we will refer to the 1992 implementing statutory instrument simply as 'the Regulations'. In the event of conflict between the Regulations and the Directive, the latter prevails in accordance with the principles of EU Law. National law continues to apply except where contradictory to the Directive (N.B. member States may adopt more stringent provisions: Art. 8).

## 8. Definitions

Unfortunately the Directive, and hence the Regulations, do not speak of tour operators and travel agents but (more broadly) of 'organiser' and 'retailer' respectively. Thus Regulation 2(1) provides:

- 'Organiser' means the person who, otherwise than occasionally, organises packages and sells or offers them for sale, whether directly or through a retailer
- 'Retailer' means the person who sells or offers for sale the package put together by the organiser.

It follows that travel agents who put together packages will be treated as organisers for the purposes of the Regulations. Similarly, volunteers who put together packages (other than *occasionally*) will be treated as organisers. 'Package' is defined below (see **9**), where the scope of the Regulations is considered. Meanwhile other important definitions to note are:

- 'Brochure' means any brochure in which packages are offered for sale
- 'Offer' includes an invitation to treat whether by means of advertising or otherwise, and cognate expressions shall be construed accordingly
- 'Contract' means the agreement linking the consumer to the organiser or to the retailer, or to both, as the case may be
- 'The other party to the contract' means the party, other than the consumer, to the contract, that is, the organiser or the retailer, or both, as the case may be.

*Note*: In the definition of *contract*, above, 'consumer' means 'the person who takes or agrees to take the package ("the principal contractor") and elsewhere in these Regulations "consumer" means, as the context requires, the principal contractor, any person on whose behalf the principal contractor agrees to purchase the package ("the other beneficiaries") or any person to whom the principal contractor or any of the other beneficiaries transfers the package ("the transferee")': reg. 2(2).

## 9. Scope of the Regulations

It is important to realise that the Regulations are only concerned with package holidays. 'Package' is defined as meaning 'the pre-arranged combination' of at least *two* of the following components 'when sold or offered for sale at an inclusive price and when the service covers a period of more than twenty-four hours or includes overnight accommodation:

**(a)** Transport

**(b)** Accommodation

**(c)** Other tourist services not ancillary to transport or accommodation and accounting for a significant proportion of the package'.

Separate billing of the components of the package does not prevent the arrangements from being a package; nor does the fact that the arrangements are made in accordance with the specific instructions of the consumer prevent the package from being treated as pre-arranged: reg. 2(1).

## 10. Compensation for misleading information

Organisers and retailers must not supply the consumer with any descriptive matter relating to a package, its price or other contractual conditions, which contains misleading information: reg. 4(1). Breach of this requirement renders the organiser or retailer liable to compensate the consumer for any loss suffered in consequence: reg. 4(2). This *civil* liability complements criminal liability under s. 14 of the Trade Descriptions Act 1968 and s. 20 of the Consumer Protection Act 1987.

## 11. Brochures

While there is no legal requirement to supply a brochure, if one is made available then by reg. 5 it must contain 'in a legible, comprehensible and accurate manner' the price and certain other matters specified in Schedule 1, viz.:

(1) The destination and the means, characteristics and categories of transport used.

(2) The type of accommodation, its location, category or degree of comfort and its main features and, where the accommodation is to be provided in an EU member State, its tourist classification under the rules of that member State.

(3) The meal plan.

(4) The itinerary.

(5) General information about passports and visa requirements which apply to British Citizens and health formalities required for the journey and the stay.

(6) Either the sum or the percentage of the price which is to be paid in advance and the timetable for payment of the balance.

(7) Whether a minimum number of persons is required for the package to take place and, if so, the deadline for informing the consumer in the event of cancellation.

(8) Any arrangements for consumers who are delayed at the outward or homeward points of departure.

(9) Arrangements for security for money paid over and for the repatriation of the consumer in the event of insolvency.

It is a *strict liability* criminal offence for an organiser to contravene these requirements as to brochures: reg. 5(3). There is the usual 'due diligence' type of defence (see **23** below). Retailers are also criminally liable *if they knew or had reasonable cause to believe* that the brochure did not comply with the requirements.

The particulars in the brochure, whether or not they are required by regulation 5, constitute implied warranties carrying strict liability in contract, except as regards the details about financial security: reg. 6. The tour operator and consumer can always agree subsequently that some or all of the particulars in the brochure shall not form part of the contract: reg. 6(3). The brochure itself may expressly reserve the right to make changes in the particulars contained in it before a contract is concluded, provided that any changes are clearly communicated to the consumer pre-contractually: reg. 6(2)(b).

## 12. Information disclosure

*Before a contract is concluded* the other party to the contract must provide the intending consumer with specified information in writing or in some other appropriate form: reg. s. 7(1). The information required is:

**(a)** general information on passport and visa requirements which apply to British Citizens, including information on the length of time likely to be needed to obtain the appropriate passports and visa

**(b)** information about health formalities required for the journey and the stay

**(c)** the arrangements for security and repatriation, where relevant, in the event of insolvency: reg. 7(2).

No civil liability arises from breach of these requirements: reg. 27. But contravention is a criminal offence: reg. 7(3).

Further, in good time *before the start of the journey* the other party to the contract must provide the consumer with the following information in writing or in some other appropriate form (reg. 8), viz.

- The times and places of intermediate stops and transport connections and details of the type of accommodation to be occupied by the traveller, e.g. cabin or berth on ship or sleeper compartment on train.
- The name, address and telephone number of the local representative of the other party to the contract, or if there is no local representative where the consumer is to stay then contact details of a local agency able to give assistance (or failing that, other emergency contact number to enable the consumer to contact the other party to the contract during the stay).
- Where [a school trip or similar] journey abroad is to be made by a minor, information enabling direct contact to be made with the child or the person responsible at the child's place of stay.
- Information about optional insurance policies to cover the cost of cancellation by the consumer or the cost of assistance, including repatriation, in the event of accident or illness.

Again, no civil liability arises from breach of these requirements: reg. 27. But contravention is a criminal offence: reg. 8(3).

## 13. Form and contents of the contract

The contract terms must be set out in writing or in such other form as is comprehensible and accessible to the consumer, and communicated to the consumer before the contract is made; and a written copy supplied: reg. 9(1)(b). This requirement does not apply in the case of last-minute bookings: reg. 9(2). Depending on the nature of the package, the contract must contain at least the matters specified in Schedule 2: reg. 9(1)(a). These elements comprise:

(1) The travel destination(s) and the relevant periods of stay, with dates.

(2) The means, characteristics and categories of transport to be used and the dates, times and points of departure and return.

(3) Where the package includes accommodation, its location, its tourist category or degree of comfort, its main features and, where the accommodation is to be provided in an EU member State, its compliance with the rules of that State.

(4) The meal plan.

(5) Whether a minimum number of persons is required for the package to take place and, if so, the deadline for informing the consumer in the event of cancellation.

(6) The itinerary.

(7) Visits, excursions or other services included in the package's agreed total price.

(8) The name and address of the organiser, retailer and any insurer.

(9) The price of the package, an indication of any possibility of price revisions [see **15** below], and an indication of any tourist taxes or landing, embarkation or disembarkation fees where these dues are not included in the cost of the package.

(10) The payment schedule and method of payment.

(11) Special requirements [e.g. dietary] which the consumer has communicated to the organiser or retailer when making the booking and which both have accepted.

(12) The periods within which the consumer must make any complaint about the failure to perform or the inadequate performance of the contract.

[On complaints, see further **19** below.]

There is an implied contractual term stipulating compliance with these requirements by the other party to the contract: reg. 9(3).

## 14. Transfer of bookings

If the consumer is *prevented* from taking the package the booking may, on reasonable notice to the other party to the contract, be transferred to another person who satisfies all the conditions [e.g. as to age] applicable to the package.

Upon such transfer, both the original consumer and the transferee become jointly and severally liable for payment of the balance due and any additional costs arising from the transfer: reg. 10.

## 15. Price revisions

Contract terms purporting to permit price revisions are automatically void unless they provide for decreases as well as increases, and unless they satisfy other conditions: reg. 11(1). These require that:

- The contract states precisely how the revised price is to be calculated; and
- The contract provides that price revisions are to be made solely to allow for variations in transport costs (including fuel), dues, taxes or fees for services, or applicable exchange rates: reg. 11(2).

No price increase may be made within 30 days before the departure date; nor may an increase be charged for increased costs of less than 2%: reg. 11(3). Increases of less than 2% have to be absorbed by the organiser. There is, however, no upper limit, though the consumer may be entitled to cancel under reg. 12 (see **16** below).

## 16. Significant alteration to essential terms and cancellation

Where the organiser is *constrained* before the departure date to alter significantly an essential term of the contract (such as a permitted price revision), he must notify the consumer as soon as possible: reg. 12. The consumer may then accept the alteration or withdraw from the contract without penalty. The consumer must notify the organiser accordingly as soon as possible (or lose the benefits of reg. 12).

Where the consumer withdraws from the contract under the term implied by reg. 12, or where the organiser by reason other than the consumer's default cancels the package before the departure date, then the consumer is entitled to choose:

**(a)** to take a substitute package of equivalent or superior quality if the other party to the contract can offer this; *or*

**(b)** to take a substitute package of lower quality if the other party to the contract can offer this, whereupon the consumer may recover the difference in price from the organiser; *or*

**(c)** to receive a total refund: reg. 13.

Upon withdrawing from the contract following significant alteration to an essential term, or on cancellation by the organiser (otherwise than due to the consumer's default), the consumer is entitled, if appropriate, to be compensated by the organiser for non-performance of the contract. The exceptions to this entitlement are cases of *force majeure* – which does *not* include overbooking! – and cases where the package is cancelled because of insufficient numbers and the consumer has been given written notice within the period indicated in the description of the package: reg. 13(3).

## 17. Default as to services to be provided

Terms are also implied if a significant proportion of the services contracted for is not provided, or if the organiser realises that he will be unable to procure a significant proportion of the services. In either eventuality the organiser must make alternative arrangements, at no extra cost to the consumer, and (where appropriate) compensate the consumer for the difference: reg. 14. If it is impossible to arrange alternative services, or if the alternatives are not accepted by the consumer for good reasons, the organiser must provide the consumer with equivalent transport back to the place of departure or other agreed returning point and (where appropriate) compensate the consumer: reg. 14(3).

## 18. Liability for proper performance of contractual obligations

The Regulations go beyond the duty of care required by the common law and the Supply of Goods and Services Act 1982 (see **5** above). *The other party to the contract is liable to the consumer for the proper performance of the contractual obligations irrespective of whether they are to be performed by that other party or by other suppliers of services*: reg. 15(1). This severe rule amounts to *strict* civil liability. Liability, though strict, is however not absolute, because the organiser (or retailer) will *not* be liable when:

- The failures in proper performance of the contract are attributable to the consumer; *or*
- The failures are attributable to a third party *unconnected* with the provision of the services contracted for, and are unforeseeable or unavoidable; *or*
- The failures are due to *force majeure*: i.e. unusual and unforeseeable circumstances beyond the control of the organiser, the consequences of which could not have been avoided; or an unforeseen event which could not have been forestalled, even if all due care had been exercised by the organiser or by the supplier of services: reg. 15(2).

Nevertheless, in these circumstances (other than fault by the consumer) the organiser is under an implied obligation to give prompt assistance to a consumer in difficulty: reg. 15(7).

> *Note*: nothing in reg. 15 affects any remedy which the other party to the contract may have against a defaulting supplier of services: reg. 15(1).

In cases of damage other than personal injury resulting from the non-performance or improper performance of the services involved in the package, the contract may include a term providing for *reasonable* limitation of liability: reg. 15(4). The contract may also limit liability in accordance with the international conventions governing such services: reg. 15(3).

## 19. Complaints

If the consumer complains about a defect in the performance of the contract, the other party to the contract is under an implied obligation to make, whether or not through his local representative, prompt efforts to find an appropriate solution: reg. 15(8). As a corollary, the contract must clearly and explicitly oblige the consumer to communicate any complaint at the earliest opportunity, and in writing or any other appropriate form, to the supplier of the services concerned and to the other party to the contract: reg. 15(9).

## 20. Financial security

The other party to the contract must at all times be able to provide sufficient evidence of security for the refund of money paid over and for the repatriation of the consumer in the event of insolvency: reg. 16. This evidential requirement is reinforced by criminal law sanctions: reg. 23 and Sched. 3. No civil liability arises from non-compliance: reg. 27. There are further detailed requirements, backed by criminal law sanctions, as to a bonding system to cover refunds and repatriation costs in the event of insolvency: regs. 17–22.

## 21. Enforcement and sanctions

Many of the requirements under the Regulations are a matter for the civil law, as noted where appropriate above. But regs. 5, 7, 8, 16 and 22 (see **11, 12** and **20** above) involve *criminal offences*. Enforcement of these criminal law sanctions is the duty of local weights and measures authorities (usually called 'Trading Standards Departments'): reg. 23 and Sched. 3. Liability is strict, subject to the usual 'due diligence' defence (see **23** below). The various offences concerned carry, on summary conviction, a fine not exceeding level 5 on the standard scale [£5,000]; and on conviction on indictment, a fine. No contract is void or unenforceable, and no right of action in civil proceedings arises, by reason only of the commission of an offence: reg. 27.

## 22. 'By-pass' provision

Where the commission by any person of an offence under the Regulations (as enumerated in **21** above) is due to the act or default committed by some other person *in the course of any business of his*, the other person is guilty of the offence and may be prosecuted and punished whether or not proceedings are taken against the first-mentioned person: reg. 25(1). Conniving directors, managers or other similar officers of bodies corporate may also be prosecuted and punished: reg. 25(2).

## 23. The 'due diligence' defence

This defence is typical in consumer protection matters and in the Regulations follows the formulation in the Consumer Protection Act 1987, s. 39. Thus the Regulations provide that in proceedings against any person for an offence [as enumerated in **21** above] it is a defence for that person 'to show that he took all reasonable steps and exercised all due diligence' to avoid committing the offence: reg. 24(1). The onus is thus on the defendant to prove his defence on the balance of probabilities, and in the absence of suitable procedures properly monitored, and adequate staff training and supervision, the court is not likely to be satisfied.

Where this defence involves alleging the act or default of another, or reliance on information given by another, seven clear days' notice before the hearing must be served on the prosecution, identifying the third party so far as this is possible: reg. 24(2), (3). Reliance on information given by another will not avail unless the defendant shows that it was reasonable in all the circumstances to have relied on the information, having regard in particular to whether there was any reason to disbelieve the information and also to the steps taken to check it: reg. 24(4).

There is also a defence of innocent publication of a brochure where an offence has been committed under reg. 5 (see 11 above), i.e. it is a defence for the person charged to prove that he is a person whose business it is to publish or arrange for the publication of brochures and that he received the brochure for publication in the ordinary course of business and had no reason to suspect that its publication would amount to an offence under the Regulations: reg. 24(5).

## Progress test 10

1. What, typically, is the legal status of the travel agent at common law? In what circumstances might the travel agent be liable to the consumer under the common law? Does self-regulation through a code of conduct have any role to play here?

2. What is the basis of liability of the tour operator under the common law? How does the ABTA Tour Operators' Code of Conduct modify the common law position?

3. For the purposes of the Package Travel, Package Holidays and Package Tours Regulations 1992, define:
   'organiser'
   'retailer'
   'brochure'
   'offer'
   'contract'
   'consumer'
   'the other party to the contract'.

4. What are the elements of a 'package' for the purposes of the 1992 Regulations?

5. What sanctions does the law impose if retail travel agents supply consumers with misleading descriptive matter relating to a package, its price or other contractual conditions?

6. Under the 1992 Regulations, what information must be contained in any brochure supplied? What are the sanctions for failure to observe the requirements?

7.  Under the 1992 Regulations, what information must the other party to the contract disclose to the intending consumer before the contract is concluded; and what information must be provided before the start of the journey? What is the sanction for failure to comply with these requirements?

8.  The 1992 Regulations stipulate an implied contractual term of compliance with certain requirements as to the contents (and form) of the contract. What are the essential elements of the contract?

9.  Is the consumer entitled to transfer his or her booking in any circumstances? If so, on what terms?

10. How do the 1992 Regulations deal with the problem of price increases?

11. In what circumstances is the organiser entitled significantly to alter an essential term of the contract? How may this be done and what then are the consumer's choices and/or rights to compensation?

12. In what circumstances (if any) do the 1992 Regulations permit a tour operator justifiably to alter the specified accommodation, or cancel the package holiday altogether, on the grounds respectively of:
    (i) overbooking; or
    (ii) insufficient numbers?

13. What duties do the 1992 Regulations impose on the organiser when a significant proportion of the services contracted for are actually or prospectively not provided?

14. In *Davey* v. *Cosmos Air Holidays* it was held that Cosmos knew, or should have known, about a reported health risk at a Portuguese resort and should have taken precautions to minimize or eliminate the risk and have warned their customers accordingly. If the facts were to recur today, how would reg. 15 of the 1992 Regulations apply to the case?

15. Consider the facts of *Wilson* v. *Best Travel*, viz: the plaintiff, while staying at a Greek hotel (in 1986) booked through Best Travel, was seriously injured after tripping and falling through glass doors at the hotel. The doors complied with Greek but not British safety standards. The plaintiff based his claim on breach of contract, either (i) breach of implied term that the hotel structure would be reasonably safe; or (ii) breach of the duty in s. 13 of the Supply of Goods and Services Act to exercise reasonable care and skill to see that the hotel was reasonably safe, i.e. to ensure that the hotel had been regularly and competently inspected for safety. The plaintiff's case, it will be recalled, failed. Do you think that a different conclusion would be reached if the case were to be decided today under reg. 15 of the 1992 Regulations?

16. Charles and Diana, who are both stressed executives, book a 'relaxing luxurious and romantic winter weekend in Paris' together, through Hopeful Holidays plc, who arrange the travel and accommodation. Unfortunately the journey on the cross-Channel ferry is marred by the presence of a drunken football crowd, and the train journey to Paris is greatly delayed when the French locomotive repeatedly breaks down. Charles and Diana arrive in Paris very late and too vexed and tired to enjoy their holiday. The accommodation turns out to be a grand but rather dilapidated hotel and its central heating system was not functioning. How should Charles and Diana complain and how should Hopeful Holidays plc respond? What is the legal liability of Hopeful Holidays in respect of the various mishaps?

17. How are consumers protected against the possibility of insolvency by the other party to the contract?

18. Identify the provisions in the 1992 Regulations which carry criminal law sanctions, and explain the 'due diligence' defence and how it may be invoked if a third party is to be blamed. Can that third party be prosecuted as well or instead?

# 11

# PRODUCT LIABILITY

## THE CONSUMER'S CONTRACTUAL RIGHTS

### 1. The statutory rights

It will be recalled that in respect of defect in title and defective goods the consumer has certain inalienable rights (or 'statutory rights') under the Sale of Goods Act and other legislation by virtue of the Unfair Contract Terms Act (*see* **6:19, 20**). These rights will be available to the consumer as against the manufacturer of the defective product if, and only if, the manufacturer is also the seller of the product direct to the consumer. Normally, of course, the product will reach the consumer indirectly, through a retailer, with whom the consumer makes the contract of sale. This result, that the statutory rights avail the consumer against the seller alone, arises by virtue of the doctrine of privity of contract.

### 2. Privity of contract

The doctrine asserts that only a party to a contract can take rights (or for that matter, obligations) under it. Therefore only a party to a contract can sue or be sued on it. In practical terms, this means that in respect of a breach of the statutory rights, the consumer can sue only the seller, and even this action is not open to the consumer unless he is also the buyer. It is not possible for a non-contracting party, such as a member of the consumer's family, or a friend, or the recipient of the goods as a gift, or a subsequent private purchaser from the consumer, to sue the original seller, unless the buyer can be construed as acting as the agent for the non-contracting party (e.g. where a wife acts as agent for her husband). The doctrine of privity is thus a severe limitation on the efficacy of the consumer's statutory rights. The consequence is that an action by the consumer against the manufacturer will normally have to be based either in contract on the manufacturer's guarantee (if any) or in tort.

> *Daniels* v. *White and Tarbard* (1938): Mr Daniels purchased some lemonade from Mrs Tarbard. The lemonade, manufactured and bottled by R. White & Sons Ltd. had somehow been contaminated by carbolic acid, which made both Mr and Mrs Daniels ill. It was held that Mr Daniels could succeed on a claim against Mrs Tarbard under the Sale of Goods Act. But note that Mrs Daniels had no claim against Mrs Tarbard as she had not bought the lemonade and so was not a party to the contract. (For her claim against the manufacturers, *see* **11**.)

*Note*: A retailer who is liable to a customer for breach of the statutory rights in the Sale of Goods Act can normally seek an indemnity from his own supplier for breach of the Act, who in turn can claim against his supplier and so on back through each link in the chain of distribution to the manufacturers (*see Godley* v. *Perry* (5:**11**)).

## 3. Manufacturers' guarantees

Provided that the consumer knows about the guarantee before he makes the contract with the retailer, and that he fulfils any requirements imposed by the manufacturer (e.g. return of a guarantee card), then the consumer can establish a 'collateral' contract with the manufacturer and can sue on it. To adopt the technical language of the law of contract, the 'offer' is found in the terms of the guarantee (which have to be communicated to the consumer before acceptance), while the act of purchasing the goods from the retailer, and the fulfilment of any other requirements of the guarantee, constitute both the 'acceptance' of and the 'consideration' for the contract of guarantee. The consumer has become privy to a contract with the manufacturer. In other words, the parties have entered into a direct and enforceable contractual relationship together. Some argue that even if the consumer's first notion of the 'offer', say the registration card from the manufacturer, is when he or she opens the box, the affixing of a stamp and the completion of all the many and detailed questions often found upon it will constitute the mechanics of a contract. Of course, they may also guarantee the inclusion of the consumer on so-called 'junk' mailing lists!

> *Note*: A manufacturer's guarantee is often called a 'warranty'. This use of the word 'warranty' must not be confused with the same word 'warranty' in its alternative meaning of minor contractual term, as opposed to a 'condition'. The meaning which the word carries will be clear from the context in which it is employed.

> *Carlill* v. *Carbolic Smoke Ball Co.* (1893): this famous case is a forerunner of the enforceability of guarantees. Mrs Carlill bought a smoke ball on the strength of an advertisement by the defendants in which they offered to pay £100 to anyone who caught influenza after using one of their smoke balls in the prescribed way. 'To show their sincerity' the defendants deposited £1,000 with named bankers. Mrs Carlill used the smoke ball in the prescribed way but nevertheless caught influenza. She sued for the £100. HELD: She was entitled to succeed. The advertisement was an offer to the world at large, which Mrs Carlill had accepted by buying and using the smoke ball as prescribed; in the absence of any requirement to the contrary, there was no need to communicate 'acceptance' of the guarantee to the defendants.

It should be clearly understood that if the consumer does sue on a guarantee, his only rights are those granted by the guarantee itself. Thus if the guarantee provides for repair of goods and replacement of defective parts, then that is all that the consumer is entitled to under the guarantee; he cannot claim as against the manufacturer that his statutory rights have been infringed, a point often misunderstood.

> *Note*: It is increasingly common to find the sellers of 'white' goods (refrigerators, cookers, freezers, etc.) and 'brown' goods (TVs, hi-fis, etc.) offering so-called 'extended

guarantees', e.g. 'five years of trouble-free viewing'. In reality these are no more than insurance contracts. They are usually expensive, say 25% of the purchase price of the goods. The wise consumer will consider the value of such a deal in the light of the *probability* likelihood of failure of the goods, and the cost of repair, at a time beyond the consumer rights attached by the SGA and whatever manufacturer's guarantee may be available to him.

*Note*: For the proposed *consumer guarantee* and the *European Commission's Green Paper on Guarantees and After-Sales Services* (COM (93) 509), *see* 5:9.

## 4. Unfair Contract Terms Act

Section 5 of the Act provides that where goods are of a type ordinarily supplied for private use or consumption, a manufacturer's guarantee cannot exclude or restrict liability for defects in the goods while in consumer use, resulting from negligence during manufacture or distribution of the goods. Goods are to be regarded as 'in consumer use' when in use otherwise than exclusively for the purposes of a business. Section 5 does not apply to a dealer's guarantee (*see* 6:**18**).

Prior to the enactment of s. 5, manufacturers' guarantees sometimes took away more rights than they actually awarded, in which case a consumer would have been well advised not to accept the guarantee by returning the guarantee card (if any). Now, however, it is impossible for the consumer, in consequence of accepting a guarantee, to lose the right to sue the manufacturer or a distributor in the tort of negligence. But s. 5 does not strictly speaking create new rights; it merely prevents the consumer from being deprived of his common law right to sue a negligent manufacturer or distributor. The manufacturer is not subjected to strict liability for defective products – negligence must still be proved as a condition of liability. Further, nothing in s. 5 alters the rule that the manufacturer is not liable (apart from any obligations specifically assumed under the guarantee) in contract, whether for breach of the statutory rights or for breach of any other contractual obligations of the seller.

## 5. Criminal law sanction

The Consumer Transactions (Restrictions on Statements) Order 1976 makes it a criminal offence for a guarantee to contain a statement describing or limiting obligations (whether legally enforceable or not) accepted by the manufacturer in relation to goods, without accompanying that statement by a further statement clearly and conspicuously to the effect that the statutory rights of the consumer against the seller are not affected (Art. 5). The law's policy here is to resort to the threat of criminal law sanctions in an attempt to prevent consumer ignorance of the statutory rights from being exploited, for example by the display of a 'no refunds' sign (*see* 6:**24**).

# THE CONSUMER'S RIGHTS IN TORT

## 6. Negligence

So far as an action against the manufacturer is concerned, at common law the alternative to suing on the guarantee (if there is one) is to sue in tort – the tort of negligence. In order to succeed in a negligence action, the plaintiff must prove more than the mere existence of carelessness. He must prove:

**(a)** that the defendant was under a duty of care to him; *and*

**(b)** that there has been a breach of that duty; *and*

**(c)** that as a result the plaintiff has suffered damage which is not too remote.

## 7. The duty of care

The leading case is *Donoghue* v. *Stevenson*.

> *Donoghue* v. *Stevenson* (1932): the assumed facts on which the decision as to legal principle was based were that Mrs Donoghue visited a cafe and there drank from a bottle of ginger beer which had been bought for her by a friend. Among the contents of the bottle Mrs Donoghue then discovered a decomposing snail, previously hidden by the opaque glass of the bottle. Mrs Donoghue became ill and claimed damages from the manufacturer. HELD (but only 3:2): The manufacturer of goods sold by him to a retailer or other distributor in circumstances which prevent the retailer or ultimate consumer from discovering by inspection any defect, is under a legal duty of care to the ultimate consumer to take reasonable care that the goods are free from any defect likely to cause injury or damage (House of Lords).

> *Note*: (1) The 'ultimate consumer' need not necessarily be a purchaser but could be anyone foreseeably injured by a dangerous product. (2) The defect need not necessarily be a defect in the actual manufacturing process; it may equally be in the design, or in the container, or even in the labelling of the goods.

*Donoghue* v. *Stevenson* is authority for the much wider proposition underlying the development of the whole concept of the duty of care in negligence, namely that . . . 'You must take reasonable care to avoid acts or omissions which you can reasonably foresee would be likely to injure your neighbour. Who, then, in law is my neighbour? The answer seems to be – persons who are so closely and directly affected by my act that I ought reasonably to have them in contemplation as being so affected when I am directing my mind to the acts or omissions which are called in question' (Lord Atkin). Students of tort, being aware of this wider 'neighbour principle', often overlook that *Donoghue* v. *Stevenson* is in essence a product liability case, authority for the narrower proposition given in the text above that a negligent manufacturer is liable to an ultimate consumer who suffers damage.

## 8. Product must be dangerous and cause injury or damage

The extent of the duty of care owed by the manufacturer to the ultimate consumer is limited by the rule that the defect must be such that it actually results in 'injury to the consumer's life or property' (Lord Atkin in *Donoghue* v. *Stevenson*). It is not enough for the product merely to be defective; it must also be dangerous. For example, if the consumer buys an iron which will not heat up, the manufacturer has no liability in the tort of negligence, whereas if the iron overheats and causes a fire, then the manufacturer, if negligent, will be liable. Stamp LJ in *Dutton* v. *Bognor Regis UDC* (1972) CA put the matter this way: 'I may be liable to one who purchases in the market a bottle of ginger beer which I carelessly manufactured and which is dangerous and causes injury to person or property; but it is not the law that I am liable to him for the loss he suffers because what is found inside the bottle and for which he has paid money is not ginger beer but water.'

> *Junior Books Ltd* v. *Veitchi* (1982): JB engaged a building company to build a factory for them. Their architect nominated specialist sub-contractors (V) to lay a concrete floor. There was no contractual relationship between JB and V. Owing to V's negligence the floor developed cracks. It was not dangerous, but it would require expensive maintenance. JB claimed the cost of replacing the floor and consequential financial loss including loss of profits from V. HELD by a majority of the House of Lords: Where, as here, the proximity between the producer of faulty work or a faulty product and the user was sufficiently close, the duty of care owed by the producer extended beyond a duty merely to prevent harm to the user's person or property but included a duty to avoid defects in the work or product itself. In such a case the cost of remedying the defects in the work or product or of replacing it, and any consequential financial loss, was recoverable by the user, notwithstanding the lack of a contractual relationship between producer and user.

> *Note*: *Junior Books* was initially regarded by many as a landmark in the development of the law of tort, extending the circumstances in which damages for pure economic loss, not consequential on personal injury or damage to property, will be recoverable (if foreseeable: *see* 13). But at present the law still stops short of creating a general manufacturer's warranty of quality in tort for a defective article which has not caused personal injury or damage to other property. 'The concept of proximity must always involve, at least in most cases, some degree of reliance . . . between an ultimate purchaser and a manufacturer [it] would not easily be found to exist in the ordinary everyday transaction of purchasing chattels when it is obvious that in truth the real reliance was on the immediate vendor and not on the manufacturer' (Lord Roskill). Indeed, the House went smartly into reverse on the *Junior Books* decision: *Leigh and Sullivan* v. *Aliakmon Shipping* (1986), and the Privy Council too: *Candlewood Navigation Corporation* v. *Mistui OSK Lines* (1985). In *Simaan General Contracting* v. *Pilkington Glass* (1988), Dillon LJ said that the *Junior Books* decision had been 'the subject of so much analysis and discussion that it cannot now be regarded as a useful pointer to any development of the law', and in *D & F Estates* v. *Church Commissioners* (1988) the House of Lords reverted to the original position regarding pure economic loss – that unless it is consequent upon physical damage it is not recoverable in tort. This has now been applied in *Department of the Environment* v. *Bates* (1989) and most importantly by a

seven-member House of Lords in *Murphy* v. *Brentwood DC* (1990), where it was firmly emphasised that recovery of pure economic loss, such as repair or replacement costs for useless or valueless goods, is to be left to contract law; even the cost of averting the risk of personal injury or damage to property is a matter of pure economic loss and is not recoverable against the manufacturer under the law of tort.

## 9. Intermediate examination

For the duty of care to arise, the defect must not be such that the manufacturer could reasonably have expected the consumer or retailer to discover and remedy it before loss was caused. There must be 'no reasonable possibility of intermediate examination' (Lord Atkin in *Donoghue* v. *Stevenson*; it will be remembered that the ginger beer bottle was opaque and so precluded intermediate examination). Where there does exist a reasonable opportunity of intermediate examination of the goods, the retailer will bear liability in negligence for defective goods. But in today's legal climate it is clear that if the manufacturer for his part is to escape liability, Lord Atkin's 'reasonable possibility of intermediate examination' requires that there is a reasonable expectation of intermediate examination.

> *Grant* v. *Australian Knitting Mills Ltd* (1936): the purchaser of a pair of underpants contracted dermatitis because the garment contained excessive sulphite. Could the consumer reasonably have been expected to wash the underpants before wearing them for the first time, and so wash out the excess sulphite? HELD: This was not to be expected.

> *Holmes* v. *Ashford* (1950): the plaintiff contracted dermatitis from hair dye. Instructions had been issued by the manufacturers that the dye might be dangerous to certain skins, and they advised a test. The hairdresser read the warning but ignored it and made no test. HELD: The hairdresser was liable but not the manufacturer.

> *Evans* v. *Triplex Glass Co. Ltd* (1936): a car windscreen suddenly and for no apparent reason shattered one year after purchase of the car, causing injury. HELD: The manufacturers of the windscreen were not liable as there was the likelihood of an intermediate examination by the makers of the car. Nor had the windscreen been proved to be defective when its manufacturers put the product into circulation.

## 10. Joint liability

Liability for a defective product may rest jointly upon both manufacturer and retailer. This possibility will be an important consideration where one defendant's financial resources are greater than the other's. The retailer will, for instance, be jointly liable in negligence (quite apart from any liability of the retailer under the Sale of Goods Act) where he sells an untested product which he has acquired from an unreliable source. In these circumstances liability would be joint and several, i.e. either or both parties could be sued. Of course the plaintiff would not obtain double damages by suing both parties. But he would have the tactical advantage of being able to obtain his damages from the defendant most likely to pay up, leaving it to the two defending parties to seek an indemnity or apportionment of loss between themselves under the Civil Liability (Contribution) Act 1978.

*Fisher* v. *Harrods Ltd* (1966): the plaintiff was injured by a bottle of cleaning fluid which exploded. The doctrine of privity of contract meant that the plaintiff had no action for breach of the statutory rights, the bottle having been purchased by a friend. But HELD: The sellers were liable in negligence for selling an untested product which they had obtained from an unreliable source. The manufacturers were not sued, otherwise they would have been found liable too. This case shows a clear policy toward retailers – that they should choose their suppliers with care.

## 11. Breach of duty of care

Given that a duty of care exists within the limitations specified in 8 and 9 above, it still does not follow that the consumer will succeed in an action for negligence against the manufacturer. He must prove that the manufacturer failed to exercise reasonable care. The test of such failure is whether, on balance of probabilities, it is a reasonable inference to be drawn from the evidence that the harm was so caused. Thus in *Grant* v. *Australian Knitting Mills Ltd* 'If excess sulphites were left in the garment, that could only be because someone was at fault. The appellant is not required to lay his finger on the exact person in all the chain who was responsible, or to specify what he did wrong. Negligence is found as a matter of inference from the existence of the defects taken in connection with all the known circumstances . . .' The point is that it would be an impossible task for a consumer to identify exactly how the defect occurred, for he has no knowledge of the defendant's manufacturing process. It is enough that the consumer can identify a defect which *prima facie* ought not to be there.

The burden of proof is then shifted on to the manufacturer to answer the inference of negligence and satisfy the court that he took reasonable care. This reversal in practice of the burden of proof led the Royal Commission on *Civil Liability and Compensation for Personal Injury* (*see* 16) to conclude that reversal of the burden by legislation would usually make no difference to the consumer. Yet even so the problem of proving breach of duty can defeat the claimant in a consumer case. In *Daniels* v. *White* (*see* 2), Mrs Daniels failed in her claim against the manufacturers because the court was satisfied, too easily perhaps, that they had answered the inference of negligence by proving the existence of a good system of work under proper supervision at their factory. So Mrs Daniels recovered no compensation from either the seller or the manufacturers.

*Note*: *Daniels* v. *White* was not followed in *Hill* v. *James Crowe (Cases) Ltd* (1978), where Mackenna J held that it was not enough for the manufacturer of a badly made wooden packing case to prove that he had a good system of work and proper supervision at his factory. In the circumstances one of the manufacturer's workmen must have been negligent, and the manufacturer was vicariously liable. *Daniels* v. *White* must now be viewed as wrongly decided, at least to the extent that it omitted to consider the issue of vicarious liability for negligence by a member or members of the workforce; after all, it seems that the judge was satisfied in that case that a proper system of checking could consist of a 14-year-old girl sniffing the bottles emerging from a cleansing process! Admittedly, it is always dangerous to judge 1930s circumstances through 1990s spectacles.

## 12. Breach of statutory duty

Contravention by manufacturer or retailer of safety regulations under the Consumer Protection Act 1987, Part II, will not only be a criminal offence but will also allow any person affected by the contravention to bring an action for breach of statutory duty. Chapter 21 treats this aspect of product liability in detail.

## 13. Remoteness of damage

The final fact that the plaintiff has to prove in a negligence action, having proved the existence of a duty of care and breach of that duty, is damage which is not too remote. In tort this means that loss will be irrecoverable unless reasonably foreseeable as a consequence of the breach of duty (the rule established by *The Wagon Mound* (1961)). But the defendant does not have to be able to foresee the precise circumstances in which the damage occurs in order to be fixed with liability. It is enough that the manufacturer or retailer foresees, or ought reasonably to foresee, the general kind of damage against which he should guard. If the damage of that kind which actually occurs is then simply more extensive than could have been anticipated, this is no defence; nor is it a defence that the precise manner in which the damage was inflicted could not have been anticipated. Damage in tort will be 'foreseeable' and not too remote, even if 'very improbable', or only 'liable to happen in the most unusual case' (to adopt expressions used by the House of Lords in *The Heron II, Koufos* v. *Czarnikow* (1969)). Again, the fact that an individual consumer may be particularly susceptible to certain kinds of injury, because he has (say) an unusually thin skull or an unusually weak heart, does not exculpate the defendant (the 'egg-shell skull' principle, which, expressed colloquially, means that 'you take your victim as you find him').

Subject to these rules, then, damages (including where appropriate loss of earnings and damages for pain and suffering) will be recoverable in respect of personal injury and death, and property damage. The measure of damages will be on an indemnity basis, i.e. the compensation needed to restore the consumer to the financial position he would have been in had the breach of duty never occurred. (Contrast this basis of assessment of damages in tort with 'expectancy damages' in contract: *see* 9:**1**.)

## 14. Contract or tort?

The great advantage of a negligence action is that it is not restricted by the doctrine of privity. On the other hand its great disadvantage is that the manufacturer may succeed in rebutting the inference of negligence (by proving that he was not to blame, he acted reasonably). Contrast a contractual action for breach of the statutory rights. While subject to limitations by the doctrine of privity, this has the great advantage that once the breach is established liability is strict, i.e. it exists whether the seller has been negligent or not. But it seems that there may be little difference between contract and tort so far as the question of remoteness of damage is concerned (*see* 9:2).

> *Frost* v. *Aylesbury Dairy Co.* (1905): typhoid germs were found in milk. The dairy as seller was held liable under what is now s. 14(3) of the Sale of Goods Act, even though the exercise of all reasonable skill by the dairy could not have detected the defect which caused the germs.

# PART I OF THE CONSUMER PROTECTION ACT 1987

## 15. Strict liability

As the foregoing paragraphs have noted, under the common law a consumer may have no remedy at all in respect of loss caused by defective goods. This may be because there is no privity of contract and the manufacturer cannot be demonstrated to have been negligent. But whatever the reason, the possible absence of an adequate remedy led to demands for reform of the law relating to product liability. These demands reflected developments in the United States, where judicial activity had imposed strict liability on manufacturers and distributors for death or injury caused by defective products.

## 16. Proposals

Four proposals should be noted as of historical interest:

**(a)** Strasbourg Convention on Products Liability in regard to Personal Injury and Death (open for signature from 1977).

**(b)** Directive on Liability for Defective Products, presented by the Commission of the EEC to the Council adopted in 1985 and implemented in the UK by the Consumer Protection Act 1987, Part I.

**(c)** Report on Liability for Defective Products by the Law Commission (Cmnd 6831, 1977).

**(d)** Report of the Royal Commission on Civil Liability and Compensation for Personal Injury (under the chairmanship of Lord Pearson, Cmnd 7054, 1978).

## 17. Recommendations of the proposals

Broadly, these proposals advocated the following:

**(a)** Producers (both of finished products and components) should be subject to strict liability in tort for death or personal injury caused by defective products. A product is to be regarded as 'defective' when it does not provide the safety which a person is entitled to expect, having regard to all the circumstances including the presentation of the product.

**(b)** Distributors should not be strictly liable, except where they fail to disclose the identity of the supplier of the defective goods, or where they sell them exclusively under their own brand name, or where they import the goods.

**(c)** The producer should have a defence where the product was not defective when he put it into circulation. His strict liability should in any event be subject to a cut-off period of ten years from the circulation of the product.

## 18. The EC Directive on Product Liability

This was implemented by Part I of the Consumer Protection Act 1987 (hereafter CPA) which was brought into force on 1 March 1988. Part I of the CPA does not apply to any product supplied by its producer before Part I was brought into force: s. 50(7).

## 19. The Part I strict liability regime

Strict civil liability – i.e. liability without proof of negligence or fault and aside from any limitations imposed by privity of contract principles – is imposed on the producer of a defective product which causes loss or damage: s. 2.

'Product' means all goods (including components or raw materials comprised in another product, but not 'primary agricultural goods' – *see* **20**) and electricity: s. 1(2). But a person who supplies a product in which components or raw materials are comprised is not to be treated by reason only of his supply of the finished product as supplying any of the components or raw materials: s. 1(3).

> *Note*: Unlike both the Council Directive on general product safety (92/59/EEC) (implemented in the UK by the General Product Safety Regulations 1994) and Part II of the CPA – which co-exist to make it a *criminal* offence to supply any unsafe consumer product – civil liability under Part I CPA covers all goods (as defined above) and is *not* restricted to consumer goods. The 1994 Regulations and Part II CPA are considered in Part Two of this book, which deals with criminal law sanctions.

## 20. Liability of 'producer' and others

Liability under s. 2 is imposed primarily on the 'producer' of the product, a term which includes within its ambit not just manufacturers but also producers of raw materials and those who carry out an industrial process on goods: s. 1(2).

Furthermore, liability under s. 2 extends beyond producers to certain other traders, namely:

**(a)** any person who holds himself out as the producer by putting his name or mark on the product ('own-brand' products)

**(b)** any person who imports the product into the Community (note not necessarily into the UK, so an injured consumer might find himself able to sue a company which imported the product from the Far East into France, from where they were further traded into England)

**(c)** the supplier of the product where he cannot identify the producer or importer or his own supplier (e.g. because his bookwork is slovenly): s. 2(2), (3).

Where two or more persons are liable under Part I for the same damage, their liability is joint and several: s. 2(5).

*Note*: Liability under s. 2 does not extend to producers of game or agricultural produce not industrially processed: s. 2(4). The UK has chosen *not* to exercise the option of derogating from the Directive here by including unprocessed agricultural produce or game within the scope of the strict liability regime.

## 21. Meaning of 'defect'

A product is defective 'if the safety of the product is not such as persons generally are entitled to expect': s. 3. In determining this question all the circumstances are to be taken into account, including:

**(a)** the manner in which, and purposes for which, the product has been marketed, its get-up, the use of any mark in relation to the product and any instructions or warnings about the use of the product

**(b)** the use to which it could reasonably be expected that the product would be put

**(c)** the time when the product was supplied by its producer.

A defect is not to be inferred from the fact alone that the safety of a product which is supplied after that time is greater than the safety of the product in question.

## 22. Defences

By virtue of s. 4, in any proceedings under Part I it is a defence for the defendant to show:

**(a)** that the defect is attributable to compliance with any requirement imposed by or under any enactment or with any Community obligation

**(b)** that the defendant did not at any time supply the product in question

**(c)** that the product was not supplied in the course of a business

**(d)** that the defect did not exist in the product at the time of supply

**(e)** 'that the state of scientific and technical knowledge' when the actual product was supplied 'was not such that a producer of products of the same description as the product in question might be expected to have discovered the defect if it had existed in his products while they were under his control': s. 4(1) (*e*)

**(f)** that, in the case of a manufacturer of a component, the defect was wholly attributable to the design of the product in which the component has been fitted or to compliance with instructions given by the producer of that product.

*Note*: The defence in s. 4(1)(*e*) above is the so-called 'development risks' or 'state of the art' defence, which the UK has chosen to include among the defences, having declined to exercise the option given in the Directive of derogating from the Directive on this point by disallowing the development risks defence. Some commentators have seen this defence as reintroducing the concept of fault by the back door. Product liability is about loss distribution (an economic concept), not fault (a moral one). In any case, Article 7(e) of the Directive is seemingly more stringent: the producer has to prove 'that the state of scientific and technical knowledge at the time when he put the product into circulation was not such as to enable the existence of the defect to be discovered' – an objective test. Under the principles of EU law (reviewed, for instance, in *Faccini Dori* v. *Recreb Sri* [ECJ]) national legislation must, as far as possible, be interpreted to comply with any relevant Directive; if not possible, the defaulting member state may be liable to make good loss caused to individuals by the failure to implement the Directive properly.

It may be added that a producer cannot avoid or reduce his liability merely because damage was caused both by a defect in his product and by the act of omission of a third party (e.g. a negligent supplier handling a defective product); but in such a case the producer may have recourse against the third party for apportionment of loss as between themselves.

## 23. Damage giving rise to liability under Part I

By virtue of s. 5 this is limited to:

**(a)** death or personal injury

**(b)** any loss of or damage to any property (including land) which at the time of the loss or damage is (*i*) of a description of property ordinarily intended for private use, occupation or consumption, and (*ii*) intended by the person suffering the loss or damage mainly for his own private use, occupation or consumption. No damages can be awarded under Part I in respect of loss or of damage to such property unless the amount to be so awarded exceeds £275.

No liability exists under Part I in respect of any loss of or damage to the defective product itself or to the whole or any part of any product which has been supplied with the defective product comprised in it.

Note: Article 16 of the Directive gives Member States an option of introducing an upper financial limit on liability, resulting from the same defect in identical items, of not less than 70 million ecu (about £40 million). The UK has decided *not* to exercise this option.

## 24. Contributory negligence

Where the person suffering the loss or damage has been contributorily negligent, damages may be reduced or disallowed under the Law Reform (Contributory Negligence) Act 1943: s. 6(4) CPA.

## 25. Limitation of actions

There is a limitation period of three years for the bringing of proceedings, commencing the day on which the claimant became aware, or should reasonably have become aware, of the damage, the defect, and the identity of the producer. There is an absolute cut-off period of ten years from the date on which the actual product was supplied, unless the claimant has in the meantime instituted proceedings: s. 6 and Sched. 1.

## 26. Exclusion clauses

The producer (or other defendant) is prevented from limiting or excluding his liability under Part I by any contract term, notice or other provision: s. 7.

## 27. Causation

While Part I of the CPA means that the claimant no longer has to prove negligence or fault in respect of damage covered by Part I, it will be appreciated that the claimant still has to prove that the product was defective (as defined in 21 above), and that the damage was caused by the defect.

## 28. Existing rights unaffected

The producer's liability under Part I is without prejudice to any right of the victim to bring a claim under the existing laws of contract or tort: s. 2(6). That is, CPA Part I is an addition to consumer protection, it does not repeal or replace rights ('as well', not 'instead').

## Progress test 11

1. What is the doctrine of privity of contract? How does it operate to restrict the consumer in seeking redress for loss caused by defective goods?

2. In what circumstances will a manufacturer's guarantee be enforceable against him by a consumer?

3. A manufacturer's guarantee reads: 'Should these goods prove to be defective in any way within twelve months from date of purchase, the manufacturer will repair them or, at his option, replace them free of charge. No further liability whatsoever can be accepted'.
   (a) Is the exclusion cause effective?
   (b) Does the issue of the guarantee with the goods constitute a criminal offence?

4. What does the consumer have to prove in order to succeed in an action in negligence against a manufacturer?

5. In what circumstances will a retailer (but not the manufacturer) be liable to the consumer in negligence? When will the retailer be jointly liable with the manufacturer? Precisely describe the nature of this claim, if one exists.

6. A student buys a pocket electronic calculator, which he is allowed to use in his examinations. The calculator does not perform certain mathematical functions properly, with the consequence that the student fails his examinations. Does the student have a good claim in law against the manufacturer?

7.  Does the consumer have to prove negligence on the part of the manu-facturer, or does the manufacturer bear the burden of disproving it?

8.  What additional remedy does the consumer have in respect of a contra-vention of safety regulations made under the Consumer Protection Act 1987?

9.  When will damages in negligence be too 'remote' to be recoverable?

10. What are the advantages and disadvantages of an action against a retailer in negligence, as opposed to an action against him for breach of the statutory rights under the Sale of Goods Act? How has the position been improved by the implementation of CPA Part I?

11. What is meant by the 'state-of-the-art' defence within CPA Part I? Why might it be subjected to the scrutiny of the European Court?

# 12

# ADVERTISING

## 1. Definitions

Advertising is a means of passively promoting products and services. It is conducted using audio and visual media, including printed material such as newspapers and magazines, posters, hoardings and leaflets. Television, whether terrestrial or satellite, radio and even the famous computer 'superhighway' are all used by advertisers.

The principal difference between media advertising and promotion is that the latter is an advertisement which is on-pack or perhaps at the point of sale and it provides an active product purchase incentive. That is, it usually involves audience participation of one sort or another! So advertising and sales promotion are functionally distinct but complementary instruments used for the publicity and promotion of products.

## 2. Self-regulation

The principal control over advertising in the UK is achieved by voluntary codes of practice: the British Code of Advertising Practice and the British Code of Sales Promotion Practice. First published more than thirty years ago, revised versions were implemented in February 1995. In a press release announcing the new version the ASA explained that 'The basic principles of the Codes, which are supervised by the Advertising Standards Authority, have remained unchanged since they were originally drawn up in 1961. These are that advertisements should be legal, decent, honest and truthful; that advertisements should be prepared with a sense of responsibility to consumers and to society; and that they should respect the principles of fair competition generally accepted in business.

The following is a selection of the new rules:

- Decency – 'Advertisements should contain nothing that is likely to cause serious or widespread offence. Particular care should be taken to avoid causing offence on the grounds of race, religion, sex, sexual orientation or disability'.
- Alcohol – 'No medium should be used to advertise alcoholic drinks if more than 25% of its audience is under 18 years of age'.
- 'Consumers should not be encouraged to drink and drive. Advertisements . . . should not suggest that the effects of drinking alcohol can be masked and should include a prominent warning on the dangers of drinking and driving'.

- 'Advertisers should ensure that low-alcohol drinks are not promoted in a way that encourages their inappropriate consumption and should not depict activities that require complete sobriety'.
- Children – 'Parental permission should be obtained before they are committed to purchasing complex and costly goods and services'.
- 'Advertisements should not actively encourage them [children] to eat or drink at or near bedtime, to eat frequently throughout the day or to replace main meals with confectionery or snack foods'.
- 'Promotions addressed to children should not encourage excessive purchases in order to participate . . . should make clear that parental permission is required if prizes and incentives might cause conflict between children and their parents, e.g. animals, bicycles, holidays'.
- Motoring – 'Advertisers . . . should not make speed or acceleration claims the predominant message of their advertisements'.
- Environmental claims – 'Claims such as "environmentally friendly" . . . should not be used without qualifications unless advertisers can provide convincing evidence that their product will cause no environmental damage'.
- 'If a product has never had a demonstrably adverse effect on the environment, advertisements should not imply that the formulation has changed to make it safe'.
- 'Advertisers must not use fear or anxiety to promote medicines or recovery from illness'.
- 'Advertisements for medicines should not be addressed to children'.
- 'Advertisements should not suggest that it is desirable to be underweight'.
- 'Promotions should be designed and conducted in a way that respects the right of consumers to a reasonable degree of privacy and freedom from annoyance'.

The Codes are administered by the CAP Committee (Committee of Advertising Practice), whose members are drawn from the advertising industry. Complaints from consumers, or bodies representing consumer interests, go to the Advertising Standards Authority, which was set up by the advertising industry. The ASA has an independent chairman, and two-thirds of its members are drawn from outside advertising.

Sanctions for breach of the Code include adverse publicity from the reports issued by the ASA in respect of complaints investigated. Ultimately the media may deny defaulting advertisers advertising space, and defaulting agencies may be denied trading facilities. Nevertheless the weakness of the Code, a weakness common to all self-regulatory codes, is that in the last resort the code is voluntary and lacks the force of law.

The system is funded by surcharges on advertising and direct marketing expenditure. The money is collected by the Advertising Standards Board of Finance. This is a body that operates independently of the ASA and the CAP, thus ensuring impartiality of judgement.

The ASA deals with advertisements in print: in newspapers and magazines, on posters and hoardings. The advertising of financial services is supervised by a number of regulatory bodies and consumer credit advertising is checked by Trading Standards officers. The ASA covers cinema and home video advertising, but we have the Radio Authority (under the Broadcasting Act 1990) dealing with commercials on radio and the Independent Television Commission handling TV. With financial and pharmaceutical adverts and those directed at children Trading Standards officers deal with the incorrect or misleading, but the ITC handles complaints suggesting that particular adverts are just objectionable.

There are also several codes of practice operated by trade associations in specific sectors, such as the British Direct Marketing Association and the Mail Order Traders' Association.

## 3. Legal sanctions

English law contains no generalized provisions controlling advertising. There are, however, numerous statutes which bear upon advertising. Since the Codes of Practice were first published the number of statutes aimed at consumer protection has greatly increased. There are now more than 100 UK statutes, orders and sets of regulations affecting advertisements and promotions.

Perhaps most significant are the Consumer Credit Act 1974 (*see* 14:**1–4**) and the Trade Descriptions Act 1968. The 1968 Act in prohibiting false trade descriptions at the same time necessarily prohibits false and misleading advertisements. False statements about the quality or price of goods, or the existence of facilities or services, can be attacked in this way. Moreover the consumer, aided by the Misrepresentation Act 1967, may be able to bring a civil claim in respect of misrepresentation if such is the effect of the advertisement. But English law is ill-adapted to deal with the more subtle case of misleading advertising – the undue emphasis, ambiguity, suggestion by association, etc. Nor is advertising 'puff' controlled.

## 4. Directive on Misleading Advertising

This Directive was adopted by the EEC Council of Ministers in June 1984 (84/450/EEC), and implemented in the UK by means of the Control of Misleading Advertisements Regulations 1988. The Regulations are intended to protect consumers, traders and the public interest from misleading advertising, defined as 'any advertising which in any way, including its presentation, deceives or is likely to deceive the persons to whom it is addressed or whom it reaches and which, by reason of its deceptive nature, is or is likely to injure a competitor of the person whose interests the advertisement seeks to promote'.

The UK has given effect to the Directive through strengthening the existing system of self-regulation. The Director General of Fair Trading now has the power, as a last resort, to seek a court order banning misleading advertising under the self-regulatory system. That is, complaints are routed through the ASA and if their self-regulatory mechanisms fail, the Director can and has acted. There have been some interesting cases so far: a misleading slimming advertisement (Tobyward) and homeworking schemes (Blinkhorn) where injunctions were obtained, a timeshare development sales campaign (Home Ownership Exchange) where the Director accepted an assurance of future good conduct drawn in the same terms as he would have requested an injunction, as he did, with claims about undistributed estates (Central Records Research), depilatory products (Antony Green & Co. and Lavery Rowe Advertising), and a variety of false assertions of relationships with the OFT (CR Properties, Hintonview Ltd. and Mercantile Corporation Ltd). In October 1994 Connell Residential, a chain of estate agents, assured the DGFT that they would desist from erecting 'sold' boards outside properties where no sale had taken place.

In 1993 the DGFT received 246 complaints about misleading advertising. This was a considerable increase on previous years. In 1994 the number declined by 43.5% to 139.

## 5. Fair trading

The Director General of Fair Trading is responsible for reviewing practices which may adversely affect the economic interest of consumers and this responsibility includes review of advertising practices.

## Progress test 12

1. How does English law presently deal with the control of advertising generally? Contrast this control with the control mandated by the EEC Directive.

2. Describe the self-regulatory system of control over advertising adopted by the UK advertising industry.

3. Does the Director General of Fair Trading have a role to play in the control of advertising?

4. What is the ASA? How is it funded?

5. What are the general principles underlying the Codes administered by the ASA?

6. Describe the correlation between the medium within which an advertisement appears and the nature of the regulatory controls that exist over that advertisement.

# 13

# CONSUMER CREDIT: INTRODUCTORY

## INTRODUCTION TO THE CONSUMER CREDIT ACT

### 1. Crowther Committee Report on Consumer Credit

English law regulating credit had developed in a characteristically *ad hoc* way, with the consequence that much depended on the legal technicalities in which a particular credit transaction was framed, irrespective of the real substance of that transaction. The Crowther Committee was appointed by the government to review the whole field of consumer credit and it reported in 1971 (Cmnd 4596). The Committee were concerned at 'the serious anomalies arising from the division of credit transactions into legally distinct compartments and from failure to accord a uniform treatment to a range of security devices all designed to achieve the same objective'. The Report's recommendations so far as they concerned the consumer credit law – as distinct from its recommendations for a separate Lending and Security Act rationalizing the law of security – received government approval in the White Paper *The Reform of the Law on Consumer Credit* (Cmnd 5472, 1973), and were duly enacted (with modifications) in the Consumer Credit Act 1974. The provisions of the Act were brought into force in stages over a period of years, the process not finally being completed until 19 May 1985. (In this and subsequent chapters the Consumer Credit Act is referred to as 'the Act' or 'CCA'.)

### 2. Scope of the Act

The Act comprehensively regulates the provision of any form of financial accommodation to individuals (including unincorporated firms), subject to a ceiling of £15,000. (On questions concerning 'extortionate credit bargains' this limit does not apply.) All methods of supplying credit are controlled. Banks, finance houses, mail order firms, retailers, moneylenders, pawnbrokers, ancillary credit businesses (credit-brokers, debt adjusters, debt counsellors, debt collectors, credit reference agencies: cf. s. 145 CCA), etc. – all are controlled by the Act and subjected to the licensing system (*see* 19:6) which it establishes.

The Act may be described as a skeleton in that it comprises the fundamental structure of the control over consumer credit, but requires for its flesh the detailed further provisions as to its operation contained in the many regulations and orders made under the Act.

## 3. Find one's way round the Act

The Act contains several helpful features of draftsmanship. These include the following:

**(a)** A comprehensive definition section (s. 189) defining, or directing the reader to the definition of, the terms used by the Act.

**(b)** A summary (Sched. 1) of the thirty-five offences created by the Act, together with an indication of the appropriate sanction to which contravention renders the wrongdoer liable.

*Note*: When construing a statute it is frequently difficult to determine whether infringement of any particular requirement allows the victim to bring a civil action against the wrongdoer for, e.g., breach of statutory duty. In this respect the Act gives specific guidance: 'A breach of any requirement made (otherwise than by any court) by or under this Act shall incur no civil or criminal sanction as being such a breach, except to the extent (if any) expressly provided by or under this Act': s. 170(1). It may be added that while breach of the CCA may carry with it no further sanction, such breach (or breaches) will be a factor to be taken into account by the Director General of Fair Trading in exercising his licensing functions under the Act: s. 170(2).

**(c)** A series of examples (Sched. 2) illustrating by a full analysis the use of the terminology employed by the Act. In the case of conflict between Sched. 2 and any other provision of the Act, that other provision prevails: s. 188(3).

# BASIC CONCEPTS AND DEFINITIONS

## 4. Consumer credit agreement

A consumer credit agreement is a personal credit agreement by which the creditor provides the debtor with credit not exceeding £15,000: s. 8(2). A personal credit agreement involves the granting of credit by the creditor to an individual (which includes a partnership or other unincorporated body: s. 189, s. 8(1)). 'Credit' includes any form of financial accommodation: s. 9(1).

## 5. Consumer hire agreement

The Act also controls consumer hire agreements because in substance a hire agreement often amounts to the giving of financial accommodation. Furthermore, many hire agreements, such as the rental of TVs, often give the hirer the use of the equipment for all, or at least most of, its useful life. A consumer hire agreement is an agreement by which goods are bailed to an individual (the 'hirer', which includes a partnership or other unincorporated body: s. 189), where the agreement is such that it:

**(a)** is not a hire-purchase agreement; *and*

**(b)** is capable of subsisting for more than three months; *and*

**(c)** does not require the hirer to make payments exceeding £15,000: s. 15.

> *Note*: (1) A consumer hire agreement need only be *capable* of lasting for more than three months – it need not necessarily do so. (2) Hire-purchase agreements fall within the definition of consumer credit agreements.

## 6. Regulated agreements

This is the key concept in the Act, for the Act controls only regulated agreements (except for the controls over advertising and extortionate credit bargains, which are of wider application). A 'regulated agreement' is a consumer credit agreement, or consumer hire agreement, other than an exempt agreement: s. 189.

Before turning to the meaning of exempt agreement (*see* **7**), we may note that the effect of the definitions considered so far is to subject to the Act's control agreements involving financial accommodation where the party accommodated is an individual (as defined above) and where the amount of the credit does not exceed £15,000. The ceiling of £15,000 refers to the amount of the credit granted, and does not take into account the interest thereon. With regard to hire-purchase agreements (defined below: *see* **14**) the Act specifically provides for the amount of credit to be computed as the total price of the goods less the aggregate of any deposit or down-payment and the total charge for credit: s. 9(3).

> *Note*: (1) By s. 189, 'total price' means 'total sum payable by the debtor under a hire-purchase agreement or a conditional sale agreement including any sum payable on the exercise of an option to purchase, but excluding any sum payable as a penalty or as compensation or damages for a breach of the agreement'; and (2) by the same provision 'total charge for credit' means a sum calculated in accordance with regulations under s. 20(1). (The regulations referred to are the Consumer Credit (Total Charge for Credit) Regulations 1983.)

In the case of conditional sale and credit-sale agreements (defined below: *see* **15, 16**) the amount of credit is similarly computed. The amount of credit provided will be the total price less any deposit and the total charge for credit. In the case of cash loans of a fixed sum the amount of credit is simply the amount of the loan.

## 7. Exempt agreements

As has just been seen, the meaning of exempt agreement is an important element in the definition of regulated agreement. An exempt agreement is not regulated by the Act. Exempt agreements are defined in s. 16 of the CCA, and fall into one of two broad categories:

**(a)** Section 16(2) exempts mortgages for the purchase of land or the provision of dwellings on land where the mortgage is granted either (*i*) by a local authority or building society; or (*ii*) by an insurance company, friendly society, organization of employers or organization of workers, charity, land improvement company, or body corporate named or specifically referred to in any public general Act. The institutions listed in (*ii*) have to be specified in an order made by the

Secretary of State if they are to be exempted. The relevant order is the Consumer Credit (Exempt Agreements) Order 1989 (as amended).

**(b)** Section 16 also gives the Secretary of State power to exempt certain other agreements where the number of payments does not exceed a specified number or the rate of interest does not exceed a specified maximum: s. 16(5). Section 16 further provides for the exemption by order from regulated consumer hire agreements of agreements covering the hire of meters for gas, electricity, or water, or equipment provided by a 'specified public telecommunications operator': s. 16(6), as amended by the Telecommunications Act 1984. The Consumer Credit (Exempt Agreements) Order 1989 gives effect to these exemptions and spells out the details (*see* **8**). The very need for such exemptions to be specified emphasizes the exhaustive nature of the Act's control over consumer credit.

## 8. The Consumer Credit (Exempt Agreements) Order 1989 (as amended)

Under this Order exempt agreements include the following:

**(a)** Debtor-creditor-supplier agreements for fixed-sum credit where payment is to be made in not more than four instalments. (The terms 'debtor-creditor-supplier' and 'fixed-sum credit' are defined below: *see* **10, 11**.) This exemption covers ordinary account or trade credit, e.g. the milkman's or newsagent's bill or the retailer's account to be settled at the end of the month. The exemption does not apply to any hire-purchase, conditional sale or pledge agreements.

**(b)** Debtor-creditor-supplier agreements for running-account credit where repayment of the whole amount of the credit taken up in each accounting period has to be made by a single payment. ('Running-account credit' is defined below: *see* **11**.) Credit cards are an example of running-account credit, and this exemption covers, for instance, Diners Club and the American Express green card (but not, e.g., Barclaycard, Access, or the American Express gold card) precisely because the terms on which the first-named cards are issued require settlement of the entire periodical account by a single payment with no facility for extended credit. The exemption would also cover, for instance, a credit account at a shop of the kind where the consumer is sent a monthly statement to be settled in full by a single payment.

**(c)** Agreements where the maximum interest does not exceed 13 per cent or 1 per cent above the highest of the London and Scottish Clearing Banks' base rates 28 days before the agreement is made, whichever is higher. This exemption is designed to cover cheap loans extended by business to employees. It applies only to debtor-creditor agreements (defined below: *see* **10**), i.e. it does not apply in cases where the credit supplied is linked with the supply of goods or services by a seller who has a business connection with the creditor. So a credit sale where, say, the retailer allows the consumer to pay off the purchase price over several months without imposing a charge for credit will be exempt (if exempt at all) under the exemption mentioned in **(a)** above.

123

## 9. No contracting out

By s. 173(1) of the CCA, any term in any agreement inconsistent with a provision in the Act for the protection of the debtor or hirer or his relative or surety, is void. But nothing in s. 173(1) prevents a thing from being done in relation to any person which would normally require the authority of an order of the court or the Director General of Fair Trading, if that person consents at the time to its being done: s. 173(3).

## 10. Debtor-creditor-supplier agreements and debtor-creditor agreements

These expressions look formidable and, indeed, the definitions (ss. 12, 13) are rather complex. They have been described as impenetrably obscure! But the essence of the matter is as follows. A debtor-creditor-supplier agreement is one where the creditor is also the supplier of the goods or services or has an existing or contemplated business connection with the supplier. A debtor-creditor agreement, on the other hand, is one where the creditor is not also the supplier and has no existing or contemplated business connection with him. In a debtor-creditor agreement the creditor merely provides the debtor with the needed credit facilities.

Examples of debtor-creditor-supplier agreements include hire-purchase, conditional sale and credit-sale agreements, and transactions whereby goods or services are paid for by credit card. Example of debtor-creditor agreements include the ordinary bank loan or overdraft, and personal loans by finance houses in cases where there is no business connection between the creditor and the supplier of any goods or services financed by the loan (i.e. the lender has no particular interest in the way the 'financial accommodation' is used).

## 11. Running-account credit and fixed-sum credit

Running-account credit is credit which is made available under a personal credit agreement where the credit fluctuates up to a permitted maximum, as is the case, for example, with credit cards. Periodical payments made by the debtor 'top-up' the amount of credit available: s. 10(1)(*a*). All credit other than running-account credit is fixed-sum credit: s. 10(1)(*b*). Hire-purchase, conditional sale and credit-sale agreements all involve fixed-sum credit.

## 12. Restricted-use credit and unrestricted-use credit

The definitions of these in s. 11 express a fairly simple concept. Restricted-use credit is a regulated consumer credit agreement involving credit which is earmarked to finance a particular transaction and the money is paid direct to the supplier of the goods or services (as for instance under hire-purchase, conditional sale and credit-sale agreements). Unrestricted-use credit involves cases where the money goes through the hands of the debtor (as for instance when a finance house gives the debtor a personal loan). In such cases the credit will still be unrestricted-use credit even though a term of the agreement requires the debtor to use the money in a certain way and any other use would be a breach of contract. For example, suppose that a finance house makes a personal loan to the debtor on condition that the money be used to finance an extension to the debtor's house. If the money is paid direct to the builder it will be restricted-use credit; whereas if the money is paid to the debtor in the first instance it will be unrestricted-use credit, and it would still be so even if another use of the money (e.g. to finance a holiday) by the debtor would amount to a breach of contract.

## 13. Linked transactions

The definition of linked transaction (s. 19) is complex. Basically, however, a linked transaction is one which is ancillary to the regulated agreement. The idea is that a linked transaction is to be treated under the Act as if it had been part of the regulated agreement itself. In particular, the debtor's right of cancellation (*see* 15:**12–15**) is to apply to a linked transaction in the same way as it applies to the regulated agreement: s. 69(1). Further, a linked transaction entered into before the making of the principal agreement has no effect until such time (if any) as that agreement is made: s. 19(3).

> *Note*: By virtue of the Consumer Credit (Linked Transactions) (Exemptions) Regulations 1983, certain linked transactions are excluded from the operation of ss. 19(3) and 69(1). The exempted linked transactions are contracts of insurance; other contracts in so far as they contain a guarantee of goods; and transactions comprising or effected under agreements for the operation of deposit and current accounts.

One type of situation caught by s. 19 is where the ancillary transaction is entered into in compliance with a term of the principal (regulated) agreement. For example, where the debtor is obligated by the principal agreement to enter into a maintenance contract in respect of consumer durables which he is acquiring under a regulated hire-purchase or conditional sale agreement, that maintenance contract would be a linked transaction. It would, therefore, be cancelled or terminated along with the principal agreement should that occur.

Another type of situation caught by s. 19 is where the principal agreement is a debtor-creditor-supplier agreement and the ancillary transaction in question is financed or to be financed by the principal agreement. For example, if the debtor uses a credit card to obtain goods or services, the contract by which he obtains them is a linked transaction.

The concept of a limited transaction is important for at least two reasons: if and when a regulated agreement can be cancelled, the limited transaction falls too, and when an evaluation is being made as to whether a credit transaction is extortionate, any linked transactions will be taken into account.

# HIRE-PURCHASE, CONDITIONAL SALE AND CREDIT-SALE AGREEMENTS

## 14. Hire-purchase agreement

This is an agreement, other than a conditional sale agreement, under which:

**(a)** goods are bailed in return for periodical payments by the bailee; *and*

**(b)** the property in the goods will pass to the bailee if the terms of the agreement are complied with and the bailee exercises an option to purchase the goods: s. 189.

The retailer may finance the hire-purchase agreement himself, but often the arrangement is a tripartite one. That is, the retailer sells goods to a finance house and the finance house lets the goods out on hire-purchase terms to the consumer. The finance house has, in effect, made a secured loan to the debtor.

## 15. Conditional sale agreement

This is an agreement for the sale of goods (or land) under which the purchase price or part of it is payable by instalments, and property is to remain in the seller (notwithstanding that the buyer is to be in possession) until such conditions as to the payment of instalments or otherwise as may be specified in the agreement are fulfilled: s. 189.

While a conditional sale at common law technically involves an agreement for *sale*, the policy of the CCA is to assimilate the legal incidents of hire-purchase and conditional sale. So far as regulated consumer credit agreements are concerned, the consumer is placed in the same position irrespective of whether the contract is technically hire-purchase or conditional sale.

## 16. Credit-sale agreement

This is 'an agreement for the sale of goods, under which the purchase price or part of it is payable by instalments, but which is not a conditional sale agreement': s. 189.

It will be noted that under a credit-sale agreement the consumer acquires title to the goods immediately upon making the contract. The creditor has, in effect, made an unsecured loan.

*Note*: Hire-purchase, conditional sale and credit-sale agreements will always be debtor-creditor-supplier agreements for fixed sum, restricted-use credit (*see* **10–12**).

## 17. Meaning of 'debtor' and 'creditor'

The CCA uses the term 'debtor' as meaning the individual receiving credit under a consumer credit agreement (s. 189), and therefore the term includes the hirer under a hire-purchase agreement and the buyer under a conditional sale or credit-sale agreement. Similarly the term 'creditor' means the person providing credit under a consumer credit agreement, and therefore includes the legal supplier of the goods (i.e. the retailer, or the finance house where the transaction is the typical tripartite one) in contracts of hire-purchase, conditional sale and credit-sale.

## 18. Terms control

Quite separate from the controls over hire-purchase, conditional sale and credit-sale agreements found in the CCA is the control over credit terms exercised by the government from time to time by orders made under the Emergency Laws (Re-enactments and Repeals) Act 1964 (as amended by Schedule 4, para. 23 of the CCA). Hire agreements are also controlled under the 1964 Act. The control is achieved by the stipulation of minimum deposits and by the limitation of the period over which repayment may be made. The object of exercising this control over credit terms is not to protect consumers by discouraging them from over-committing themselves, but rather to achieve a measure of monetary control over the economy. No credit restrictions under the 1964 legislation are currently in force.

## Progress test 13

1. How many offences does the CCA create? Where may a summary of them be found? Can the legal adviser know for certain whether contravention of any of the offences will allow the consumer to sue for breach of statutory duty?

2. Define (a) 'consumer credit agreement'; and (b) 'consumer hire agreement'. ✓

3. C agrees to bail goods to D (an individual) in return for periodical payments. The agreement provides for the property in the goods to pass to D on payment of a total a £22,500 and the exercise by D of an option to purchase. The sum of £22,500 includes a down-payment of £3,000. It also includes an amount which, according to the regulations made under s. 20(1) of the CCA, constitutes a total charge for credit of £4,500.
(a) Is this a hire-purchase, credit-sale, or conditional sale agreement?
(b) How much credit is provided under the agreement?
(c) Is the agreement a consumer credit agreement?
(cf. example 10, Sched. 2, CCA.)

4. Define 'regulated agreement', and consider whether the agreement in question 3, above, is such an agreement.

5. Consider whether the following agreements are regulated under the CCA:
(a) a building society mortgage
(b) rental of a British Telecom telephone
(c) newspaper deliveries, the account for which is presented monthly

(*d*) agreement for the use of a credit card

(*e*) a credit-sale agreement where the consumer has to pay the purchase price in six equal monthly instalments, no charge being made for credit.

6. Is it possible to contract out of the provisions of the CCA?

7. Explain the distinction between debtor-creditor-supplier agreements and debtor-creditor agreements.

8. (*a*) Consider whether the following agreements are debtor-creditor-supplier agreements or debtor-creditor agreements: (*i*) hire-purchase agreement; (*ii*) agreement for the use of a credit-card; (*iii*) a bank overdraft.

(*b*) Consider whether the agreements in (*i*), (*ii*) and (*iii*) above will involve running-account credit or fixed-sum credit.

(*c*) Consider whether the agreements in (*i*), (*ii*) and (*iii*) above will involve restricted-use credit or unrestricted-use credit. (Cf. examples 10, 16–18, Sched. 2, CCA.)

9. Give an example of a linked transaction and explain the significance of the concept.

10. Define and distinguish between (*a*) hire-purchase agreement; (*b*) conditional sale agreement; (*c*) credit-sale agreement.

# 14

# SEEKING CREDIT BUSINESS

## ADVERTISING CREDIT FACILITIES

### 1. Part IV Consumer Credit Act: its scope

Part IV applies to persons who:

**(a)** carry on a consumer credit business; *or*
**(b)** carry on a consumer hire business; *or*
**(c)** carry on a business in the course of which they provide credit to individuals secured on land: s. 43(2).

Part IV controls advertisements by such persons for business purposes, where the advertisement indicates that the advertiser is willing (*i*) to provide credit, or (*ii*) to enter into agreements for the bailment of goods by him: s. 43(1).

*Note*: 'Advertisement' is very broadly defined in s. 189 to include every form of advertising.

### 2. Exempt advertisements

Part IV does not control advertisements which indicate that the credit must exceed £15,000 and that no security is required, or that the security is to consist of property other than land, or that the credit is available only to a body corporate: s. 43(3). (Note that, subject to s. 43(3), the advertisement will be controlled under Part IV even if it does not relate to a regulated agreement.) An advertisement for the bailment of goods (i.e. for hire facilities) is outside Part IV if it indicates that the advertiser is not willing to enter into a consumer hire agreement: s. 43(4). The Secretary of State may by order provide that Part IV shall not apply to other advertisements of a description specified in the order: s. 43(5). Very broadly, regulations have exempted advertisements relating to agreements which are exempt agreements by virtue of the Consumer Credit (Exempt Agreements) Order 1989 (*see* 13:**7, 8**).

*Note*: The exemptions mentioned above are conferred by the Consumer Credit (Exempt Advertisements) Order 1985. It may be added that the figure of £15,000 mentioned above was raised from the original figure of £5,000 by the Consumer Credit (Increase of Monetary Limits) Order 1983.

## 3. Part IV controls

The controls, designed to secure 'truth in lending' (the basic policy behind the whole CCA), comprise the following:

**(a)** The Secretary of State is required to make regulations concerning the form and content of advertisements to which Part IV applies, with a view to ensuring that the advertisement conveys a fair and reasonably comprehensive indication of the nature of the credit or hire facilities offered by the advertiser and of their true cost to persons using them: s. 44(1).

> *Note*: Detailed regulations have been made pursuant to s. 44(1), namely the Consumer Credit (Advertisements) Regulations 1989. These regulations control the form and content of credit advertisements, dividing them into three distinct categories: simple, intermediate and full. They replaced earlier regulations and introduced new provisions which require advertisers to publish specified warnings in relation to loans secured on the debtor's home. In particular the warning: 'YOUR HOME IS AT RISK IF YOU DO NOT KEEP UP REPAYMENTS ON A MORTGAGE OR OTHER LOAN SECURED ON IT'. This, obviously, is designed to warn borrowers of the potentially dire consequences which can arise if they fail to repay a secured loan.

**(b)** In addition to the particularized disclosure requirements to be imposed under the regulations referred to in **(a)** above, the Act makes it an offence for advertisements to convey information which is in a material respect false or misleading: s. 46(1). Information stating or implying an intention on the advertiser's part which he has not got will be 'false' for this purpose: s. 46(2).

**(c)** It is an offence for an advertisement to which Part IV applies to indicate that the advertiser is willing to provide credit under a restricted-use credit agreement relating to goods or services, if the advertiser does not hold himself out as prepared to supply the goods or services for cash: s. 45.

**(d)** Advertisements by ancillary credit businesses (*see* 13:**2**) are covered (subject to exemptions) by the relevant parts of the above-mentioned controls: s. 151.

## 4. Advertising infringements

Where the advertiser commits an offence, a like offence is committed by the publisher, the deviser, and the person who procured the publication of the advertisement: s. 47(1). The publisher will have a defence if he proves that the advertisement was published by him in the course of a business and that he did not know or suspect that its publication would be an offence: s. 47(2). Further, the CCA contains the usual 'due diligence' type of defence (applicable generally to offences under the Act), i.e. it is a defence for the person charged to prove:

**(a)** that his act or omission was due to a mistake, or to reliance on information supplied to him, or to an act or omission by another person, or to an accident or some other cause beyond his control; *and*

**(b)** that he took all reasonable precautions and exercised all due diligence to avoid such act or omissions: s. 168(1).

Infringement does not affect the validity of any agreement subsequently entered into by the consumer (*see* s. 170(1)), unless of course the advertisement constitutes a misrepresentation or misdescription.

# CANVASSING

## 5. Canvassing off trade premises

The Act contains provisions designed to control the doorstep selling of credit. It is an offence to canvass debtor-creditor agreements off trade premises: s. 49(1). Canvassing involves making oral representations during visits made otherwise than in response to a previous request: s. 48(1). The request should also be in writing and signed, otherwise the salesman commits the offence of soliciting debtor-creditor agreements during visits made in response to a previous oral request: s. 49(2). Section 49 does not apply to debtor-creditor-supplier agreements, so canvassing of such agreements off trade premises is permissible, but only if the supplier of the credit has a licence specifically so providing: s. 23(3). (The debtor will have the benefit of the statutory 'cooling-off' period in cases where he signs a regulated agreement elsewhere than on business premises: *see* 15:**12–15**.)

## 6. Circulars to minors

A person commits an offence if, with a view to financial gain, he sends to a minor (i.e. someone under age eighteen) any document inviting him to:

**(a)** borrow money; *or*
**(b)** obtain goods on credit or hire; *or*
**(c)** obtain services on credit; *or*
**(d)** apply for information or advice on borrowing money or otherwise obtaining credit, or hiring goods: s. 50(1).

It is a defence for the person charged to prove that he did not know, and had no reasonable cause to suspect, that the recipient of the document was a minor: s. 50(2).

## 7. Unsolicited credit-tokens

It is an offence to deliver or send by post an unsolicited credit-token to a person: s. 51(1). This means that now it is, for instance, an offence for a bank to post unsolicited credit cards to its customers. (Credit-tokens also include checks, vouchers, coupons, stamps, etc., as defined in s. 14 of the CCA, and *see Re Charge Card Services Ltd* (1988).) Except in the case of a small (*see* 15:**1(c)**, *Note*) debtor-creditor-supplier agreement, the credit-token will be unsolicited unless the recipient has made a prior request for the token in a document signed by him: s. 51(2). Unsolicited credit-tokens are permissible, however, where the credit-token is for use under an existing agreement or in renewal or replacement of a previous token: s. 51(3).

> *Elliott* v. *DGFT* (1980): the Divisional Court upheld the conviction under s. 51(1) of footwear retailers who mailed to prospective customers an unsolicited plasticized card purporting to be a credit card valid for immediate use. The card was still a credit-token within s. 14, notwithstanding that it was not capable of contractually binding the issuer.

> *Note*: Under the CCA the debtor's liability for unauthorized use of a credit card (or other credit token) cannot commence before he either signs it (or a receipt for it), or first uses it: s. 66. Under s. 84, liability for misuse cannot exceed £50 (the limit imposed by the Consumer Credit (Increase of Monetary Amounts) Order 1983). The debtor is, however, liable without limit for loss arising from misuse of the credit-token by a person who acquired possession of it with the debtor's consent. No liability can arise after the creditor has been given notice of loss or theft. Nor can liability arise if the credit-token agreement does not contain the name, address and telephone number of the person to be contacted on loss of the credit-token. The Consumer Credit (Credit-Token Agreements) Regulations 1983 prescribe that these contact particulars have to be prominent and easily legible.

## 8. Quotations

Regulations may be made as to the form and content of quotations to customers by a person who carries on a consumer credit or consumer hire business, or a business in the course of which credit is provided to individuals secured on land: s. 52. The Consumer Credit (Quotations) Regulations 1989 have been made under this power. The regulations contain broadly similar provisions to those relating to the form and content of advertisements. The regulations also prescribe that a quotation must be provided in response to a request for written information made in writing, orally on the trader's premises or, in certain circumstances, by telephone.

## 9. Duty to display information

Regulations may be made requiring a person who carries on a consumer credit or consumer hire business, or a business in the course of which he provides credit to individuals secured on land, to display in the prescribed manner, prescribed information about the business at any premises where the business is carried on and to which the public have access: s. 53. No such regulations have been made.

# CREDIT-BROKERS AND CREDIT REFERENCE AGENCIES

## 10. Recovery of credit brokerage fees

The consumer may approach a credit-broker for introduction to a source of credit. By s. 155 of the CCA, a credit-broker is only entitled to a nominal sum of

£3 by way of fee or commission for his services, unless a 'relevant agreement' (which includes a regulated agreement) is entered into within six months of the broker introducing the consumer to the prospective source of credit.

*Note*: The sum of £3 mentioned above, and the sum of £1 mentioned in **11(b)** below, are the revised amounts as stipulated in the Consumer Credit (Increase of Monetary Amounts) Order 1983.

## 11. Credit reference agencies

During the process of negotiating an agreement a creditor or owner is likely to check up on the credit rating of the prospective debtor or hirer with a credit reference agency. The CCA protects consumers in the following ways:

**(a)** *Disclosure of identity of agency.* A creditor, owner or negotiator, at the request of a debtor or hirer received not more than twenty-eight days after the end of the antecedent negotiations, must disclose the name and address of any credit reference agency consulted about the debtor's or hirer's financial standing: s. 157.

*Note*: The Consumer Credit (Conduct of Business) (Credit References) Regulations 1977 contain additional disclosure requirements as to credit reference agencies consulted, where the negotiations have been conducted through credit-brokers.

**(b)** *Disclosure of filed information.* A credit reference agency is under a duty to give the consumer a copy of the file relating to him, the particulars being reduced into 'plain English' where necessary. The consumer must pay a fee of £1. The agency must send the consumer a statement in the prescribed form of his rights to have wrong information corrected: s. 158.

*Note*: The prescribed form, *inter alia*, may be found in the Consumer Credit (Credit Reference Agency) Regulations 1977.

**(c)** *Correction of wrong information.* A consumer given information under s. 158 may, if he thinks it is incorrect and likely to be prejudicial, require it to be removed or corrected. The agency has to inform the consumer within twenty-eight days whether it has removed the entry or amended the file (or taken no action), and if it has amended the file a copy of the amended entry must be supplied to the consumer. Within a further twenty-eight days a dissatisfied consumer may require the agency to add to the entry a notice of correction (not exceeding 200 words) supplied by the consumer. If the matter is then still in dispute, either the consumer or the agency may apply to the Director General of Fair Trading for his determination: s. 159.

## 12. Sanctions

Breach by the agency of any of the duties imposed by ss. 157–159 is an offence triable summarily.

## Progress test 14

1. What advertisements are controlled by Part IV of the CCA?

2. What are the Part IV controls over advertising?

3. Will (a) the advertiser, (b) the publisher, (c) the deviser, be liable for an advertisement which infringes the Part IV controls? What defence(s) will be available to these respective parties?

4. How (if at all) does the commission of an offence against the Part IV controls over advertising affect the legal position of the consumer?

5. How does the CCA attempt to curb the doorstep salesman?

6. A firm distributes from door to door throughout its locality circulars inviting applications to the firm for advice on borrowing money. A proportion of the circulars fall into the hands of young people under age eighteen. Has the firm committed an offence?

7. If the banks promoting the Access credit card were today to send a mass mailing of credit cards to customers, would that be an offence?

8. (a) AB Bank plc send C a credit card in renewal of a credit-token agreement. The card is lost in the post. What is C's liability (if any) under the CCA?
   (b) D's credit card is stolen by E, who uses it to make purchases totalling £100. What is D's liability (if any) under the CCA?

9. How is the giving of quotations controlled under the CCA?

10. How are (i) credit brokers and (ii) credit reference agencies controlled under the CCA?

# 15

# ENTRY INTO CREDIT OR HIRE AGREEMENTS

## 1. Exemptions

Part V of the CCA is concerned with entry into credit or hire agreements. Certain agreements, however, are exempted (by s. 74) from the Part V requirements, including:

**(a)** Non-commercial agreements (i.e. a consumer credit or consumer hire agreement not made by the creditor or owner in the course of a business carried on by him): s. 189.

**(b)** Debtor-creditor agreements for overdrafts on current accounts, where the Director General of Trading so determines.

**(c)** Small debtor-creditor-supplier agreements for restricted-use credit.

> *Note*: Section 17(1) defines a 'small agreement' as (*i*) a regulated consumer credit not exceeding £50, other than a hire-purchase or conditional sale agreement, *or* (*ii*) a regulated consumer hire agreement which does not require the hirer to make payments exceeding £50, being (in either case) an agreement which is either unsecured or secured by a guarantee or indemnity only (whether or not the guarantee or indemnity is itself secured). The sum of £50 mentioned here is the revised limit set by the Consumer Credit (Increase of Monetary Limits) Order 1983.

But while the above agreements are generally exempt from Part V, note that:

(*i*) the provisions as to antecedent negotiations (s. 56: *see* 16:3) apply to agreements within **(b)** and **(c)** above; *and*

(*ii*) in the case of **(c)** above, the provisions as to disclosure of information (s. 55) also apply;

(*iii*) in cases **(b)** and **(c)** above, regulations under s. 60 as to form and content of agreements (*see* 6) apply to any term of the agreement which is expressed in writing: s. 74.

## 2. Disclosure of information

Regulations may require specified information to be disclosed in the prescribed manner to the debtor or hirer before a regulated agreement is made. If the regulations are not complied with the agreement will be improperly executed: s. 55. No regulations under s. 55 have in fact been made.

(For the legal effects of improper execution of an agreement, *see* **9, 10**.)

## 3. Form and content

The Secretary of State is required to make regulations as to the form and content of regulated agreements: s. 60(1). The object of the regulations is to ensure that the debtor or hirer is made aware of his rights, duties, remedies, and the amount and rate of the total charge for credit. The regulations may require specified information to be included in the prescribed manner in documents, and other specified material to be excluded: s. 60(2). (The Director has power to waive any of the requirements in particular cases: s. 60(3).) Legibility is required: s. 61(1)(*c*). Breach of any of the requirements renders the agreement improperly executed: s. 61.

The detailed regulations required by s. 60 have been made. They are the Consumer Credit (Agreements) Regulations 1983 (as amended). The regulations provide that the agreement must be easily legible and must state the following information (*inter alia*):

**(a)** the amount of credit or credit limit

**(b)** the total charge for credit

**(c)** the amounts and timing of repayments

**(d)** the APR (Annual Percentage Rate)

**(e)** details of any security provided by the debtor.

The agreement must also contain prescribed statements of the protection and remedies available to the debtor under the CCA, chiefly in relation to cancellation (*see* **12–15**), termination (*see* 17:**4–6**), and repossession (*see* 18:**10, 11**), in so far as relevant to the type of agreement concerned.

## 4. Prescribed terms and express terms

The Consumer Credit (Agreements) Regulations 1983 also prescribe certain terms to be contained in the signed document itself (cf. s. 61(*a*) CCA). The prescribed terms relate to the amount of credit or credit limit; the rate of interest; and obligations as to repayments. All other terms (apart from implied terms) must be embodied in the agreement: s. 61(1)(*b*). 'Embodied' means that the agreement either sets out the terms or refers to another document in which they are set out: s. 189(4).

## 5. Signature

The agreement must be signed by the debtor or hirer *personally*, and it must also be signed by or on behalf of the creditor or owner: s. 61(1)(*a*). (Where the debtor or hirer is a partnership or unincorporated body, the agreement may be signed by or on behalf of such debtor or hirer: s. 61(4).) Improper signature means that the agreement is improperly executed: s. 61(1).

The Consumer Credit (Agreements) Regulations 1983 prescribe a form of signature box for the different types of regulated agreements. For example, the prescribed signature box in relation to hire-purchase agreements is as follows:

> This is a Hire-Purchase Agreement regulated by the Consumer Credit Act 1974. Sign it only if you want to be legally bound by its terms.
>
> Signature(s)
> of Debtor(s)
>
> Date(s) of signature(s)
>
> The goods will not become your property until you have made all the payments. You must not sell them before then.

If the agreement is a cancellable one (*see* **12**), immediately above, below or adjacent to the signature box there must appear a separate box containing prescribed statement of protection (cf. **6**):

> YOUR RIGHT TO CANCEL
>
> Once you have signed this agreement, you will have for a short time a right to cancel it. Exact details of how and when you can do this will be sent to you by post by the creditor.

## 6. Copies

Sections 62 and 63 of the CCA contain detailed provisions to ensure that the debtor or hirer receives at least one (and usually two) copies of the agreement (and any document referred to in it). Broadly, the position is as follows. If the unexecuted agreement is personally presented to the debtor or hirer for his signature, he must be given a copy there and then. If the unexecuted agreement is sent to the debtor or hirer for his signature, he must be sent a copy at the same time. If the agreement is not executed on signature by the debtor or hirer, he must be given a second copy within 7 days of the agreement being executed. In the case of a cancellable agreement (*see* **12**), the second copy must be sent by post (*see* **7** for further requirements).

Copies have to comply with regulations as to form and content: s. 180(1). The regulations which prescribe (in detail) the form and content of copies are the Consumer Credit (Cancellation Notices and Copies of Documents) Regulations 1983 (as amended). Copies must be easily legible.

Breach of any of the requirements as to the supply of copies renders a regulated agreement improperly executed: ss. 61–63.

## 7. Notice of cancellation rights

The Act contains special provisions as to notices where the agreement is cancellable (*see* **12**), with a view to ensuring that the debtor is informed about the right to cancel. If the agreement is cancellable, all copies referred to in **6** above must contain a notice in the prescribed form setting out the rights of cancellation: s. 64(1)(*a*). If only one copy of the agreement is required by the rules, a separate notice of cancellation rights must be sent by post within 7 days following the making of the agreement: s. 64(1)(*b*). (It has already been mentioned that in the case of a cancellable agreement, if a second copy is required it must be sent by post: s. 63(3).)

A notice of cancellation rights must indicate:

**(a)** the right of the debtor or hirer to cancel the agreement; *and*

**(b)** how and when to cancel it; *and*

**(c)** the name and address of a person to whom notice of cancellation may be given: s. 64(1).

The Consumer Credit (Cancellation Notices and Copies of Documents) Regulations 1983 (as amended) prescribe (in detail) the form and content of copies in conformity with s. 64.

A cancellable agreement is improperly executed if the requirement as to notices are not met: s. 64(5).

*Note*: By virtue of the Consumer Credit (Cancellation Notices and Copies of Documents) (Amendment) Regulations 1984, agreements which are not cancellable agreements within the meaning of the CCA but which confer on debtors or hirers similar rights of cancellation are to be treated as cancellable agreements for the purposes of giving copies under ss. 62 and 63 of the Act, and, under the Consumer Credit (Cancellation Notices and Copies of Documents) (Amendment) Regulations 1989, there are certain dispensations granted regarding copies of agreements relating to land.

## 8. Securities

The Act requires any security provided by a person other than the debtor or hirer in relation to a regulated agreement to be expressed in writing and in the prescribed form: s. 105 (and cf. the Consumer Credit (Guarantees and Indemnities) Regulations 1983). There are also provisions as to copies. Breach of these requirements means that the security is not properly executed.

## 9. Effect of improper execution of the agreement

The agreement will be enforceable against the debtor or hirer only on an order of the court: s. 65(1). The court must dismiss an application for enforcement if, but only if, it considers it just to do so having regard to the prejudice caused by the contravention and the degree of culpability for it. The court must also have regard:

**(a)** to its powers on making an order to impose conditions or suspend the operation of the order, and to vary any agreement or security; *and*

**(b)** to its powers to compensate the debtor or hirer by reducing or discharging any sum payable by him: s. 127.

## 10. Cases where no enforcement order can be made

In the following cases no enforcement order can be made whatever the other circumstances:

**(a)** where no agreement containing all the prescribed terms was signed by the debtor or hirer: s. 127(3)

**(b)** in the case of a cancellable agreement, where the debtor or hirer is not supplied with a (proper) copy of the executed agreement before the commencement of the proceedings: s. 127(4)(*a*)

**(c)** in the case of a cancellable agreement, where the requirements as to notice of cancellation rights were not complied with: s. 127(4)(*b*).

> *Note*: If the court declines to enforce an agreement (*see* **9**), or cannot make an order for its enforcement, one consequence is that the consumer can retain without further payment any goods in his possession under the agreement, for the reason that a retaking of goods is an 'enforcement' of the agreement: s. 65(2).

# THE RIGHT OF CANCELLATION

## 12. Cancellable agreements

A regulated agreement may be cancelled by the debtor or hirer if:

**(a)** there were antecedent negotiations;
**(b)** which included oral representations;
**(c)** which were made in the presence of the debtor or hirer; *and*
**(d)** the agreement was signed by the debtor or hirer otherwise than on permanent or temporary business premises of

(*i*) the creditor or owner, *or*

(*ii*) any party to a linked transaction (other than the debtor or hirer or relative of his), *or*

(*iii*) the negotiator in any antecedent negotiations: s. 67.

> *Note*: It appears from Example 4, in Sched. 2 to the Act, that negotiations by telephone are not made 'in the presence of' the debtor or hirer, and so if all the negotiations take place by telephone the agreement will not be cancellable. This is regarded as unfortunate by those who are depressed by the increasing use of telephones as marketing tools.

## 13. Cooling-off period

Cancellation may be effected by notice given by the debtor or hirer at any time between his signing of the unexecuted agreement and:

**(a)** the end of the fifth day following the day on which the debtor or hirer received the second statutory copy of the agreement, or, if no second copy was required, the statutory notice of cancellation rights

**(b)** alternatively, if the need for the statutory notice has been waived by the Director in the exercise of his powers (cf. s. 64(4)), the cooling-off period will terminate at the end of the fourteenth day following the day on which the debtor or hirer signed the unexecuted agreement: s. 68.

## 14. Notice of cancellation

By s. 69, the agreement is cancelled by the debtor or hirer serving notice ('however expressed') to that effect within the cooling-off period. Notice may be served on:

**(a)** the creditor or owner; *or*
**(b)** the person specified in the notice under s. 64(1) (*see* **7**); *or*
**(c)** the creditor's or owner's agent (including a credit-broker or supplier who is the negotiator in antecedent negotiations); *or*
**(d)** any person who, in the course of a business carried on by him, acts on behalf of the debtor or hirer in any negotiations for the agreement.

A notice of cancellation sent by post to a person is deemed to be served on him at the time of posting whether or not it is actually received: s. 69(7).

*Note*: No special form is mandatory for giving notice of cancellation, but the Consumer Credit (Cancellation Notices and Copies of Documents) Regulations 1983 (as amended) do prescribe an optional form of cancellation for use by the debtor or hirer. The creditor or owner must include the form in the second statutory copy of the agreement, or, if no second copy was required, in the statutory notice of cancellation rights.

## 15. Effects of cancellation

The notice operates to cancel the agreement and any linked transaction, save for those excepted by the Consumer Credit (Linked Transactions) (Exemptions) Regulations 1983 (*see* 13:**13**, *Note*): s. 69(1). The effects are as follows:

**(a)** All sums paid by the debtor or hirer are repayable, and all sums due cease to be payable: s. 70(1).

**(b)** The debtor or hirer has a lien over goods in his possession for any sum repayable to him on cancellation: s. 70(2).

**(c)** Under a restricted-use debtor-creditor-supplier agreement, or a consumer hire agreement, or a linked transaction, a debtor or hirer who is in possession of the goods is under a duty to restore them after cancellation of the agreement (subject to any lien he may have). The consumer may if he wishes send the goods back, but he need only redeliver the goods at his own premises. Meanwhile the consumer must take reasonable care of the goods, though this duty ceases after twenty-one days following the cancellation: s. 72.

**(d)** Where goods were taken in part-exchange, the negotiator (defined in s. 56(1) to include credit-brokers and suppliers) must return them to the consumer (in substantially as good a condition as when the consumer delivered them to the negotiator) within ten days of cancellation, otherwise a part-exchange allowance must be paid. The consumer has a lien over goods in his possession in respect of this obligation: s. 73.

**(e)** Except in the case of a debtor-creditor-supplier agreement for restricted-use credit, an agreement which has been cancelled continues in force as far as it relates to payment of credit and interest. But no interest is payable by the debtor on any sum repaid within one month of cancellation or, in the case of credit repayable by instalments, before the date on which the first instalment is due: s. 71. If credit repayable by instalments has not been wholly repaid by this date, the creditor must make a written and signed request in the prescribed form recalculating the remaining instalment: s. 71(3) and Consumer Credit (Repayment of Credit on Cancellation) Regulations 1983.

> *Note*: The effect of exercising a right to cancel was illustrated in *Global Marketing Europe v. Berkshire County Council Dept. of Trading Standards* (1994) where a timeshare agreement, which would otherwise have been subject to the cancellation rights contained within The Timeshare Act 1992, was held to have constituted a 'linked transaction' to the credit agreement which financed it. Thus the exercise of the cancellation rights under the CCA effectively cancelled the timeshare agreement as well.

## 16. Withdrawal from prospective agreement

If offer and acceptance have not yet taken place according to the normal rules of contract, the prospective debtor or hirer can withdraw by written or oral notice, however expressed: s. 57(1), (2). Withdrawal has the same effect as cancellation, even where the agreement if made would not have been cancellable. A notice to the debtor's or hirer's own negotiating agent will be sufficient: s. 57(3). An agreement purporting to bind a prospective debtor or hirer to entering into a future regulated agreement is void: s. 59. (There are certain very limited exceptions to s. 59: cf. Consumer Credit (Agreements to enter Prospective Agreements) (Exemptions) Regulations 1983.)

## 17. Prospective land mortgages

The right to cancel does not apply to prospective land mortgages on account of the technical difficulties which would be involved. Instead, provision is made in certain types of prospective land mortgage for a compulsory seven-day 'consideration period' during which the creditor or owner must not approach the debtor or hirer at all, except in response to a specific request. The consumer is by this means to be afforded opportunity to reflect upon and, if he so decides, to withdraw from the prospective agreement. These provisions are not applicable to bridging loans or mortgaged land. (Cf. ss. 58 and 61 of the CCA.)

> *Note*: The Consumer Credit (Cancellation Notices and Copies of Documents) Regulations 1983 (as amended) prescribe the form of withdrawal notice which must be

included in the copy of the agreement to be given to the debtor or hirer under the CCA at the commencement of the consideration period.

## 18. Extending the right of cancellation to cash sale

It had long been regarded as extraordinary that a policy consideration extending consumer protection to those who enter into 'doorstep' agreements' on credit should not have been available to those who enter cash agreements as well. The opportunity to extend this protection, indeed the obligation to do so, arose with the adoption by the EC of a Directive which was implemented by the UK by means of the 'Consumer Protection (Cancellation of Agreements Concluded away from Business Premises) Regulations 1987. The effect of these regulations is (broadly) to give the consumer a seven-day cooling off period if he agrees to a 'doorstep' sale for cash after an 'unsolicited' visit by the trader or his representative.

*Note*: The Director General of Fair Trading has expressed concern about some of the methods used to promote the sale of 'timeshare' interests in property ('I find some of the techniques used to sell timeshare wholly unacceptable . . . there is a section of the industry that has rejected ethical practice and appears to hold the public in contempt.'). Following his 1990 Report on timeshares, the Timeshare Act 1992 was enacted, a key element of which is a 14-day 'cooling-off' period. Thus, the idea of consumers having the right to cancel, to think again, has been further extended.

# VARIATION OF AGREEMENTS

## 19. Formal requirements on variation

Where the creditor or owner, in exercise of a power contained in the agreement, varies a regulated agreement, the variation will not take effect before written notice of it is given to the debtor or hirer in the prescribed manner: s. 82(1). The effect of variation is to revoke the earlier agreement, and the modifying agreement is treated as reproducing the combined effect of the two agreements: s. 82(2). If the earlier agreement is a regulated agreement but the modifying agreement is not, the modifying agreement is nevertheless to be treated as a regulated agreement unless it is for running-account credit: s. 82(3). The Consumer Credit (Notice of Variation of Agreements) Regulations 1977 prescribe the manner in which notice of variation must be given: generally seven days' notice must be served on the debtor or hirer.

## Progress test 15

1. What regulated agreements are exempted from the Part V CCA requirements? How completely are such agreements exempted from the requirements?

2. What information must a regulated agreement provide by virtue of the Consumer Credit (Agreements) Regulations 1983?

3. Mr A proposes to enter into a regulated hire-purchase agreement in respect of certain hi-fi equipment. The agreement is signed by his wife on his behalf. Mr A obtains possession of the equipment. He then decides that he cannot afford to pay the agreed instalments, but he wishes to have the equipment. What is his legal position?

4. At what stage or stages in the formation of a regulated consumer credit or hire agreement should the debtor or hirer receive copies of the agreement?

5. When will a regulated agreement be cancellable? If it is cancellable, how does the CCA seek to ensure that the consumer will be aware of his rights and how to exercise them? Describe the ways in which the right to cancel has been extended in recent years. What further extensions are proposed?

6. What factors must the court take into account in deciding whether to accede to an application for enforcement of an agreement which has been improperly executed? In what cases can no enforcement order be made whatever the other circumstances?

7. If an agreement is cancellable, how much time is the consumer given in which to cancel? To whom may notice of cancellation be given? Is there any prescribed form for cancellation?

8. What are the effects of cancellation of an agreement? On cancellation, what is the legal position with regard to:
   (a) goods in the consumer's possession;
   (b) goods given in part-exchange;
   (c) the payment of credit and interest?

9. A trader persuades a customer to sign on his premises an immediately binding agreement to enter into future regulated consumer credit agreement. Later, when the customer reads the information contained in the prospective agreement, he does not wish to proceed with the transaction. Can the consumer withdraw and get the deposit back?

10. How does the CCA operate to give a 'cooling-off' period in the case of prospective land mortgages?

11. Where a regulated agreement may be varied under a power contained in the agreement, what requirements must the creditor or owner observe in order effactually to exercise the power? What is the legal effect of variation?

# 16

# CONSUMER CREDIT: LIABILITY FOR DEFECTIVE GOODS AND SERVICES

## A SUMMARY

### 1. Review of liability

The following may be liable for defective goods or services which the consumer purchases with the aid of some form of financial accommodation.

**(a)** *The supplier of the goods*, who may be liable for:

(*i*) misrepresentation (*see* Chap. 4)

(*ii*) breach of express term (condition, warranty intermediate stipulation (*see* Chap. 4))

(*iii*) breach of implied term (title, description, quality, fitness, samples (*see* Chap. 5))

(*iv*) breach of duty of care in the tort of negligence (*see* Chap. 9).

**(b)** *The supplier of the services*, who may be liable under the Supply of Goods and Services Act 1982 (*see* Chap. 5).

**(c)** *The manufacturer of the goods*, who may be liable for:

(*i*) breach of obligations assumed by him in a guarantee

(*ii*) breach of duty of care in the tort of negligence (*see* Chap. 11).

Note: Exclusion of liability arising in the above cases is prevented or, as the case may be, subjected to a reasonableness test, by the Unfair Contract Terms Act (*see* Chap. 6).

**(d)** *Persons conducting antecedent negotiations* (*see* **2**).

**(e)** *The supplier of the credit* (*see* **4–6**).

# PERSONS CONDUCTING ANTECEDENT NEGOTIATIONS

## 2. Credit-brokers

The category of persons who may conduct antecedent negotiations with the consumer (*see* s. 56) comprehends credit-brokers. 'Credit-brokers' is widely defined in ss. 189 and 145, and includes persons who effect introductions of individuals desiring to obtain credit to persons carrying on a consumer credit business. So dealers who introduce customers to a finance company are credit-brokers, whether the credit provided is a personal loan, or takes the form of hire-purchase, conditional sale or credit-sale.

A dealer may be liable to the consumer in the following ways:

**(a)** *Breach of a collateral warranty. Andrews* v. *Hopkinson* (1957): a dealer told a consumer that a certain car was 'a good little bus; I'd stake my life on it. You will have no trouble with it.' The consumer entered into a hire-purchase agreement with a finance company, to whom the dealer sold the car. The car had a steering defect which caused the consumer serious injury. At the time of this case it was possible to exclude liability much more easily than it is now. Here, and for that reason, no claim could be brought against the finance company (the other party to the contract). So, unless a contract could be argued as having been made between the consumer and the dealer there could be no redress (*Drury* v. *Victor Buckland Ltd* (1941) CA). The dealer had made an oral promise ('a good little bus', etc.) but the consumer had given nothing in exchange. Thus no contract because there was no consideration? It was HELD that the dealer had obtained enough benefit out of the deal, taken as a whole, because in reliance on the oral promise the consumer had entered into a contract with the finance company, which had bought the vehicle from the dealer.

So 'collateral contract' theory in this context is something of a fiction, but one with a good cause! Now that much less liability can be excluded much less often, consumers are rarely put to such elaborate reasoning.

**(b)** *Breach of duty of care in the tort of negligence.* In *Andrews* v. *Hopkinson* (above) the dealer was also held to be liable in negligence, as the steering defect could have been discovered by the exercise of reasonable care on the dealer's part.

*Note*: The supplier of the goods may be liable to the supplier of the credit under the terms of a contract (e.g. a recourse agreement) between them.

## 3. Agency under s. 56 of the CCA

Under common law principles a statement by the credit-broker will not bind the creditor unless the relationship of agency exists between them. Thus a dealer's representations will not generally bind the finance company at common law. This normal outcome at common law is altered by s. 56 of the CCA. Section 56(2) provides that in the case of debtor-creditor-supplier agreements, negotiations 'shall be deemed to be conducted by the negotiator in the capacity of agent of the creditor as well as in his actual capacity.' This deemed agency would apply typically in hire-purchase, conditional sale and credit-sale transactions. Antecedent negotiations include any representations made by the negotiator to the consumer and any other dealings between them. It follows from s. 56(2) that the creditor (e.g. a finance company) will be liable for misrepresentations made by a dealer. Notice of rescission may be given to the dealer as agent of the creditor for this purpose: s. 102.

Any attempt to contract out of s. 56, whether by providing that the negotiator is to be treated as agent of the consumer, or by purporting to exclude the creditor's liability for the negotiator's act or omissions, is nullified by s. 56(3).

*Note*: Non-commercial agreements and small agreements are not excluded from the operation of s. 56 (*see* 15:7). Contrast the position with regard to s. 75 CCA (*see* 5).

# SUPPLIER OF CREDIT

## 4. Where the supplier of credit also supplies the goods or services

In these cases the liability of the supplier will be as above (*see* 1, 3). Typical examples of such 'two-party' credit transactions are hire-purchase, conditional sale and credit-sale agreements. It will be recalled (*see* 5:13) that the Supply of Goods (Implied Terms) Act 1973 (as amended) imposes the same implied terms in hire-purchase agreements as are imposed by the Sale of Goods Act in contracts of sale, namely:

**(a)** title (s. 8 of 1973 Act)

**(b)** description (s. 9)

**(c)** satisfactory quality (s. 10(2))

**(d)** fitness for purpose (s. 10(3))

**(e)** samples (s. 11).

Further, the restrictions on exclusion clauses in hire-purchase agreements and contracts of sale are identical (s. 6 of the Unfair Contract Terms Act: *see* 6: 19).

Liability for breach of the above implied terms lies with the legal supplier of the goods, i.e. the dealer if he finances his own hire-purchase transaction, but otherwise the finance company (cf. *Drury* v. *Victor Buckland Ltd: see* 2(a) note).

*Note*: The implied terms in hire-purchase agreements apply whatever the amount of credit involved and whatever the status of the customer – they are not confined to regulated agreements.

## 5. Joint liability under s. 75 of the CCA

Section 75 applies to all debtor-creditor-supplier agreements where the creditor and the legal supplier of the goods are *not* one and the same person. This is the so-called 'connected lender' type of transaction, as for instance where the debtor's contract to buy goods from a retailer is financed by a loan agreement with a finance house with whom the retailer has a business connection. In such cases, where the debtor has, in relation to a transaction financed by the agreement, any claim against the supplier in respect of a misrepresentation or breach of contract, he has 'a like claim' against the creditor: s. 75(1). Creditor and supplier are jointly and severally liable (s. 75(1)), though by s. 75(2) the creditor has a statutory right of indemnity against the supplier for loss suffered in satisfying his liability. Section 75 applies notwithstanding that the debtor, in entering into the transaction, exceeded the credit limit or otherwise contravened any term of the agreement: s. 75(4). Contracting out of s. 75 is ineffective by virtue of s. 173(1) (*see* 13:**9**).

The s. 75(1) liability does not apply to:

**(a)** a non-commercial agreement (defined in 15:**1(c)**)

**(b)** a claim in so far as it relates to a single item to which the supplier has attached a *cash* price not exceeding £100 or more than £30,000 (s. 75(3); nor of course would s. 75(1) apply if the *credit* ceiling of £15,000 were exceeded).

In *Porter* v. *General Guarantee Corporation Ltd* (1982), the court wrongly applied s. 75 to a hire-purchase agreement. The truth is that s. 75 can never apply to hire-purchase or to conditional sale or credit-sale, because in these transactions the supplier of the credit also supplies the goods to the consumer. But the consumer is adequately protected in such contracts since both s. 56(2) (*see* **3**) and the statutory rights (*see* **4**) will be applicable. Indeed, a prime consequence of s. 75 is to impose on the connected lender effectively the same liability for defects in respect of a transaction financed by a personal loan as is imposed on the creditor by other means in a transaction financed by hire-purchase, conditional sale or credit-sale. The provisions of s. 56 overlap, however, with those in s. 75 governing connected lender transactions. This could be significant, for instance, in cases of misrepresentation where the supplier of an item has attached a cash price not exceeding £100; here the connected lender would be liable only under the deemed agency provisions of s. 56. The connected lender's liability under s. 75 (where applicable) is, however, potentially more extensive than his liability under s. 56 would be, inasmuch as s. 75 will include liability for breach of the statutory rights by the supplier under the supply contract.

It is a general point of policy behind ss. 56 and 75 that since the creditor has an interest in the transaction financed by him then he should share in any liability which arises under it. Furthermore, an extension of this leads to the creditors, in a sense, 'policing' the traders with whom they are connected.

*U.D.T.* v. *Taylor* (1980): in this Scottish case the facts were that the consumer (T) bought a motor car from dealers with finance supplied by U.D.T., who had business arrangements with the dealers. The car turned out to be un-roadworthy and T rejected it for misrepresentation and breach of contract. U.D.T. nevertheless sued T to enforce the loan agreement. HELD on appeal to the Sheriff Principal: Where the debtor had the right to rescind the supply contract, he could also rescind the credit contract ('a like claim'), and would therefore have a good defence to an action by the creditor.

*Note*: It is questionable whether the 'like claim' does extend to the right to *rescind* the credit contract as well as the supply contract; but the actual result in the above case must be correct because the consumer's claim against the dealer would include his wasted expenditure under the loan agreement and that claim for damages would be 'a like claim' and valid as a counterclaim to the creditor's action.

## 6. Credit cards and s. 75

Where the consumer purchases goods with a cash price of over £100 using a credit card, the credit card company is at first sight liable under s. 75 for misrepresentation or breach of contract by the supplier of the goods. But the application of s. 75 to credit cards presents anomalies. First, certain credit cards (e.g. the American Express green card and Diners Club) are exempt from s. 75 altogether because they require payment of the whole amount of the credit provided in each billing period to be made by a single payment (*see* 10:8). These cards (and some others) are often referred to as 'charge' cards, but there is no magic in the name. The distinction is made between cards inside and outside s. 75 by reference to the obligation to repay, not by the naming of the card. Secondly, s. 75 came into operation on 1 July 1977, but only in relation to regulated agreements made on or after that day: Sched. 3, para. 16. The effect of this seems to be that the statutory protection is not available to cardholders who first obtained their cards before 1 July 1977. After discussions with the Office of Fair Trading, however, Barclaycard and Access voluntarily agreed to accept liability to such cardholders in circumstances where s. 75 would otherwise have applied. But this voluntary acceptance of liability is limited to the amount of the transaction charged to the cardholder's account. This limitation could in practice reduce the cardholder's protection, since damage caused by defective goods (e.g. a television set which bursts into flames) could well exceed their purchase price. Even should the cardholder have recourse to s. 56 (in cases involving misrepresentation, for example), there is still the problem that s. 56 itself will probably not apply to cardholders who first obtained their cards before April 1977: cf. Sched. 3, para. 1. There are, therefore, a number of 'classes' of credit card holders, each protected to a different extent. It is anticipated that this situation will recede as the years go by.

There are alternative interpretations of the 'connected lender' liability under s. 75. It could be that each use of the credit card creates a new contract in that it constitutes an acceptance of a standing offer of credit. Every couple of years or so new credit cards are issued. This might be the performance of a contract made long ago, as a result of which the first card was issued – or it could be that every time a card is renewed a new contract is made.

If either of these alternatives is correct, and so far there is no judicial reasoning to help us, then there are not 'two classes of card holder'. It is time that such matters were formally clarified. Indeed the Office of Fair Trading has conducted an extensive Review of consumer credit, and reform may follow.

## 7. Section 75, problem areas, the OFT Review, deregulation and possible reform

The UK government has been looking to 'deregulate' the framework within which business must operate. This is obviously intended to stimulate economic recovery, but there is a danger that consumer protection may be reduced or lost as sets of regulations are repealed.

As part of this process the OFT conducted a series of public hearings to gather evidence and reported in 1994. A large number of recommendations for change were made. The less technical of these include:

**(a)** The upper limit for the operation of most of the CCA should be raised from £15,000 to £25,000, and certain other levels altered too, such as the minimum for the operation of 'connected lender liability' raised from £100 to £150 and the maximum reduced from £30,000 to £25,000.

**(b)** The obligation to show the APR for credit agreements up to £150 should be removed, and the regulations concerning credit and hire advertisements should be simplified.

**(c)** The right to cancel an agreement that was negotiated on trade premises but signed elsewhere should be removed.

**(d)** The various categories of credit licences should be removed. Licences should cover all credit and hire trading activities.

On 15 May 1995, the then DGFT, as he was on the point of leaving, published 'a further report' on s. 75. His parting proposals for change include that joint and several liability continue, with no obligation on the card holder to go first to the supplier of the goods or services involved, but that this liability be limited to the amount of credit involved in the transaction. It is currently unlimited. This would considerably reduce both issuers' exposure and consumer protection; the lower limit should remain at £100, but the upper limit should be £15,000 (unless and until the general upper limit is raised to £25,000). It is currently £30,000. He announced that card issuers had agreed to accept liability for overseas credit card transactions – on an *ex gratia* basis (but see (d) below).

There is no doubt that 'deregulation' of commercial law will take place on a fairly massive scale over the next few years, but it is thought unlikely that very much will be done to the regulatory framework surrounding consumer credit.

If nothing much is done we may celebrate the preservation of consumer protection, but we will be left with some of the noise which has appeared in the system since s. 75 was implemented in 1977. As examples:

**(a)** It has been argued that there should be no liability for finance companies where the particular dealer was not signed up by them but by 'merchant acquirers' on their behalf. This has been dismissed by the OFT as just wrong, and criticised by the Consumer and Commercial Law Committee of the Law Society as uncertain, but the point is still made.

**(b)** It is argued, and probably correctly, that in the increasingly common circumstances where an extra card is issued on an account, say for the use of another family member, then the liability cannot attach to losses incurred by that second person because it only extends to the 'debtor', and further that if injury is caused to the debtor by defects in goods supplied to the extra cardholder then liability cannot extend that far either because the debtor was no part of the transaction! It is thought that where the goods are obviously for household or shared use then liability would be acknowledged, but it would take some establishing were the point to be tested in court.

(c) It has been argued, and this time probably wrongly, that once the credit has been paid off then the exposure to liability ceases. It is surely unacceptable that those who pay off early should be less protected than those who do not.

(d) It has been argued that liability is not extended to transactions effected abroad, say on holiday. Given the sales pitch that is used to attract cardholders, such an argument has a cynical ring. The OFT has asserted that it is wrong. The CCA makes no statement about geographical limitation. The Law Society has commented that 'there is significant backing for the view that the place where the card is used is irrelevant for the purposes of s. 75'.

## 8. 'Connected lender liability' and Europe

Directive 87/102 requires member states to implement 'connected lender' liability such that, as clause 1 of Article 11 states, a consumer should not be disadvantaged in relation to his or her rights against a supplier for defective goods and services merely by virtue of the fact that he or she has made a credit agreement which is used to finance the purchase of those goods or services.

The CCA already gives wider protection than this. Here the liability is restricted to that for breach whereas UK law extends to misrepresentation too. Here the extra target only arises after the consumer has unsuccessfully claimed against the supplier, whereas UK law provides joint and several liability – consumers can claim against either or both the supplier and the finance company.

Implementation across the member states has been uneven. In Holland it seems that creditor liability only arises where there has been no delivery at all. In Germany the debtor can simply refuse to pay the creditor if the dealer is in breach. In the UK the position is simple and clear, as was intended by the Crowther Committee in 1971. Some issues need clarification, but there is much to lose if the rush to deregulate leads to the repeal of s. 75.

## Progress test 16

1. Summarize the ways in which the undermentioned persons may be liable to the consumer for the supply of defective goods or services which the consumer has purchased with the aid of some form of financial accommodation:
   (a) the supplier of the goods;
   (b) the supplier of the services;
   (c) the manufacturer of the goods.

2. A dealer introduces a consumer to a finance company, who then let the goods sold to them by the dealer to the consumer under a regulated hire-purchase agreement. Is the dealer a 'credit-broker' within the meaning of the CCA?

3. B, a motor-dealer, tells C that a certain second-hand car 'goes like a bomb'. The D Finance Co., pursuant to a pre-existing arrangement with B, then lends money to C under a regulated agreement so that C can buy the car from B. The car's brakes are defective and C is seriously injured.
   (a) Has C any cause of action against B?
   (b) Do the D Finance Co. have any liability towards C?

4. E, a motor-dealer, tells F that a certain used car is 'a good runner'. The G Finance Co. subsequently buys the car from E and lets it under a regulated hire-purchase agreement to F. The car's gearbox jams as F is driving the vehicle away from E's premises.
   (a) Has F any cause of action against E?
   (b) Does the G Finance Co. have any liability towards F?
   Would it make any difference if the hire-purchase agreement contained a clause stating: 'the credit-broker introducing the prospective debtor to (the Finance Co.) shall be deemed to be the agent of the debtor'?

5. The H Finance Co., which has a pre-existing arrangement with J, a dealer, lends K £14,500 under a regulated agreement to enable K to purchase a yacht from J. K does purchase the yacht, at £31,000. The yacht proves to be unseaworthy and it sinks and is not salvageable. Has K any cause of action against the H Finance Co.?

6. L buys an electric kettle, manufactured by M, from N, a retailer, financing the transaction on L's Access credit card. The purchase price of the kettle is £18. The kettle short-circuits, causing L a severe electric shock. Consider the respective liabilities (if any) of M, N, and Access.

7. P has Diners Club and Barclaycard credit cards, both first obtained in 1976, and American Express and Access credit cards, both first obtained in 1978. P contemplates (i) buying a video cassette recorder and (ii) paying for a package holiday against one of the credit cards. Are there any consumer protection reasons why P should use any one credit card in preference to the others?

# 17

# TERMINATION OF CREDIT AGREEMENT BY THE DEBTOR

## REBATE ON EARLY SETTLEMENT

### 1. Early settlement

The debtor under a regulated consumer credit agreement is entitled at any time, by written notice to the creditor, to discharge his indebtedness under the agreement by paying all amounts payable to the creditor: s. 94.

### 2. The statutory rebate

The debtor is entitled, under regulations made pursuant to s. 95, to a statutory rebate of charges for credit if he discharges his indebtedness earlier than the time fixed by the agreement. The Consumer Credit (Rebate on Early Settlement) Regulations 1983 give detailed formulae for calculating the rebate.

### 3. Duty to give information

In order to bolster up the right to a statutory rebate, the creditor is placed under a duty, on receipt of a written request, to give the debtor a statement indicating the amount of payment required to discharge his indebtedness under the agreement: s. 97. By virtue of the Consumer Credit (Settlement Information) Regulations 1983, the creditor must provide the settlement information in the prescribed form within 12 working days after receiving the written request. The information given must include, in particular, details of any rebate to which the debtor is entitled.

Furthermore, it would be as well for the creditor if the information given is accurate. In *Lombard North Central plc* v. *Stobart* (1990) the creditor informed the purchaser of a car (orally and in writing) that £1,003 was required to settle his account. Relying upon this, the car was sold for £5,100. In fact the settlement figure had been understated by £4,710. The Court of Appeal refused to over-rule a County Court judgement rejecting the creditor's claim for the rest of the money. The reliance was shown to have been honest. There is, it seems, no requirement that it be reasonable as well!

*Note*: Sections 77–79 give the debtor or hirer a general right during the currency of the agreement, on payment of a fee (now 50p), to a copy of the executed agreement and to information from the creditor or owner as to the state of the account between them. Regulations prescribe that the information must be provided within 12 working days after receipt of the written request by the debtor or hirer. (The relevant regulations are the Consumer Credit (Prescribed Periods for Giving Information) Regulations 1983, and the Consumer Credit (Running-Account Credit Information) Regulations 1983.)

# VOLUNTARY TERMINATION OF HIRE-PURCHASE OR CONDITIONAL SALE AGREEMENTS

## 4. The right to terminate

At any time before the final payment under a regulated hire-purchase or conditional sale agreement falls due, the debtor is entitled by giving written notice to terminate the agreement: s. 99. This right is quite separate from the right to early settlement under s. 94 (*see* 1).

## 5. The '50 per cent' provision

The liability of the debtor terminating an agreement under s. 99 is to pay the following:

**(a)** All sums accrued due: s. 99(2).

**(b)** Any additional sum needed to bring the total paid to one-half of the total price, unless

   (*i*) the agreement provides for a smaller payment, *or*

   (*ii*) the court is satisfied that a lesser sum would be equal to the loss sustained by the creditor: s. 100(1), (3) (and *see Yeoman Credit* v. *Waragowski* (1961), 18:**5**).

**(c)** Damages if the debtor has failed to take reasonable care: s. 100(4).

> *Note*: Where an installation charge has been specified in the agreement as part of the total price, one-half of the total price means the whole installation charge plus one-half of the remainder of the total price: s. 100(2).

## 6. Return of goods

It will be appreciated that where the debtor exercises the right to terminate in s. 99, as opposed to the right of early settlement in s. 94 (*see* 1), then the goods have to be returned to the creditor. If the debtor wrongfully retains them the court, unless satisfied that it would not be just to do so, must order the goods to be delivered to the creditor without giving the debtor an option to pay the value of the goods instead: s. 100(5).

# VOLUNTARY TERMINATION OF HIRE AGREEMENTS

### 7. The right to terminate

The hirer under a regulated hire agreement is entitled by giving written notice to terminate the agreement prematurely. Notice cannot be given to expire earlier than eighteen months after the making of the agreement. The minimum period of notice, unless the agreement provides for a shorter period, is the length of the shortest agreed interval between the making of rental payments by the hirer, or three months, whichever is less. Premature termination of a hire agreement in this way does not affect any liability which has already accrued under the agreement (cf. s. 101).

> *Note*: Section 101(7), (8) provides for the exemption from these termination provisions of certain commercial leasing transactions and, more generally, of any agreement where the annual payments exceed the sum of £900 (as now stipulated by the Consumer Credit (Increase of Monetary Amounts) Order 1983).

### Progress test 17

1. How can a debtor obtain a rebate of credit charges under a regulated consumer credit agreement?

2. How can the debtor, if he is unsure, ascertain the amount that is payable in order to discharge his indebtedness under a regulated consumer credit agreement?

3. D, a debtor, does not wish to continue payments under a regulated hire-purchase agreement. Can D return the goods and terminate the agreement? If so, how much must D pay?

4. Explain how the CCA provides for the premature termination by the hirer of a regulated hire agreement.

# 18

## CONSUMER CREDIT: REMEDIES

### 1. Jurisdiction

The county court has exclusive jurisdiction to determine all disputes relating to regulated agreements: s. 141.

## CREDITOR'S REMEDIES

### 2. The remedies

Breach of a credit agreement may lead to the creditor or owner pursuing one or more of the following remedies (the list is not exhaustive), depending upon the circumstances:

**(a)** Action for arrears

**(b)** Termination of the contract

**(c)** Action for damages

**(d)** Action for repossession of goods.

### 3. Action for arrears

Whatever the type of credit agreement, the creditor may always sue at common law for any arrears in the repayments as they fall due. The following points in the CCA should be noted:

**(a)** The agreement may provide for the payment of interest on arrears (default interest). The Act provides that the debtor under a regulated consumer credit agreement shall not be obliged to pay any such default interest at a higher rate of interest than that charged in the agreement: s. 93.

**(b)** The court is given wide powers, on application in appropriate cases by either party to the agreement, to make a 'time order', i.e. an order giving the debtor or hirer the opportunity to pay arrears by such instalments, payable at such times, as the court considers reasonable having regard to the means of the debtor or hirer: s. 129. In the case of a hire-purchase or conditional sale agreement a time order may also deal with sums which, although not payable by the debtor at the time the order is made, would become payable if the agreement continued in force: s. 130(2).

**(c)** The agreement may contain an acceleration clause, i.e. a clause providing for immediate payment of the entire outstanding balance on default by the debtor or hirer, or on the occurrence of other stated contingencies (e.g. execution levied by another creditor against the debtor's goods). Such an acceleration clause is a perfectly valid device provided that it is not construed as a penalty clause, a result which can be avoided by the inclusion of provision for an appropriate rebate on early settlement (cf. 17:2). Under the Act at least seven days' notice in writing of the intention to operate any acceleration clause is required: ss. 76(1), 87(1). In default cases the debtor or hirer may then rectify the matter within the specified time, in which case the acceleration clause does not become operative: s. 89. If the default is not rectified within the specified time, it will then be too late for the debtor to exercise his right to terminate under s. 99 (*see* 17:4): *Wadham Stringer Finance Ltd* v. *Meaney* (1980). In this eventuality a time order (*see* **3(b)**) could still avail the debtor.

**(d)** The court may find the credit bargain to be extortionate (*see* **16**).

## 4. Termination

A credit arrangement may expressly provide for its termination by the creditor or owner on default by the debtor or hirer or on the occurrence of other stated contingencies. Further, under the common law the creditor or owner will be entitled to treat the agreement as terminated if the debtor or hirer defaults and the default is sufficiently serious to amount to repudiation of his obligations. Whatever the reason for termination the CCA affords the consumer some protection in the case of a regulated agreement.

**(a)** *Default cases.* At least seven days' written notice ('default notice') is necessary before the creditor or owner can become entitled to terminate the agreement: s. 87. The default notice must be in the prescribed form and specify:

(*i*)  the nature of the breach, *and*

(*ii*)  the action required to remedy it, or (if the breach is not capable of remedy) the sum (if any) required as compensation for the breach: s. 88.

The default notice must also contain information in the prescribed terms about the consequences of failure to comply with it: s. 88(4). If the debtor or hirer takes the specified action the breach is treated as not having occurred: s. 89. Or the debtor may apply for a time order.

Note: The prescribed form and content for default notices will be found in the Consumer Credit (Enforcement, Default and Termination Notices) Regulations 1983.

**(b)** *Non-default cases.* Even in non-default cases at least seven days' written notice, in the form prescribed by the above-mentioned regulations, is necessary before the creditor or owner can become entitled to terminate an agreement of specific duration in exercise of a contractual right to do so: s. 98. Here the debtor's or hirer's only protection (unless the credit bargain is extortionate: *see* **16**) is to apply for a time order under s. 129 (*see* **3(b)**).

## 5. Action for damages

The creditor may wish to bring an action for damages on breach by the debtor of a hire-purchase or conditional sale agreement. (Breach of a credit-sale or loan agreement normally only allows the creditor to sue for instalments in arrears; an acceleration clause can be invoked if the agreement contains one.) Faced with an action for damages, the debtor's legal position will depend upon whether the agreement has been repudiated or terminated.

**(a)** *Repudiation.* It has already been noted that if the debtor terminates a regulated hire-purchase or conditional sale agreement pursuant to s. 99 (*see* 17:4), then his liability is generally limited to payment of arrears plus such additional sum as is needed to bring the total paid up to one-half of the total price (*see* 17:5). But the debtor may not exercise his statutory right to terminate under s. 99. He may instead simply go into arrears or otherwise be in breach of contract. If the breach is a major one it will amount to repudiation of the debtor's obligations and will entitle the creditor to treat the agreement as terminated and to sue for damages. In such a case the measure of damages is governed by the common law and will be based upon the decision of the Court of Appeal in *Yeoman Credit Ltd* v. *Waragowski* (1961). This case held that the creditor is entitled to be compensated for his loss of profit on the transaction, i.e. to be put in the same position as he would have been in if the contract had been fulfilled. Thus the debtor will have to pay:

(*i*)  all sums accrued; plus

(*ii*)  the balance of the total price; but less

(*iii*)  the proceeds of resale of the repossessed goods (the creditor must sell at the best price reasonably obtainable);

(*iv*)  the sum (usually nominal) payable for the option to purchase;

(*v*)  a discount for accelerated receipt (*Overstone Ltd* v. *Shipway* (1962) CA).

**(b)** *Termination.* In contrast to the heavy measure of damages imposed by the *Waragowski* decision, if the debtor is merely in breach of contract in circumstances not amounting to repudiation, and the creditor is provoked into exercising a contractual right to terminate the contract, then the measure of damages will be much less. Here the debtor will only be liable to pay:

(*i*)  instalments in arrear at the date of termination plus interest (*Financings Ltd* v. *Baldock* (1963) CA);

(*ii*)  damages if the debtor has failed to take reasonable care of the goods.

The reason given for this lesser liability is that the creditor's loss results not from the debtor's breach but from the creditor's decision to terminate the contract.

It is apparent from the above rulings that a game of cat and mouse is to be played out between creditor and debtor. In order to minimize his liabilities a debtor who has fallen into arrears must not repudiate the contract or even terminate it under s. 99; he must instead provoke the creditor into terminating the contract (or seek a time order). In *Waragowski* the debtor paid the initial deposit but no more. The creditor terminated the agreement six months later. This amounted to repudiation by the debtor. On the other hand, in *Financings Ltd* v. *Baldock* the debtor failed to pay the first two instalments, and although he expressed a willingness to try and pay, the creditor terminated the agreement. The Court of Appeal held that this did *not* amount to repudiation by the debtor (cf. *Lombard North Central plc* v. *Butterworth* (1987) CA). It may be added that wrongful disposition of the goods by the debtor will always amount to repudiation.

# DEBTOR'S PROTECTION AGAINST 'SNATCH BACK'

## 6. Repossession

Termination of a hire-purchase agreement terminates the bailment of the goods so that the creditor, as legal owner, is entitled to repossession. Likewise under a conditional sale agreement the seller on termination will be entitled to repossession, because the property in the goods will have remained with the seller as the conditions as to instalments or otherwise will not have been fulfilled. This outcome – repossession – could, and frequently did, work injustice to the debtor, who might have paid much of the total price under the contract only to see the legal owner retake ('snatch back') the goods in consequence of termination of the agreement through breach (possibly purely technical) by the debtor. The CCA contains provisions protecting the debtor against snatch back, and this protection is considered in the following paragraphs.

## 7. The protection

The protection is threefold:

**(a)** Notice is required.

**(b)** Entry on premises to take possession is restricted.

**(c)** The goods may be 'protected'.

## 8. Notice

It will be recalled that notice prior to termination is required in both default and non-default cases (*see* **4**). In default cases this affords the debtor the opportunity of remedying the default and so nullifying the threatened termination; or the debtor may apply for a time order (possible too in non-default cases) under s. 129.

> *Note*: By virtue of the Consumer Credit (Enforcement, Default and Termination Notices) Regulations 1983 (as amended in 1984), the default notice must contain a statement in the prescribed form as to the debtor's right under the Act to get back all the money he has paid under the hire-purchase or conditional sale agreement if the creditor retakes protected goods without the debtor's consent or a court order (*see* **10, 11**).

## 9. Entry on premises

The creditor or owner is not entitled 'to enter any premises' to take possession of goods subject to a regulated hire-purchase, conditional sale or consumer hire agreement, without a court order: s. 92(1). Entry in contravention of this requirement is actionable as a breach of statutory duty: s. 92(3).

> *Note*: The debtor or hirer may always consent at the time of entry to entry without a court order: s. 173(3) (*see* 13:9); the point is that consent cannot validly be given in advance.

## 10. Protected goods

The creditor is not entitled to recover possession of protected goods without a court order. Goods are 'protected goods' at any time when:

**(a)** the debtor is in breach of a regulated hire-purchase or conditional sale agreement relating to goods; *and*

**(b)** the debtor has paid to the creditor one-third or more of the total price of the goods; *and*

**(c)** the property in the goods remains in the creditor: s. 90(1).

> *Note*: Where an installation charge has been specified in the agreement as part of the total price, one-third of the total price means the whole or the installation charge plus one-third of the remainder of the total price: s. 90(2).

## 11. Contravention of s. 90

The consequences of contravention are that:

**(a)** the agreement is terminated

**(b)** the debtor is released from all liability

**(c)** the debtor is entitled to recover from the creditor all sums paid by the debtor under the agreement: s. 91.

The following points should be noted:

**(a)** The debtor is not entitled to recover possession of the goods themselves, as the agreement is terminated (*Carr* v. *James Broderick & Co. Ltd* (1942)). Nor can the creditor revive the agreement by returning the goods to the debtor (*Capital Finance Co. Ltd* v. *Bray* (1964) CA).

**(b)** Section 90 aims at preventing protected goods from being retaken, without a court order, 'from the debtor'. so s. 90 will not be contravened if the debtor has parted with possession of the goods by (say) selling them to a third party (but note that delivery up of the goods by the debtor to a third party for some limited purpose, e.g. repairs, will not be parting with possession of the goods).

**(c)** Section 90 does not apply where the debtor terminates or has terminated the agreement: s. 90(5).

**(d)** Section 90 is not contravened if the debtor consents at the time to the creditor retaking possession of the goods: s. 173(3) (*see* 13:9). The consent must be genuinely voluntary: cf. *Mercantile Credit Co. Ltd* v. *Cross* (1965) CA.

> *Bentinck Ltd* v. *Cromwell Engineering Co. Ltd* (1971): the debtor was in possession of a car on hire-purchase terms. After a serious road accident he left the car at a garage and, three months later, disappeared without trace. Nine months after the accident the creditors retook possession of the car with the consent of the garage proprietor and sold it. HELD: As the car had been abandoned the protected goods provisions in the Hire-Purchase Act 1965 had not been contravened. It is thought that the same result would ensue under s. 90 of the CCA, because (*i*) if the goods have been abandoned, the creditor does not repossess 'from the debtor', (*ii*) alternatively, the debtor in abandoning the goods consents to repossession under s. 173(3).

## 12. Financial relief under consumer hire agreements

Section 90 applies only to goods under regulated hire-purchase and conditional sale agreements. A different form of protection is afforded in the case of consumer hire agreements. Where the owner under a regulated consumer hire agreement recovers possession of goods other than by court action, the hirer may apply to the court under s. 132 for an order that:

**(a)** the whole or part of any sum paid by the hirer to the owner in respect of the goods shall be repaid; *and*

**(b)** the obligation to pay the whole or part of any sum owed by the hirer to the owner in respect of the goods shall cease. The court must grant the application in full or in part if it appears to it to be just to do so, having regard to the extent of the enjoyment of the goods by the hirer.

These provisions are strengthened by the further power granted to the court to make an order for financial relief along the above-mentioned lines wherever the court makes an order in proceedings relating to a regulated consumer hire agreement for delivery of the goods to the owner: s. 132(2).

## 13. Protection orders

The court, on the application of the creditor or owner under a regulated agreement, has power to make such orders as it thinks just for protecting the creditor's or owner's property from damage or depreciation pending the determination of proceedings under the Act: s. 131.

# SPECIAL ORDERS IN RELATION TO HIRE-PURCHASE OR CONDITIONAL SALE AGREEMENTS

## 14. Return orders

The court has power to make a 'return order', i.e. an order for the return of the goods to the creditor, in relation to a regulated hire-purchase or conditional sale agreement, where:

**(a)** an application is made for an enforcement order or a time order; *or*

**(b)** an action is brought by the creditor to recover possession of the goods: s. 133.

The order, like all orders in relation to regulated agreements, may be conditional or suspended: s. 135. The court will frequently combine a suspended return order with a time order; in other words, the operation of a return order will be suspended for so long as the debtor observes the requirements of a time order by paying the specified instalments at the specified times.

## 15. Transfer orders

The court also has power in relation to a regulated hire-purchase or conditional sale agreement to make a 'transfer order': s. 133. This is an order for the transfer to the debtor of the creditor's title to certain of the goods included in the agreement, and the return to the creditor of the remainder of the goods.

# EXTORTIONATE CREDIT BARGAINS

## 16. Reopening of credit bargains

The Moneylenders Acts of 1910 and 1927 gave the court power to reopen 'harsh and unconscionable' moneylending transactions by money-lenders, there being a rebuttable presumption under the 1927 Act that interest of or above 48 per cent was harsh and unconscionable. The CCA (ss. 137–140) gives the court much wider powers, which apply where a credit bargain is held to be 'extortionate' (*see* **17**). If extortionate, any credit bargain may be reopened where the debtor is an individual, *whatever the amount of credit involved*. The debtor, or a surety, need not wait to be sued by the creditor under the credit agreement before applying to the court for relief (cf. s. 139(1)).

'Credit bargain' is defined to include not only the credit agreement itself, but also other transactions where those other transactions are to be taken into account in computing the total charge for credit: s. 137(2). Hiring agreements, however, cannot be reopened under these provisions (but cf. s. 132: *see* **12**).

## 17. When bargains are extortionate

A credit bargain is extortionate if it requires the debtor or a relative of his to make payments which are 'grossly exorbitant', or it otherwise 'grossly contravenes ordinary principles of fair dealing': s. 138.

*Note*: (1) There is under the Act no threshold above which a rate of interest is presumed to be exorbitant. Indeed, in *Ketley Ltd* v. *Scott* (1981) a short-term secured loan at an equivalent annual rate of interest of 48 per cent was held on the facts not to be extortionate.

(2) During 1991 the Office of Fair Trading conducted an extensive survey of the nature and extent of extortionate credit bargains. Legislative change may well follow if the present DGFT is convinced that consumers are being exploited by moneylenders.

## 18. Guidelines

The Act contains guidelines (in s. 138) relating to both objective and subjective factors which the court is to take into account in determining whether a credit bargain is extortionate. Regard is to be had to 'all relevant considerations' including:

**(a)** interest rates prevailing when the credit bargain was made

**(b)** the age, experience, business capacity and state of health of the debtor, and the nature and degree of financial pressure which he was under when he made the credit bargain

**(c)** the degree of risk accepted by the creditor, his relationship to the debtor, and whether or not a colourable cash price was quoted for any goods or services included in the credit bargain.

> *Wills* v. *Wood* (1984): Mr Wills, a retired hotelier, deposited £11,000 with his solicitors to be lent to their clients from time to time. In this way he lent sums totalling £3,000 to Miss Wood, a spinster aged 57. The loans were secured on a second mortgage at 12.5 per cent interest per annum. At the time money-lenders generally were charging 18–24 per cent on second mortgages. HELD by the Court of Appeal: The credit bargain was not extortionate. The word was 'extortionate', not 'unwise'. There must at the least be a substantial imbalance in bargaining power of which one party had taken advantage before a credit bargain could be considered extortionate. The debtor was of full age and capacity and capable of taking professional advice, which she had done. There was nothing oppressive or objectionable about the loans. (Nor was Mr Wills an unlicensed moneylender under the Moneylenders Acts; he was not carrying on the business of a moneylender, but was merely investing his savings in secured loans. Cf. now s. 21 CCA: *see* 19:6.)

## 19. Onus of proof

Once the debtor has raised the issue by alleging that a credit bargain is extortionate, it is for the creditor to prove the contrary: s. 171(7).

## 20. Nature of relief available

The court has wide powers under s. 139(2) to make orders 'for the purpose of relieving the debtor or a surety from payment of any sum in excess of that fairly due and reasonable'. For example, the terms of the credit agreement may be altered, or the creditor may be required 'to repay the whole or part of any sum paid under the credit bargain or any related agreement by the debtor or surety, whether paid to the creditor or any other person'.

> *Note*: The court's powers outlined above apply to agreements and transactions 'whenever made' (Sched. 3, para. 42). But an order 'shall not alter the effect of any judgment': s. 139(4).

## Progress test 18

1. Which courts have jurisdiction to determine disputes relating to regulated agreements?

2. If a debtor falls into arrears in the payment of instalments due under a regulated hire-purchase agreement, can the creditor (*a*) claim default interests; and (*b*) invoke an acceleration clause?

3. What is a time order?

4. How many day's notice must a default give? What must it specify where the agreement is an hire-purchase or conditional sale agreement?

5. What steps can a debtor take to protect his interests when he has been served with (*a*) a default notice; or (*b*) a notice of termination in a non default-case?

6. What is the measure of damages to which a debtor is liable on (*a*) repudiation of a hire-purchase agreement by the debtor; or (*b*) termination by the creditor of a hire-purchase agreement for breach by the debtor?

7. How does the CCA seek to protect the debtor against 'snatch back'?

8. When are goods 'protected'?

9. What are the legal consequences of the creditor retaking protected goods without a court order?

10. The protected goods provisions in the CCA do not apply to consumer hire agreements. What form does the protection take when the owner repossesses for default by the hirer?

11. What is (*a*) a protection order; (*b*) a return order, (*c*) a transfer order? In what circumstances are they available? Explain how the court is likely to combine a return order with a time order.

12. What is a 'credit bargain'? When may the court find it to be 'extortionate'? What guidelines are given to aid the court in determining whether a credit bargain is extortionate?

**13.** Is the burden of proof on the debtor to satisfy the court that a credit bargain is extortionate?

**14.** If the court does find that a credit bargain is extortionate, what is the nature of the relief that it can order? Give examples.

**15.** A finance company let a car to D under a regulated hire-purchase agreement. D pays a deposit and the first two instalments, but fails to pay the next two instalments. The finance company find the car parked in the road outside D's house and they take it away. D then sees it advertised for sale outside a local garage and, without anyone's consent, retakes the car. The finance company now propose to sue D for damages. What is the legal position between D and the finance company under the CCA?

# Part Two

# ADMINISTRATIVE REMEDIES AND CRIMINAL LAW SANCTIONS

## Introductory note

In Part Two of this book we leave consideration of the consumer's private law rights and turn to administrative remedies and criminal law sanctions. The consumer's private law rights can often be rather illusory: he may be ignorant of his rights; he may lack the initiative or confidence to seek a civil law remedy; he may lack time or money to seek proper legal advice and then to institute civil proceedings, with the attendant delays and risks. So regulation by administrative authority offers better prospects for the protection of consumers at large. The trader's liability to criminal law sanctions will normally reinforce the powers possessed by administrative authorities. Administrative remedies will thus combine with criminal law sanctions to have a preventative effect in consumer protection.

Administrative remedies and civil law remedies will often overlap. For example, a misdescription will be likely to involve the commission of an offence under the Trade Descriptions Act as well as amounting to breach of contract by virtue of the Sale of Goods Act. On the other hand, it must be stressed that the consumer's contractual position will not generally be affected by reason only of the commission of a criminal offence by the trader, as we shall see. Individual consumers who are prejudiced by a trader's default, however, may succeed in obtaining an indirect remedy, in the form of a compensation order (*see* Chap. 24), after a successful prosecution has been brought by the administrative authority. The significance of this is that resort to an administrative authority is frequently the consumer's most practicable remedy.

Part Two concludes with a survey of the institutional framework, largely provided by the state, for the settlement of individual consumer disputes.

# 19

# FUNCTIONS OF THE DIRECTOR GENERAL OF FAIR TRADING UNDER THE CONSUMER CREDIT ACT

## 1. Introduction

The post of Director General of Fair Trading was created by the Fair Trading Act 1973. The Director's consumer protection functions under that Act are dealt with in Chapter 20. It is convenient to deal first in this chapter with the additional duties imposed upon the Director by the Consumer Credit Act.

## GENERAL FUNCTIONS OF DIRECTOR UNDER THE ACT

### 2. Part I Consumer Credit Act

Part I imposes upon the Director the following duties in connection with credit:

**(a)** to administer the licensing system set up by the CCA (*see* **6**)

**(b)** to superintend the working and enforcement of the CCA

**(c)** to keep social and commercial developments relating to the provision of credit or bailment under review, and to advise the Secretary of State: s. 1

**(d)** to arrange for the dissemination of information and advice to the public about the operation of the CCA and the availability of credit facilities: s. 4.

### 3. Enforcement

The Director is responsible for superintending the enforcement of the CCA and regulations made under it, and he can, where necessary or expedient, take enforcement steps himself: s. 1(1). But day-to-day enforcement is the responsibility of the local weights and measures ('trading standards') authority: s. 161. The local weights and measures authority must give notice to the Director of an intended prosecution for an offence under the Act, and they must wait for an acknowledgment from the Director, or for twenty-eight days, before proceeding:

s. 161(2). In addition they must, as and when required, report to the Director on the exercise of their functions under the Act: s. 161(3). In these ways is a balance achieved between centralized enforcement of the Act, and efficient local enforcement in cases of only local significance.

Finally, it may be noted that where a person is convicted of an offence, or a judgment given against him, the court may make arrangements to bring the conviction or judgment to the Director's attention: s. 166. Information of this kind may influence the Director in the exercise of his licensing functions under the Act.

# INTRODUCTORY NOTE ON LICENSING

## 4. Licensing as a means of control

Licensing of business is a flexible yet powerful means of control. A trader or organization persistently infringing the criminal law, or deliberately breaking contracts, in the expectation of showing a profit despite the loss of the odd criminal prosecution or civil suit, may find the threat of withdrawal of a trading licence a stronger stimulus to fairer dealing. A licence revoked, or not renewed, effectively prevents further trading on account of the criminal law sanctions and civil law disabilities which unlicensed trading is likely to incur.

In 1991 the DGFT announced his intention to remove credit licences from rogue traders, such as second-hand car dealers convicted of offences within the Trade Descriptions Act, particularly 'clocking', and in 1992 he extended his gaze towards photocopier leasing firms using unfair selling practices.

Between 1977 and 1994 the DGFT had stated that he was 'minded to revoke, suspend or vary compulsorily' the licences held by these numbers of members of the following trades: motor dealers – 836; debt collectors and investigators – 64; estate, insurance and mortgage agents – 222; finance companies – 460; retail trades and commercial leasing – 318; and building and home improvements companies – 121.

## 5. Examples of licensing

Licensing in the field of credit has been previously attempted, namely the licensing of moneylenders. This licensing was ineffective because it was not systematically enforced. There are many examples of licensing intended to protect both consumers and honest traders. Recent developments are the registration of insurance brokers under the Insurance Brokers (Registration) Act 1977; the registration under the Data Protection Act 1984 of data users who hold personal data and of persons carrying on computer bureaux who provide services in respect of personal data; and the licensing of non-solicitor conveyancers. Perhaps of greatest significance for the consumer in the area of licensing is the system for licensing consumer credit business, in operation under the CCA.

*Note*: An interesting scheme of *negative licensing* was introduced under the Estate Agents Act 1979, which empowers the Director General of Fair Trading to prohibit unfit persons from doing 'estate agency work': s. 3. By the end of 1994, 219 traders had been banned entirely.

# LICENSING FUNCTIONS OF DIRECTOR

## 6. Licensing under Part III

Part III of the CCA sets up a licensing system. A licence is required to carry on a consumer credit or consumer hire business: s. 21(1). Any such business – whether carried on by sole trader, partnership, limited liability company, or other body – requires a licence, but not a local authority, or body corporate empowered by a public general Act to carry on a business: s. 21(2), (3). The scope of the licensing control is therefore extensive (cf. 13:**2**), and by s. 147(1) it includes ancillary credit businesses (credit brokerage, debt-adjusting, debt-counselling, debt-collecting, credit reference agencies, all defined in s. 145). However, a person is not to be treated as carrying on a particular type of business merely because occasionally he enters into transactions belonging to a business of that type: s. 189(2). (Cf. *Willis* v. *Wood* (1984): *see* 18:**18**.)

> *Note*: The activities which arise in the normal course of a solicitor's practice comprehend credit brokerage, debt-adjusting, debt-counselling, and debt-collecting; a licence is therefore required, and in fact a group licence is in operation (*see* **9**).

## 7. Standard licences

These are issued to a named person, or to a named partnership, or unincorporated body of persons, for a period of five years. Before 1 June 1991 the period of validity was 15 years.

In 1991 the DGFT said that the estimate of the number of businesses which would be affected by the licensing system when it was introduced in 1976 was 50,000. His Annual Report for 1994 reveals that between 1976 and 1994 388,497 applications were received and 371,626 licences issued.

The licence covers such activities as are described therein. A licence covers the canvassing off trade premises of debtor-creditor-supplier agreements or regulated consumer hire agreements only to the extent that it specifically so provides: s. 23(3). (*See* 14:**5**.)

## 8. Fitness

A standard licence is to be issued by the Director to an applicant who satisfies the Director that he is a fit person and that a name under which he applies to be licensed is not misleading or otherwise undesirable: s. 25(1). In determining fitness the Director must have regard to any relevant circumstances, in particular to evidence tending to show that the applicant has been involved in fraud or other breach of the law, or in practices which, while not necessarily unlawful, are deceitful, oppressive, unfair or improper: s. 25(2).

*Note*: In his June 1991 statement about licensing the DGFT commented: 'Central to licensing is the requirement that traders should be able to demonstrate their fitness. There is a significant deterrent in having a licensing system. Traders who are aware that they are unfit are prevented from entering the credit industry and those who have been granted licences and are dealing in credit are less likely to stray from the straight and narrow'.

## 9. Group licences

A group licence may be issued by the Director if it appears to him that the public interest would be better served by doing so than by obliging the persons concerned to apply separately for standard licences: s. 25(5). The Director must give general notice of the issue of any group licence: s. 22(8). Group licences have been issued in respect of:

**(a)** solicitors holding a practising certificate

**(b)** liquidators and executors appointed to take temporary charge of a business involved in consumer credit activities

**(c)** Citizens' Advice Bureaux registered with the National Association of Citizens' Advice Bureaux

**(d)** Age Concern and other old people's welfare organizations

**(e)** chartered accountants and certified accountants holding a practising certificate

**(f)** The Institute of Business Counsellors

**(g)** a number of Enterprise Agencies and Institutions of Higher Education.

## 10. Conduct of business

Further control through licensing may be achieved by regulations made by the Secretary of State as to the conduct by a licensee of his business: s. 26.

## 11. Register

The Director maintains a register in Acton in London, which is open to public inspection on payment of a fee, containing, *inter alia*, particulars of licences applied for or in force; revocations, suspensions and variations of licences; and decisions of the Director and appeals therefrom: s. 35.

## 12. Sanctions

It is a criminal offence to engage in activities requiring a licence when not a licensee, or to carry on a business under a name not specified in the licence, or to fail to notify changes in the registered particulars: s. 39.

The enforcement of regulated agreements by an unlicensed credit or hire trader requires an order of the Director: s. 40. In determining whether to make an order, the Director must have regard to any relevant factors including the prejudice caused to debtors or hirers by the trader's conduct, and the trader's degree of culpability in failing to obtain a licence: s. 40(4). Further, the enforcement of regulated agreements made by a credit or hire trader through the agency of an unlicensed credit-broker likewise requires an order of the Director: s. 149.

## 13. Appeals

If the Director refuses to issue, renew or vary a licence, or compulsorily varies, suspends or revokes it, or refuses to make an enforcement order under ss. 40 or 149 (*see* 12), then appeal lies to the Secretary of State (ss. 41 and 150), with further appeal on a point of law to the High Court: s. 42.

## Progress test 19

1. Summarize the duties of the Director General of Fair Trading under the Consumer Credit Act.

2. (*a*) How does the CCA seek to ensure that local weights and measures authorities liaise with the Director in the enforcement of the Act? When can the Director take enforcement steps himself?
(*b*) If a trader is convicted of an offence, or has a judgment given against him, is the matter likely to come to the Director's attention?

3. Why is licensing thought to be a good method of controlling business? Give examples of the use of licensing.

4. What businesses require a licence under the CCA? What reforms have been proposed?

5. What is a standard licence? How long does it last? What activities does it permit?

6. What factors must the Director take into account in determining the fitness of an applicant for a standard licence?

7. When may the Director issue a group licence? What group licences have been issued?

8. How may a member of the public ascertain whether a particular trader is duly licensed?

9. What sanctions does the CCA impose in respect of unlicensed trading?

10. What right of appeal is open to a licensee or applicant for a licence who is dissatisfied with a decision of the Director concerning the licence?

# 20

# FAIR TRADING

## DIRECTOR GENERAL OF FAIR TRADING

### 1. The post of Director General of Fair Trading

This post was created by s. 1 of the Fair Trading Act 1973 (in this chapter referred to as 'the Act' or 'FTA'). Much of the FTA is concerned with competition law, a subject which is outside the scope of this book. Our present concern is with the consumer protection powers of the Director.

### 2. The Consumer Protection Advisory Committee

This Committee, which as its name suggests is purely advisory in function, was created by s. 3 of the FTA. The Committee had so few references made to it, and took so long about its consideration of them, that it has now been disbanded.

### 3. Powers and duties of Director

Apart from his powers under Part II and Part III of the FTA (*see* below), the Director has the following powers and duties under the Act:

**(a)** He must keep under review and collect information relating to the carrying on of commercial activities in the UK which relate to goods or services supplied to consumers in the UK, with a view to his becoming aware of practices which may adversely affect the economic interests of UK consumers: s. 2(1)(*a*) FTA.

**(b)** The Director must receive and collate evidence of practices which may adversely affect the interests (whether economic interests *or* interests with respect to health, safety or other matters) of UK consumers: s. 2(1)(*b*).

> *Note*: Section 2(1)(*a*) imposes an active duty to collect information; whereas s. 2(1)(*b*) imposes the purely passive duty to receive evidence. On the other hand, the s. 2(1)(*a*) duty relates only to practices which adversely affect the economic interests of consumers, whereas s. 2(1)(*b*) relates to practices which may adversely affect a much wider range of consumer interests.

**(c)** The Director can arrange for the publication of information and advice for consumers: s. 124(1). Among other publications put out by the Office of Fair Trading (OFT) are the many free leaflets for the guidance of consumers, obtainable in public libraries, Citizens' Advice Bureaux and elsewhere.

**(d)** The Director must encourage trade associations to prepare codes of practice: s. 124(3). This aspect of the Director's duties is considered further below (*see* **5**).

**(e)** The Director can make recommendations to the Secretary of State as to any action which he thinks it would be expedient for the Secretary of State or any other Minister to take: s. 2(3)(*b*). This power is quite separate from the recommendations which the Director can make under Part II of the FTA (*see* **9**. It was under s. 2, following publication in 1975 by the OFT of its Consultative Document entitled *Bargain Offer Claims*, that the Director recommended action against all sorts of bargain offers. In due course the Price Marking (Bargain Offers) Order 1979 was made under the Prices Act 1974, incorporating some of the recommendations. This Order proved unsatisfactory in practice and has now been repealed and replaced by the Consumer Protection Act 1987, Part III (*see* 22:**11**).

**(f)** Mention may be made here of the Estate Agents Act 1979, which empowers the Director to prohibit unfit persons from doing 'estate agency work' (*see* 19:**5**) and of the Control of Misleading Advertisements Regulations 1988 which enable the Director to obtain injunctions in order to prohibit misleading advertisements (*see* 12:**4**).

**(g)** Finally, it should be noted that the OFT does *not* act on behalf of individual consumers to resolve disputes.

# VOLUNTARY CODES OF PRACTICE

## 4. Codes of practice as an instrument of consumer protection

A code of practice, provided it is precise and does not merely contain vague generalizations, is a useful and flexible instrument of consumer protection. If voluntary, it may gain added strength by having the support of the industry whose practice it regulates, and it may also contain provisions which it would be impractical to reduce into inflexible legislative requirements. For example, the availability of spare parts and servicing facilities is one problem (*see* 5:**10**) which can be dealt with by voluntary codes, as in the AMDEA and RETRA (*see* 5:**10**), which have the approval of the OFT.

There is obviously a fine line between improving consumer protection and pure publicity. There is no doubt that one of the primary purposes of trade associations is to improve the public image of the trade in question. A clear example of this is the implementation of 1 July 1990 of a new code of standards aimed at improving the (sometimes woeful) reputation of second-hand car dealers and garages. The code lays down new conditions for the issue of warranties for used cars and repair work and sets out standards for the facilities available at garages. The trade association took the opportunity to change its name too – from the Motor Agents' Association to the Retail Motor Industry Federation (it has some 13,500 member companies). The Federation intends the new code to separate the reputable trade from what it called the 'back street and bombsite boys'. There are to be minimum warranty periods for second-hand cars: ranging from 90 days (or 3,000 miles) for cars with less than 20,000 miles on the clock to 30 days (or 1,000 miles) for cars with between 40,000 and 60,000 miles on them. Furthermore, the mileages should be guaranteed, and if there is any doubt about it, then this should be made clear to customers. There are further provisions regarding estimates and quotations for repair work, and so on. The new code received a guarded welcome from such organisations as the Consumers' Association.

Of course, a code of practice need not necessarily be voluntarily produced by industry. It may have a statutory status in giving the guidance which it does, as for example, the code of conduct drawn up under the Insurance Brokers (Registration) Act 1977 by the Insurance Brokers Registration Council and approved by the Insurance Brokers Registration Council (Code of Conduct) Approval Order 1978.

The major problem with a voluntary code of practice is that in the last resort it lacks adequate sanctions for its enforcement, though it may be enforceable as a collateral warranty if a trader has publicly claimed to honour a particular code. Adverse publicity, emanating either from the trade association responsible for the code, or from the OFT, may be a partial deterrent to breaches of the code, and the threat of expulsion from membership of a trade association may also work in the same direction. But expulsion will not necessarily deter the rogue trader, who may not even be a member of the association in the first place.

## 5. The role of the OFT

The Director is under a duty to encourage trade associations to prepare, and to disseminate to their members, codes of practice for guidance in safeguarding and promoting the interests of consumers in the UK: s. 124(3). FTA. While some voluntary codes of practice owe their existence to other sources of encouragement than the OFT (e.g. the British Code of Advertising Practice: *see* 12:2), the OFT acting under s. 124(3) is proving an active source of encouragement for voluntary codes. Commencing with the AMDEA Code (*see* 4) in 1974, over thirty codes – and the number is growing – have now been negotiated and approved by the OFT. These codes cover such matters as electrical goods, servicing of electrical appliances, shoes, sale and repair and servicing of new and used cars and motorcycles, dry cleaning and laundries, mail order catalogues and publishing of mail order advertisements, package holidays, funeral services, photography, and mechanical breakdown insurance. The Post Office and British Telecom also have codes approved by the OFT, and published leaflets about them.

A feature of the codes is that most of them contain provision for conciliation or independent low-cost arbitration of unresolved disputes. The consumer retains the right, however, to take his case to court instead; indeed, the small claims arbitration procedure in the county court (*see* Chap. 25) may well be cheaper than arbitration under the code where the dispute is not capable of proper resolution on a documents only basis and requires an oral hearing. New or revised codes will incorporate a new model arbitration scheme agreed between the OFT and the Chartered Institute of Arbitrators in 1983. The scheme provides that arbitration shall normally and unless otherwise agreed be on a documents only basis (which places a predetermined limit on costs). The Consumer Arbitration Agreements Act 1988 provides that any contract term which stipulates for arbitration rather than recourse to the courts is unenforceable against anyone 'dealing as a consumer'.

Finally, it should be noted that the OFT monitors the operation of the codes of practice. A code must be properly publicized, and must be observed. If a code is not seen to be working satisfactorily, revision of the code, and reform by the industry concerned in putting it into practice, will be required. If necessary, the OFT's approval of a code would be withdrawn.

## 6. Statutory general duty to trade fairly

The creation of such a duty has been proposed by the Director General of Fair Trading. The duty would be enforceable through codes of practice, applying to all traders within a particular sector and prepared by the OFT after consultation with appropriate trade associations. Persistent breaches of the statutory duty could lead to proceedings under Part III of the FTA (*see* **16–19**). However it now seems very unlikely that such a general duty will be created. At the end of 1994 the DTI launched another consultation exercise (*see* **20**).

# REFERENCE OF CONSUMER TRADE PRACTICES TO ADVISORY COMMITTEE UNDER PART II OF THE FAIR TRADING ACT

## 7. Reference to Advisory Committee

The Director, or the Secretary of State or other minister, may refer to a formally established Committee (i.e. the FTA provides for reference to the CPAC, although it has been disbanded with a promise of resurrection should the need arise) the question whether a consumer trade practice (defined below: *see* **8**) adversely affects the economic interests of consumers in the UK: s. 14(1) FTA. The Advisory Committee then considers the question and reports on it: s. 14(3).

> *Note*: No reference to the Advisory Committee can be made in the case of certain professions (including law, medicine, architecture and accounting) where a monopoly situation exists or may exist: s. 15; nor (except with the consent of the appropriate minister) in the case of nationalized industries: s. 16.

## 8. Consumer trade practice

For the purposes of s. 14 (*see* **7**) and the FTA generally, 'consumer trade practice' means any practice which is for the time being carried on in connection with the supply of goods (whether by sale or otherwise) or services to consumers and which relates:

**(a)** to the terms or conditions (whether as to price or otherwise) on or subject to which goods or services are or are sought to be supplied; *or*

**(b)** to the manner in which those terms or conditions are communicated to persons to whom goods or services are or are sought to be supplied; *or*

**(c)** to promotion (by advertising, labelling or marking of goods, canvassing or otherwise) of the supply of goods or services; *or*

**(d)** to methods of salesmanship employed in dealing with consumers; *or*

**(e)** to the way in which goods are packaged for the purpose of being supplied; *or*

**(f)** to methods of demanding or securing payment for goods or services supplied: s. 13.

> *Note*: 'Consumer' means any person to whom goods or services are or are sought to be supplied in the course of a business carried on by the person supplying or seeking to supply them, and who does not receive or seek to receive the goods or services in the course of a business carried on by him. 'Business' includes a professional practice; and 'goods' includes buildings: s. 137.

## 9. Proposals for the making of an Order

Under s. 17 of the FTA, a reference by the Director to the Advisory Committee under s. 14 (*see* **7**) may include in certain circumstances proposals for recommending that the Secretary of State should exercise his powers (under s. 22: *see* **11**) to make an order preventing or modifying a consumer trade practice. Proposals of this kind may only accompany the reference if the Director considers that the consumer trade practice has, or is likely to have, the effect:

**(a)** of misleading consumers as to, or withholding from them adequate information as to, their rights and obligations under a consumer transaction; *or*

**(b)** of otherwise misleading or confusing consumers with respect to any matter in connection with consumer transactions; *or*

**(c)** of subjecting consumers to undue pressure to enter into consumer transactions; *or*

**(d)** of causing the terms or conditions, on or subject to which consumers enter into consumer transactions, to be so adverse to them as to be inequitable: s. 17.

The proposals may recommend the imposition of prohibitions or requirements, particular examples of which are contained in a non-exhaustive list in Schedule 6 to the Act, namely:

**(a)** prohibition of the consumer trade practice either generally or in relation to specified consumer transaction

**(b)** prohibition of specified consumer transaction unless carried out at specified times or at specified places

**(c)** prohibition of terms or conditions purporting to exclude or limit the liability of a party to a specified consumer transaction in respect of specified matters

**(d)** a requirement that contracts relating to specified consumer transactions shall include specified terms or conditions

**(e)** a requirement that contractual documents relating to specified consumer transactions shall comply with specified provisions as to the size, type, colouring, etc., of lettering

**(f)** a requirement that specified information shall be given to parties to specified consumer transactions.

References with proposals for the making of an order must be published in full in the *London, Edinburgh* and *Belfast Gazettes*: s. 17(4).

## 10. Report of the Advisory Committee

The Committee must report on a reference which includes proposals for the making of an order within three months unless the Secretary of State allows a further period: s. 20. The Committee must take into consideration representations by interested persons: s. 81. The report must be published and laid before parliament: s. 83.

By s. 21, the committee must state in their report whether they find that the consumer trade practice specified in the reference does in fact adversely affect the economic interests of consumers in the UK, and whether it does so wholly or partly by reason of having one or more of the effects specified in s. 17 (*see* **9**). If the Committee do so conclude, their report must go on to state whether the Committee:

**(a)** agree with the proposals set out in the reference; *or*

**(b)** would agree with those proposals if they were modified in a specified manner; *or*

**(c)** disagree with the proposals.

## 11. Orders under s. 22

If the Committee agree with the proposals set out in the reference, or would agree with modified proposals, the Secretary of State may, if he thinks fit, give effect to them (either as set out in the reference, or, at his discretion, as modified in the report) by an order made by statutory instrument. The draft order must be laid before Parliament and approved by resolution of each House: s. 22.

## 12. Orders made to date

Since 1973 only the following orders have been made under the Part II procedure as described in the preceding paragraphs. (There are unlikely to be any more.)

**(a)** The Mail Order Transactions (Information) Order 1976. This Order applies to advertisements, circulars, catalogues, etc., in which persons in the course of a business invite orders by post for goods for which a payment is to be made before the goods are dispatched. Such advertisements, etc., must contain a legible statement of the name of the person carrying on the business, and the address at which the business is managed (and not just a box number, for instance). The Order does not apply to advertisements, etc., which are expressly directed at persons who are not consumers. (The government did not adopt the Director's further recommendation that it should be a criminal offence for a mail order company to fail to supply goods ordered or return money paid in advance within a specified period.)

**(b)** The Consumer Transactions (Restrictions on Statements) Order 1976, and the Consumer Transactions (Restrictions on Statements) (Amendment) Order 1978. For the provisions of these Orders, *see* 6:**24**; 11:**5**.

**(c)** The Business Advertisements (Disclosure) Order 1977. This Order deals with 'disguised business sales' by providing that a person who is seeking to sell goods that are being sold in the course of a business shall not advertise to consumers that the goods are for sale unless it is reasonably clear from the advertisement that the goods are to be sold in the course of a business.

## 13. Efficiency of Part II procedure

The object of the Part II procedure was to establish a responsible mechanism for the control as they emerge of consumer trade practices prejudicial to the consumer. Action through Act of Parliament, dependent as it is upon time being found in a crowded timetable, was thought to be too lengthy and unpredictable a process. But in the event much delay has been experienced between the Advisory Committee's several reports and their translation into law by statutory instrument. Both the present Director and his predecessor are on record as expressing their disappointment with the working of Part II of the Act.

## 14. Sanctions

Contravention of an Order under s. 22 of the FTA is an offence: s. 23. Maximum penalties are:

**(a)** on summary conviction, a fine of £5,000

**(b)** on conviction on indictment, imprisonment for a term not exceeding two years, or a fine, or both: s. 23, as amended.

Enforcement is by the local trading standards authority: s. 27. Duly authorized officers have the necessary enforcement powers, including power to make test purchases, to enter premises, and to inspect and, if needed for testing, etc., seize and detain goods or documents: ss. 28, 29. Wilful obstruction of a duly authorized officer acting in the exercise of his powers is an offence: s. 30.

Contravention of an Order under s. 22 does not of itself render a contract void or unenforceable, nor does it confer a right of action for breach of statutory duty (s. 26), but a compensation order may be available to the consumer at the discretion of the criminal court following conviction of the trader (*see* Chap. 24).

## 15. Defences

The Act contains a 'due diligence' type of defence for a person charged under s. 23 (*see* **14**), i.e. it is defence for a person charged to prove:

**(a)** that the commission of the offence was due to a mistake, or to reliance on information supplied to him, or to the act or default of another person, an accident or some other cause beyond his control, *and*

**(b)** that he took all reasonable precautions and exercised all due diligence to avoid the commission of such an offence by himself or any person under his control': s. 25(1).

If this defence involves the allegation that the commission of the offence was due to the act or default of another person, or to reliance on information supplied by another person, the defendant must, at least seven days before the hearing, serve the prosecutor with written notice giving such information identifying or assisting in the identification of that other person as the defendant possesses: s. 25(2). That other person may then be charged with and convicted of the offence: s. 24.

Publishers, advertising agents and others whose business it is to arrange for the publication of advertisements have a separate defence where contravention of an Order under s. 22 arises by virtue of the publication of an advertisement. The defendant in such a case must prove that he received the advertisement for publication in the ordinary course of business and did not know and had no reason to suspect that its publication would be an offence: s. 25(3).

# ACTION AGAINST PERSISTENTLY UNFAIR TRADERS UNDER PART III OF THE FAIR TRADING ACT

## 16. Written assurances by traders

Where it appears to the Director that the person carrying on a business has in the course of that business persisted in a course of conduct which:

**(a)** is detrimental to the interests of consumers in the UK, whether those interests are economic interests or interests in respect of health, safety or other matters; *and*

**(b)** is unfair to consumers,

the Director must use his best endeavours to obtain from that person a satisfactory written assurance that he will discontinue that course of conduct: s. 34(1).

A course of conduct is 'unfair to consumers' if it consists of:

**(a)** contravention of duties, prohibitions or restrictions enforceable by criminal proceedings, whether or not the contraventions have led to a conviction: s. 34(2); *or*

**(b)** breaches of contract or other duty enforceable by civil proceedings, whether or not proceedings have been brought; s. 34(3).

## 17. Proceedings before the Restrictive Practices Court

The Director may bring proceedings against a person before the Restrictive Practices Court if:

**(a)** the Director is unable to obtain from the person in question the required assurance to discontinue the unfair course of conduct, *or*

**(b)** that person has given the required assurance but it appears to the Director that he has failed to observe it: s. 35.

The court may:

**(a)** make an order prohibiting the course of conduct; *or*

**(b)** accept an undertaking that the course of conduct will be discontinued: s. 37.

Appeal lies to the Court of Appeal: s. 42. Breach of a court order, or undertaking given to the court, is contempt of court.

1994 saw 15 assurances given and 9 court orders. The first assurance was given in October 1974:

I, Robert James Pickersgill, of Import House, Northallerton Road, Croft on Tees, Nr. Darlington trading as Solaire Electric, hereby give to the Director General of Fair Trading written assurances sought by him pursuant to section 34(1) of the Fair Trading Act 1973:
'That I will use all reasonable precautions and exercise all due diligence to avoid continuing the following course of conduct or any similar course of conduct in the course of my business, namely:
(1) Committing offences under section 1 of the Trade Descriptions Act 1968 by applying false trade descriptions to goods or by supplying or offering to supply goods to which a false trade description is applied.
(2) Committing offences under section 11(2) of the Trade Descriptions Act 1968 by giving indications likely to be taken as indications that goods offered by me are being offered at a price less than that at which they are in fact being offered.
(3) Committing breaches of contract with consumers by supplying goods:

**(a)** which do not correspond with any description by which they are sold as required by subsection (1) of the amended section 13 of the Sale of Goods Act 1893, *or*
**(b)** which are not fit for a particular purpose for which they are being bought as required by subsection (3) of the amended section 14 of that Act.

(4) Failing to return to consumers money to which they are legally entitled, that has been received from them in the course of mail order transactions.'

For the purpose of these assurances the word 'goods' means lamps intended to emit ultra violet rays and/or to emit infra red rays and any accessory supplied or offered for supply with such a lamp. Seven hundred and sixty nine other assurances, court undertakings and orders had followed by the end of 1994.

## 18. Proceedings in the county court

Where the person against whom the proceedings are brought is not a body corporate having a share capital exceeding £10,000, and the proceedings do not involve a question of law or fact of such general application as to justify it being determined by the Restrictive Practices Court, the Director may, if he thinks fit, bring the proceedings in the county court instead: s. 41.

> *Note*: It was a county court which, in August 1983, gaoled (for 14 days) the first trader to be committed to prison for breach of a Part III undertaking. Each year only a handful of cases in connection with the Part III procedure will reach court, and when they do it is likely in practice to be the county court.

## 19. Action against an accessory

The Director can proceed against an 'accessory' where the accessory has consented to or connived at the course of conduct in question: s. 38. An 'accessory' is a director, manager, secretary or other similar officer of a company, or a person or body of persons, corporate or unincorporate, holding a controlling interest in a company. Orders by the court may bind both an accessory and an interconnected company: ss. 39, 40.

## 20. Proposals for change

It has been argued by the DGFT that the ability to act against rogue traders is unduly limited by the FTA. Some malpractices, such as extreme high pressure selling, are not in themselves unlawful, so the FTA cannot be used against them. Further, the Act requires that a 'persistent' course of improper conduct be established and that voluntary assurances should have been sought. The process is too long.

The manifesto upon which the Government was elected in 1992 contained a commitment to strengthen the powers to deal with rogue traders. In December 1994 the DTI launched a consultation exercise on proposals to increase the powers of the DGFT by reforming Part III of the FTA.

However, changes have been repeatedly proposed since the report of the then DGFT in 1986. In the current climate of deregulation it will be interesting to observe the preparedness of Government for law-making.

### Progress test 20

1. Summarize the powers and duties of the Director General of Fair Trading.

2. What are the advantages and disadvantages of voluntary codes of practice as an instrument of consumer protection?

3. Explain the role of the Office of Fair Trading in encouraging voluntary codes of practice. What success has the OFT had to date in this regard? What reform has been proposed?

4. Define 'consumer trade practice'.

5. What is the Consumer Protection Advisory Committee? What is its function in consumer protection?

6. In what circumstances may the Director, in making a reference to the Advisory Committee, include proposals for recommending that the Secretary of State should exercise his powers to make an order preventing or modifying a consumer trade practice?

7. List the prohibitions and requirements contained in Sched. 6 to the FTA as examples of recommendations which the Director might make in proposals to the Advisory Committee.

8. When must the Advisory Committee report on a reference which includes proposals for the making of an order? What must their report state?

9. In what circumstances may the Secretary of State make an order under s. 22 of the FTA? What Orders have been made to date? Summarize the respective provisions of these Orders.

10. What was the object in setting up the Part II procedure in the FTA? Has this object been achieved in practice?

11. What sanctions is a trader liable to incur by contravention of an order under s. 22 of the FTA by virtue of (a) the criminal law; and (b) the civil law? What particular defence is open to a person charged with contravention of an order? Is it possible to be imprisoned for denying consumers' rights under the Sale of Goods Act 1979?

12. In what circumstances must the Director use his best endeavours to obtain from a person a written assurance that a course of conduct will be discontinued? If the assurance sought is not given, or once given is broken, before what court or courts may the Director bring the matter, and what powers and sanctions does the court which hears the matter have?

13. When can the Director proceed against an 'accessory' under Part III of the FTA? What is an 'accessory'?

# 21

# CONSUMER SAFETY

## INTRODUCTION

### 1. Safety through criminal sanctions

The legislation governing consumer safety is now to be found in Part II of the Consumer Protection Act 1987, which consolidates with amendments the previous legislation. The CPA Part II came into force on 1 October 1987. It is intended that regulations made under the Consumer Safety Act 1978 – and its predecessor the Consumer Protection Act 1961 – will remain in force (modified as appropriate) until superseded by new regulations made under the CPA 1987 or otherwise revoked: cf. s. 50(4), (5) CPA 1987. The object of the consumer safety legislation, and of the regulations and notices made or served under it, may be encapsulated in the maxim, 'prevention is better than cure'. There are some 7,000 deaths each year in Great Britain arising from home accidents, and the safety legislation is primarily concerned with preventing such accidents through the use of criminal sanctions imposed on manufacturers, retailers, and indeed all those businesses involved in the chain of distribution. These criminal sanctions, detailed in the following paragraphs, complement the consumer's civil remedies, not least the new strict liability regime contained in Part I of the Consumer Protection Act 1987 (*see* 11: **19**).

## STATUTORY GENERAL SAFETY REQUIREMENT

### 2. General safety requirement

It is an offence to supply, offer or agree to supply, or expose or possess for supply, any consumer goods which fail to comply with the general safety requirement: s. 10(1). This provision implements the general safety requirement foreshadowed in the White Paper, *The Safety of Goods* (Cmnd. 9302) published in July 1984.

> *Note*: 'Supply' (as used here and elsewhere in the CPA) is widely defined and includes (*inter alia*) sale, hire-purchase transactions, and providing the goods under a contract for work and materials: s. 46. The supply must be in the course of a business, though it is immaterial whether the business is a business dealing in the goods: s. 46(5).

Goods fail to comply with the general safety requirement if they are not reasonably safe having regard to all the circumstances including their presentation (e.g. instructions for use), any published safety standards, and the existence of any reasonable means – taking into account the cost, likelihood and extent of any improvement – for making the goods safer: s. 10(2).

'Consumer goods' means 'any goods which are ordinarily intended for private use or consumption' except growing crops, water, food, feeding stuff or fertilizer, gas, aircraft (other than hang-gliders) or motor vehicles, drugs, medicines and tobacco: s. 10(7).

For the purposes of Part II of the CPA, 'safe', in relation to any goods, is defined as meaning that there is no risk, or no risk apart from one reduced to a minimum, that the goods will cause death or personal injury to any person: s. 19(1).

Prosecutions for offences under s. 10 have been brought recently in connection with: dangerous tools, Christmas decorations, 'vanity' cases, frying pans, moneyboxes, luggage straps, glass oil lamps, and even bath mats! In order to set 'bench marks' for the courts in assessing whether goods do meet the general safety requirement it has been the practice of the Secretary of State to 'adopt' sets of British Standards Institution ('kitemark') standards. This has been done at least a dozen times. Some would argue that this amounts to the creation of safety regulations by the back door. However, the statutory power which gave effect to this strategy has now been abrogated by the General Product Safety Regulations 1994, and no further safety standards will be approved for this purpose.

*Note*: The general safety requirement in s. 10 of the CPA is disapplied in so far as it overlaps with the General Product Safety Regulations 1994 (see **19** below). Thus in future prosecutions will usually be brought under the new (and expanded) general safety requirement in the 1994 Regulations.

## 3. Defences

Consumer goods do not fail to comply with the general safety requirement if they comply with any safety regulations, approved safety standards or relevant subordinate legislation: s. 10(3). It is a defence to show that the goods were second-hand or intended for export: s. 10(4). Retailers have a special defence: in proceedings against a retailer it is a defence for him to show that he neither knew nor had reasonable grounds for believing that the goods failed to comply with the general safety requirement: s. 10(4)(*b*). (This defence apart, liability under s. 10 is strict, though there is the usual 'due diligence' type of defence, applicable to all the offences created by the various safety provisions in the CPA (*see* **17** below).)

# SAFETY REGULATIONS

## 4. Power to make safety regulations

The Secretary of State may make regulations ('safety regulations') containing such provision as he considers appropriate for the purposes of approving safety standards in relation to the general safety requirement, and of securing that goods are safe, or not made available to persons in whose hands they would be unsafe, and that appropriate information is provided in respect of goods: s. 11(1).

Note: 'Goods' means any goods except growing crops, water, food, feeding stuff or fertilizer, gas, drugs and medicines: s. 11(4).

Over two dozen safety regulations have been made under Part II of the 1987 Act. They involve such matters as benzine in toys, furniture and furnishings, ceramic ware, gas cookers, 'low voltage' electrical equipment, toys, imitation food, cosmetics, 'all terrain' vehicles, tobacco products and heating appliances.

There are currently in force some twenty sets of regulations made under the broadly similar provisions of the previous consumer safety legislation. These regulations remain in force for the time being – until revoked or replaced by new regulations made under s. 11 of the CPA 1987. The extant regulations govern such matters as asbestos, bicycles, filament lamps for vehicles, fireworks, night-wear, certain novelties, pushchairs, and child-resistant packaging for certain toxic or corrosive products.

## 5. Provisions which may be contained in safety regulations

The CPA gives a non-exhaustive list of the matters for which safety regulations may make provision. We may note in particular that s. 11(2) allows safety regulations to contain, *inter alia*, provision:

**(a)** with respect to the 'composition or contents, design, construction, finish or packing of goods' or with respect to standards and other matters relating to goods

**(b)** for requiring goods to be approved or to conform with approved standards

**(c)** with respect to the testing or inspection of goods

**(d)** for requiring a warning or instruction or other information to be marked on or to accompany goods

**(e)** for banning the supply of particular goods or components outright.

## 6. Consultation

Before making safety regulations the Secretary of State must consult such organizations as appear to him to be representative of interests substantially affected by the proposed regulations and such other persons as he considers appropriate; in the case of proposed regulations relating to goods suitable for use at work he must consult the Health and Safety Commission: s. 11(5). Consultation is not required in urgent cases where the regulations provide that they will not last for more than twelve months (during which period the appropriate consultations can take place before further safety regulations, if necessary, are made in the normal way).

*Note*: Regulations are subject to annulment by resolution of either House of Parliament: s. 11(6).

The importance of proper consultation was emphasised in *R* v. *Secretary of State for Health ex p United States Tobacco International Inc.* (1992) where a set of regulations concerning 'oral snuff' were quashed.

# PROHIBITION NOTICES, NOTICES TO WARN AND SUSPENSION NOTICES

## 7. Prohibition notices

Where the Secretary of State considers specified goods to be unsafe, he may serve a notice ('prohibition notice') on a particular person prohibiting him from supplying the goods except with the consent, which may be conditional, of the Secretary of State: s. 13(1)(*a*).

## 8. Notices to warn

Where the Secretary of State considers specified goods which a person supplies or has supplied to be unsafe, the Secretary of State may serve on that person a notice ('notice to warn') requiring him to publish in the specified form and manner and on the specified occasions and at his own expense, a warning about the goods: s. 13(1)(*b*). It will be observed that a notice to warn stops short of giving the Secretary of State power to require those responsible for supplying unsafe goods to *recall* them.

## 9. Procedure

Schedule 2 to the CPA sets out the respective procedures which the Secretary of State must observe in serving a prohibition notice or notice to warn. These procedural requirements relate to such matters as the giving of notice by the Secretary of State of his proposed action, and the consideration by him of any representations made in respect thereof.

## 10. Notice requiring information

Where the Secretary of State requires information for the purpose of deciding whether to make, vary or revoke safety regulations, or to serve, vary or revoke a prohibition notice or notice to warn, then the Secretary of State may serve on any person a notice requiring:

(a) the furnishing of specified information; *or*
(b) the production of specified documents: s. 18(1).

Any person who fails, without reasonable cause, to comply with a notice under s. 18(1), or who knowingly or recklessly furnishes false information, commits an offence: s. 18(3). Improper disclosure of information obtained by virtue of these powers is an offence: s. 38(1).

## 11. Suspension notices

Where an officer of an enforcement authority (*see* **12** below) has reasonable cause to believe that any safety provision has been contravened, he may serve a notice ('suspension notice') prohibiting the supply (except with consent, which may be conditional) of specified goods: s. 14(1). A suspension notice cannot extend beyond six months. A further notice can only be served in respect of the same goods if proceedings have first been instituted for contravention of a safety provision or for forfeiture (*see* **16** below): s. 14(4). Any person having an interest in suspended goods may appeal to court against the suspension: s. 15. Compensation is payable to any person having an interest in goods in respect of any loss or damage caused by a suspension notice if there has been no contravention of any safety provision and no neglect or default by that person: s. 14(7).

> *Note*: 'Safety provision' used here and elsewhere in the CPA means the general safety requirement or any provision of safety regulations, a prohibition notice or a suspension notice: s. 45(1).

# ENFORCEMENT AND SANCTIONS

## 12. Enforcement

Enforcement of the various safety provisions is the duty of local authority Trading Standards or Consumer Protection departments (technically, the weights and measures authorities): s. 27(1). The Secretary of State, however, may by regulations transfer this duty to another person: s. 27(2).

## 13. Powers of enforcement authorities

Enforcement authorities may make test purchases: s. 28. A duly authorized officer of an enforcement authority may enter any premises used for business to inspect goods: s. 29(2). If the officer has reasonable grounds for suspecting that any goods are manufactured or imported and have not been subsequently supplied in the UK, he may seize and detain them for the purpose of testing whether there has been any contravention of any safety provision: s. 29(4). Any person having an interest in detained goods may appeal to the court for the goods to be released: s. 33. Compensation is payable to any person having an interest in goods in respect of any loss or damage caused by the exercise of the power to seize and detain them if there has been no contravention of any safety provision and no neglect or default by that person: s. 34. Intentional obstruction of an authorized enforcement officer is an offence: s. 32.

## 14. Dangerous imported goods

The Commissioners of Customs and Excise may disclose information obtained by them in the exercise of their functions to an enforcement authority: s. 37. Customs officers may seize and detain goods for up to two working days, during which examination can be made by an enforcement authority: s. 31. Thereafter the goods may be seized and detained by the enforcement authority under its normal powers (*see* 13).

## 15. Sanctions

Contravention of the general safety requirement, or of any safety regulations, prohibition notice, notice to warn, or suspension notice, is an offence punishable on summary conviction by imprisonment for a term not exceeding six months and/or a fine not exceeding £5,000: s. 10(6), s. 12(5), s. 13(4), s. 14(6). In the case of a corporate offender, conniving officers (e.g. directors) are also guilty and liable to prosecution and punishment: s. 40(2). A court may order reimbursement of the expenditure of the enforcement authority incurred in connection with seizing and detaining goods or in connection with their forfeiture by court order: s. 35.

## 16. Forfeiture

A court may order the forfeiture and destruction (or other disposal for repair or scrap) of goods where any safety provision has been contravened: s. 16. Forfeiture may extend to the whole batch or consignment on the basis of contravention of any safety provision by a representative sample of the goods: s. 16(4). Appeal may be made against a court order for forfeiture: s. 16(5).

## 17. Due diligence defence

Contravention of any safety provision is a strict liability offence. Nevertheless it is a defence for the defendant to show that he took all reasonable steps and exercised all due diligence to avoid committing the offence: s. 39(1).

It seems from the cases that the expression 'reasonable precautions' involves setting up a system to see that things will not go wrong, and 'due diligence' means seeing to it that the system works properly. So, set up a system (reasonable precautions) and make sure it works (due diligence). In *P & M Supplies (Essex)* v. *Devon County Council* (1992) a conviction for breach of the Toys (Safety) Regulations 1974 was upheld. It was established that of 76,960 imported toys only 378 had been tested (0.49%), and that this was insufficient.

Whilst the conviction was upheld, it was remarked that Magistrates should be assisted with independent statistical evidence to show how a reasonable trader could avoid committing an offence.

If the defence involves the allegation that the commission of the offence was due to the act or default of another person or to reliance on information supplied by another person, the defendant must at least seven days before the hearing serve the prosecutor with written notice giving such information identifying or assisting in the identification of the other person as the defendant possesses: s. 39(2), (3).

*Note*: The due diligence defence will not be available in cases of reliance on information supplied by a third party unless the defendant can show that he acted reasonably in relying on the information, in particular by taking reasonable steps to verify it: s. 39(4).

*Taylor* v. *Lawrence Fraser (Bristol) Ltd* (1978): the defendant company was prosecuted for supplying to a shop a toy which contravened the Toys (Safety) Regulations 1974 by having too high a lead content. The company's practice was to require manufacturers to guarantee that the goods supplied complied with the current regulations. Officers of the local Trading Standards department were also invited to take samples at any time for analysis. The toy in question was not covered by guarantee as the regulations had been altered in 1974 and no subsequent steps (such as analysing the paint on some of the toys in the consignment) had been taken to ensure that old stock complied with the new requirements. The company's defence, accepted by the justices, was that it had taken all reasonable precautions to avoid the commission of an offence under the Consumer Protection Act 1961 (which contains a defence corresponding to, but not identical with, that contained in the 1987 Act). On appeal by the prosecutor by way of case stated, a Divisional Court of the QBD held that the justices were bound as a matter of law to convict the defendant company, which could not by maintaining friendly relations with the local Trading Standards department avoid its responsibility for taking precautions. Lord Widgery CJ added that reliance on guarantee of compliance with the regulations was unlikely to be sufficient by itself in the absence of analysis of samples by the company. (Cf. now s. 39(4) CPA, in *Note* above.)

## 18. The 'by-pass' provision

Where the contravention by any person of a safety provision is due to an act or default committed by some other person in the course of any business of his, that other person is guilty of the offence and may be proceeded against and punished whether or not proceedings are taken against the first-mentioned person: s. 40(1).

## 19. Consumer safety: the European dimension

The General Product Safety Regulations 1994 are now in force. They implement the European Council Directive 92/59 1992 on General Product Safety. Whilst they are designed to harmonise European Community law on product safety, as far as the law in the United Kingdom is concerned, they disapply the general safety requirement in s. 10 CPA 1987 where it overlaps with the new and more extensive Regulations. They impose upon producers and distributors a duty to monitor the safety of goods by, for example, sample testing and the investigation of complaints.

They also provide for a mechanism by which member states inform each other when unsafe goods have been discovered and the action that has been taken. This exchange of information is, of course, intended to reflect the harmonisation of the law. There is to be a more collective and uniform approach to protect the people within the EU from the dangers posed by unsafe goods.

These are important new Regulations. They came into force on 3 October 1994 and they should concern all suppliers of products *intended for consumers or likely to be used by consumers.*

The new Regulations apply both to new and secondhand goods, but not to antiques, nor to products supplied on the clear understanding that they need repair or reconditioning. These Regulations do not apply to products which are specifically covered by another product directive.

Where there is no specific European directive, safety is presumed where there is compliance with member states' safety laws. Where there is neither European nor domestic law, such matters as the state of scientific and technical knowledge and compliance with codes of good practice are to be taken into account, not as conclusive of safety, but as an indication of preparedness to maintain proper standards.

Where the new Regulations apply they require that no product shall be placed on the market unless it is a 'safe product'. This will be any product which under normal or reasonably foreseeable conditions of use, including duration, does not present any risk or only minimal risks compatible with the product's use, considered as acceptable and consistent with a high level of protection for the safety and health of persons.

In order to establish whether or not a product is 'safe' these factors are to be taken into account:

- The characteristics of the product, such as its composition, packaging and instructions for its assembly and maintainence
- The effect on other products, where its use with them is reasonably forseeable
- The product's presentation, labelling, instructions for use and/or disposal and any other indication or instruction provided by the producer
- The categories of consumers who might be at risk in using the product, particularly, of course, children.

The liability attaches to 'producers' rather than distributors, 'own branders', reconditioners and, if the manufacturer is outside the EU and has no representative within the EU, the importer. Furthermore, any other party whose activities may affect the safety properties of the product may be included within the definition of 'producer'.

Distributors must 'help' assure compliance by not circulating unsafe goods or repackaging where this affects safety.

There is a defence of 'due diligence', but it will provide no excuse for those who unreasonably rely on information supplied by others.

# CIVIL LIABILITY

## 20. Validity of contracts

Contravention of a safety provision does not affect the validity of any contract unless otherwise agreed: s. 41(3).

## 21. Action for breach of statutory duty

Unless otherwise provided in the regulations, contravention of an obligation imposed by safety regulations is actionable, by any person affected by the contravention, as a breach of statutory duty: s. 41(1). Liability for breach of statutory duty is strict. Privity of contract is not a prerequisite of liability.

*Note*: This right of action for breach of statutory duty is unique in criminal statutes involving consumer protection. The corresponding provision in the previous consumer safety legislation, however, has not apparently been tried in the courts. The claimant, of course, will generally have an equally efficacious right of action under the new strict liability regime contained in Part I of the CPA 1987 (*see* 9: **19**).

## Progress test 21

1. Summarize the provisions of the Consumer Protection Acts 1961 and 1971, and indicate some of the regulations in force thereunder.

2. Is there a general prohibition against the supply of unsafe goods? How do the General Product Safety Regulations 1994 affect matters?

3. For what purpose may the Secretary of State make safety regulations? What is the procedure for making them?

4. Indicate some of the provisions which may be contained within safety regulations.

5. What is (a) a prohibition order; (b) a prohibition notice; (c) a notice to warn; (d) a suspension notice?

6. What is the extent of the power which is given to the Secretary of State to serve a notice on a person requiring information? Does the power extend to the requiring of information from lawyers? What criminal law sanctions (a) reinforce the use, and (b) protect against abuse, of this power?

7. What sanctions is a person who contravenes safety regulations liable to incur under the criminal law? What is the legal position where the commission of an offence by such a person is due to the act or default of some other person?

8. (a) A retailer who sells furniture wishes to ensure that if the goods should contravene the Furniture and Furnishings (Fire) (Safety) Regulations 1988, then he would have a defence to a prosecution brought against him in respect of the contravention. What kind of steps must he take to protect himself against criminal liability for an unwitting contravention of the regulations if such should occur?

(b) If an item of upholstered furniture sold by the retailer should, unknown to him, be so manufactured that it would fail the smouldering cigarette test imposed by the current regulations, could the purchaser of the furniture rescind the contract on that account?

(c) If not, would the purchaser have any other right of action in respect of the contravention? If the facts were that the furniture was given by the purchaser to a relative as a gift, would the recipient have any right of action in respect of the contravention?

9. What authority is responsible for the enforcement of safety regulations, prohibition orders, prohibition notices and notices to warn? What is the role of the Secretary of State as regards enforcement?

# 22

# TRADE DESCRIPTIONS

## THE LEGISLATION

### 1. Trade Descriptions Act 1968

The main thrust of the Trade Descriptions Act 1968 (in this chapter referred to as 'the Act' or 'TDA') is to prohibit:

**(a)** false trade descriptions as to goods; *and*

**(b)** false or misleading statements about services.

> *Note*: The Act does not apply to misdescriptions of the location, price or physical characteristics of land or houses. However, the Property Misdescriptions Act 1991 introduced the offence of making false or misleading statements about a prescribed matter made in the course of an estate agency or a property development business (*see* **22**).

The TDA is designed to protect the public, and does not control purely private transactions, nor a statement made by a private seller to a dealer. The Act does, however, extend to the control of statements made by one trader to another in the course of business.

> *John* v. *Matthews* (1970): a member of a working man's club bought from the club a packet of cigarettes marked '*3d*. off'. He was nevertheless charged the full recommended retail price. HELD: The object of the Act was the protection of the public, and the Act did not apply to domestic situations such as private members' clubs (Divisional Court).

### 2. Trade Descriptions Act 1972

This Act was held to be in conflict with European Community law so was repealed by the CPA, s. 48(2)(*a*).

## FALSE TRADE DESCRIPTIONS AS TO GOODS

### 3. Prohibition of false trade descriptions as to goods

Section 1 of the TDA 1968 provides: 'Any person who, in the course of a trade or business

**(a)** applies a false trade description to any goods; *or*

**(b)** supplies or offers to supply any goods to which a false trade description is applied,

shall, subject to the provisions of this Act, be guilty of an offence': s. 1(1).

The various elements comprised in the two offences created by s. 1(1) are explored in the following paragraphs (*see* **4–8**). But it may be noted at this point that the courts have glossed s. 1 by adding the requirement that though the false trade description need not induce a contract, it does have to be connected with the supply of goods before an offence under s. 1 can be committed. Not that the supplier is the only person who can commit an offence under s. 1 – it could be the buyer. The following two cases illustrate the position.

*Wickens Motors (Gloucester) Ltd* v. *Hall* (1972): car dealers sold a car to a consumer, who some forty days later returned to complain about its steering and other matters. The consumer was then told: 'There is nothing wrong with the car'. This was untrue, the car in fact being unroadworthy both then and when sold. HELD: No offence had been committed as the false statement was not connected with the sale of the car (DC).

*Fletcher* v. *Budgen* (1974): a car dealer told a private seller that there was no possibility of repairing his car and that it was fit only for scrap. The dealer then bought the car for £2, repaired it at a cost of £56, and advertised it for sale at £315. HELD: An offence could be committed by a buyer who applied a false trade description to goods on purchasing them in the course of a trade or business (Court of Appeal).

*Note*: Misdescribed motor vehicles and accessories comprise by far the largest category of convictions obtained under the Act, partly because the motor vehicles consume sufficient cash to provoke dissatisfied purchasers into complaining.

*Lewin* v. *Fuell* (1990): a stall holder at an open market was convicted of an offence under s. 1 in that the misdescribed cheap watches with expensive brand names. The court was not impressed with his assertion that nobody would take him seriously.

## 4. Meaning of false trade descriptions

Section 2 of the Act explains that a trade description is an indication, direct or indirect, and by whatever means given, of any of the following matters with respect to any goods or parts of goods, namely:

**(a)** quantity, size or gauge

**(b)** method of manufacture, production, processing or reconditioning

**(c)** composition

**(d)** fitness for purpose, strength, performance, behaviour or accuracy

**(e)** any other physical characteristics

**(f)** testing by any person and results thereof

**(g)** approval by any person or conformity with a type approved by any person

**(h)** place or date of manufacture, production, processing or reconditioning

**(i)** person by whom manufactured, produced, processed or reconditioned

**(j)** other history, including previous ownership or use: s. 2(1).

*Note*: It will be observed that matters (a)–(e) above deal with physical characteristics, while matters (f)–(j) deal with the history of the goods.

The Act goes on to provide that a trade description is false if it is false to a material degree (s. 3(1)), or likely to be misleading to a material degree: s. 3(2). Further, anything which, though not a trade description, is likely to be taken as one, is deemed to be a false trade description if false to a material degree: s. 3(3).

*Denard* v. *Smith and Dixons Ltd* (1991): here a computer was offered together with a joystick and a collection of software. The deal was advertised on a placard at the point of sale, and also in a mailshot. A customer was told that the whole package was available. When she took the goods home the software was missing. The package was advertised and not delivered. It was a false trade description.

*Robertson* v. *Dicicco* (1972) (DC): the defendant car dealer advertised a car in a newspaper as a 'beautiful car'. The car was pleasing to the eye but unfit for use. HELD: 'beautiful' (and similar adjectives) when applied to a car was likely to be taken as an indication of running quality as well as description of appearance, and so, if inaccurate, was a misleading indication within s. 3(2) of the car's performance within s. 2(1)(*d*).

*Kensington and Chelsea (Royal) London Borough Council* v. *Riley* (1973) (DC): here the expression used with respect to a car was 'immaculate'. HELD: This was likely to be taken as a description of running quality by the ordinary man and was therefore a trade description as to such quality, even if more experienced buyers would not in fact be taken in by it.

*Cadbury Ltd* v. *Halliday* (1975): on the abolition of purchase tax and the introduction of VAT the appellants were able to supply more chocolate for the same price. They accordingly supplied chocolate bars with the words 'extra value' printed on the wrappers. In due course these wrappers were discontinued and cheaper bars were introduced. For a period bars were available in both old and new wrappers, but the bars in the old wrappers no longer represented additional value. The appellants appealed against a conviction under s. 1(1) and 23 (*see* **21**). HELD: The words 'extra value' were not a trade description because they were not an indication of any matters within s. 21(1), the truth or falsity of which could be established. 'To say of an article that it is valuable is, of course, to apply a description to it, but in my view such description is not a trade description within the meaning of s. 2. In this case the alleged trade description consists of the words "extra value" and the additional "extra value" only increases the difficulty: inevitably one asks "extra of what"?' (per Ashworth J, who also thought s. 11 of the TDA (*see* **11**) inapplicable to 'worth' and 'value' claims) (Divisional Court).

*Horner* v. *Kingsley Clothing Co. Ltd* (1989): this case concerned the misdescription of sweatshirts bearing the name 'Marc O'Polo'. The justices dismissed the case on the basis that no buyer would be misled. The prosecutor's appeal was upheld. No reasonable bench could have reached that conclusion.

## 5. 'In the course of a trade or business'

The goods supplied must form an integral part of the defendant's trade or business.

*Havering London Borough Council* v. *Stevenson* (1970): the defendant ran a car hire business. His practice was to sell off cars used in the business when they were about two years old. One car so sold had a false trade description as to mileage applied to it. HELD: Although the defendant was not a car dealer, the sale had taken place as an integral part of the business carried on as a car hire firm. The defendant had accordingly contravened s. 1(1) (Divisional Court).

*Davies* v. *Sumner* (1984): a self-employed courier traded in his one-year-old motor car in part-exchange for a new vehicle. The trade-in car had travelled 118,100 miles, but its five-digit odometer read only 18,100. The courier received the appropriate credit against the price of the new car. HELD: The courier had not contravened s. 1(1)(*a*) because the trade-in transaction did not form an integral part of his business as a self-employed courier. The courier had not established a normal practice of buying and disposing of cars, a factor which distinguished the Havering case, where the defendant's business as part of its normal practice bought and disposed of cars (House of Lords).

*Devlin* v. *Hall* (1990): a taxi-driver who sold a car was not acting in the course of business because he lacked a sufficient 'degree of regularity' in such sales.

## 6. Applying a false trade description

The Act gives guidance as to when a false trade description is applied to goods. In short, a person applies a false trade description to goods if he uses the trade description in any manner likely to be taken as referring to the goods, for instance by marking the goods or their packaging, or by means of an advertisement: ss. 4(1), 5. An oral statement may amount to the use of a trade description: s. 4(2). Further, where goods are supplied in pursuance of a request which uses a trade description, the supplier is deemed to apply that trade description to the goods if the circumstances are such that it is a reasonable inference that the goods are supplied as corresponding to that trade description: s. 4(3).

*R.* v. *Ford Motor Co. Ltd* (1974) (CA): in this case Ford were deemed under s. 4(3) to have applied the trade description 'new' to a Cortina even though the order form completed by the dealer did not use the word 'new'; the form clearly contemplated a new car from Ford's stock or production line. (The court went on to hold that although the car had sustained minor damage prior to delivery to the dealer, it was still 'new' as it had been perfectly repaired.)

Compare *Raynham Farm Co. Ltd* v. *Symbol Motor Corpn Ltd* (1987): this case on

s. 13 of the Sale of Goods Act shows the limit of the court's generosity – a burnt out and refurbished Range Rover was not 'new', or even 'as new'!

*Gale* v. *Dixons Stores Group* (1993): Here a computer was supplied as new when it had in fact been returned by a previous customer as defective. This amounted to a false trade description.

## 7. Offering to supply goods

A person exposing goods for supply or having goods in his possession for supply is deemed to offer to supply them: s. 6. This provision avoids the technical difficulty that use of the phrase 'offers to supply' in s. 1 would otherwise involve. (Cf. *Fisher* v. *Bell* (1961) DC, where flick-knives displayed in a shop window constituted an invitation to treat and not an 'offer for sale' contrary to the Restriction of Offensive Weapons Act 1959; the actual decision was later reversed by statute.) The word 'supply' is wider than 'sale' and would include hire-purchase transactions, etc.

## 8. Disclaimers

Subject to certain defences (*see* **21, 22**), liability under s. 1 is strict. But such liability can nevertheless be avoided by the appropriate use of a disclaimer. The effect of a disclaimer is to neutralize a trade description; in other words by virtue of the disclaimer no trade description is regarded as having been applied to the goods at all. A disclaimer can therefore be an effective device in avoiding liability under the Act, even though the Act nowhere expressly recognizes disclaimers. Car dealers in particular have used disclaimers to neutralize false odometer readings. However, if it is to be effective a disclaimer must be 'as bold, precise and compelling as the trade description itself' (per Lord Widgery CJ in *Norman* v. *Bennett* (1974) DC). A motor dealer not wanting prospective customers to take any notice of odometer readings must take positive and effective steps to ensure that the customer understands that the reading is meaningless; 'small print' disclaimers will be ineffective to neutralize a trade description (*R.* v. *Hammertons Cars Ltd* (1976) CA). Moreover, a motor dealer will have difficulty relying on the 'due diligence' defence (*see* **21**) unless he has displayed a prominent disclaimer (*L.B. Ealing* v. *Taylor* (1995)). In *May* v. *Vincent* (1990) it was held that the TDA extends to auctioneers and that a disclaimer in an auction catalogue was ineffectual.

## 9. Disclosure of information

The Secretary of State for Trade has power to make orders requiring goods to be marked with or accompanied by information or instruction relating to goods: s. 8. Similarly, orders can be made requiring advertisements of goods to contain or refer to information relating to the goods: s. 9. The only order which was made under s. 8 and remains in force is the Trade Descriptions (Sealskin Goods) (Information) Order 1980.

## 10. False indications of approval by Royalty

It is an offence to give a false indication that any goods or services are of a kind supplied to or approved by the Queen or any member of the Royal Family: s. 12(1). Further, unauthorized use of a device or emblem signifying or deceptively resembling the Queen's Award to Industry is an offence: s. 12(2).

# FALSE OR MISLEADING INDICATIONS AS TO PRICE OF GOODS

## 11. Misleading indications as to price

The legislation on pricing and bargain offers was reworked in April 1989 with the repeal of TDA s. 11 and the infamous Price Marking (Bargain Offers) Orders 1979. These provisions have been replaced by the Consumer Protection Act (CPA) 1987, Part III. It is now an offence for a person, in the course of any business of his, to give (by whatever means) to any consumers a misleading indication as to the price of any goods, services, accommodation or facilities: s. 20(1) CPA.

The phrase 'in the course of any business of his' lay at the heart of the important recent decision in *R* v. *Warwickshire County Council ex p. Johnson* (1992) where it was held that if an employee of a company (here a Dixons store manager) gives a misleading indication of a price (here 'we will beat any TV, hi-fi and video price by £20 on the spot') he does not commit an offence under the Act because he was not the owner of the business, nor did he have a controlling interest in it.

With this decision the House of Lords seems to have held that where an employee acts in contravention of orders and gives a misleading price indication he cannot be convicted and neither can the company because, provided that they have an adequate system to provide against committing such offences, they can rely on the 'due diligence' defence.

It is also an offence to fail to take reasonable steps to correct an indication as to the price of any goods, services, accommodation or facilities, given to consumers in the course of a business of his, where the indication has subsequently become misleading: s. 20(2).

(a) 'Consumer' means, in relation to goods, any person who might wish to be supplied with the goods for his own private use or consumption; and in relation to services or facilities or accommodation, it means any person who might wish to be provided with the services or facilities, or to occupy the accommodation, otherwise than the purposes of any business of his: s. 20(6).

(b) 'Services' or 'facilities' include 'any services or facilities whatever', but not services provided to an employer under a contract of employment or services or facilities provided by an authorized person or appointed representative in the course of the carrying on of an investment business: s. 22.

(c) 'Accommodation' or 'facilities' do not include accommodation or facilities being made available by means of the creation or disposal of an interest in land (except in the case of the sale, or lease for more than 21 years, of new homes): s. 23.

> *Note*: Subject as above, s. 20 CPA covers services, accommodation or facilities as well as goods, in contrast to the old s. 11 Trade Descriptions Act 1968. Cf. too s. 14 TDA, which does not cover matters of price in relation to services, accommodation or facilities (*see* **17**).

## 12. Meaning of 'misleading' in relation to price

An indication is misleading as to price if what it conveys or implies includes any of the following, namely:

**(a)** that the price is less than in fact it is

**(b)** that the applicability of the price does not depend on facts or circumstances on which its applicability does in fact depend

**(c)** that the price covers matters in respect of which an additional charge is in fact made

**(d)** that a person expects the price to be increased, reduced or maintained (as the case may be) when in fact he has no such expectation

**(e)** that the facts or circumstances by reference to which the validity of a price comparison is to be judged are not what in fact they are: s. 21(1).

## 13. Meaning of 'misleading' in relation to method of determining a price

An indication is misleading as to a method of determining a price if what it conveys or implies includes any of the following, namely:

**(a)** that the method is not what in fact it is

**(b)** that the applicability of the method does not depend on facts or circumstances on which its applicability does in fact depend

**(c)** that the method takes into account matters in respect of which an additional charge will in fact be made

**(d)** that a person expects the method to be altered, or remain unaltered (as the case may be), when in fact he has no such expectation

**(e)** that the facts or circumstances by reference to which the validity of a comparison is to be judged are not what in fact they are: s. 21(2).

## 14. Code of Practice

The offences created by s. 20 have been backed up by a Code of Practice, which the Secretary of State approved after consultation: s. 25(1). The object of the Code is to give practical guidance on the requirements of s. 20 and to promote desirable practices as to the circumstances and manner in which price indications are given. The *legal status* of the proposed Code was the subject of some considerable debate. It is now provided that contravention of the Code will not of itself give rise to any criminal or civil liability; but in proceedings for an offence under s. 20 any contravention of the code by the defendant may be relied on – as evidence only – to establish that he committed the offence, and to the same extent the defendant may rely on compliance with the Code as evidence of a defence: s. 25(2).

The Code itself is long and detailed, but it includes:

**(a)** A general statement that indications which give only the price of the goods are unlikely to be misleading if they are accurate and cover the total charge that is being made.

**(b)** The general rule that price comparisons must be clear, e.g. higher prices should always be stated ('Sale price £150' alone will not do).

**(c)** The nature of the higher price should be clear, e.g. 'normal' or 'regular' price, and whose 'normal' or 'regular' price it is! 'Reduced from' should only refer to the seller's own previous price.

**(d)** Initials such as 'ASP' and 'RAP' (i.e. 'after sale price' and 'ready assembled price') should not be used, although 'RRP' is alright (MRP, however, is not! 'Man. Rec. price' is suggested).

**(e)** When comparing with his own previous price, and unless clearly stated otherwise, the previous price should (*i*) be shown and (*ii*) have been the price at the same outlet within the past six months for at least 28 consecutive days. (This is all that survives of the so-called '28-day rule' which existed under TDA s. 11.)

There are a great number of other details, elaborations and suggestions in the Code, but it must be borne in mind that contravention is not a crime, only evidence of an offence under CPA s. 20. In practice it is highly unlikely that compliance will attract a Trading Standards Officer's attention, whereas contravention might!

## 15. Power to make regulations

The Secretary of State is empowered to make regulations, after consultation, to regulate the circumstances and manner in which price indications may be given or to facilitate enforcement: s. 26. This regulation-making power is envisaged as a reserve power to be used only if continuing abuses are identified which are not adequately being regulated by the general provisions of s. 20 and the code of practice. The code has not proved popular with TS Departments. It is argued that prosecutions have been made very difficult. The area is currently under detailed review.

> *Note*: CPA Part III requires that where a price indication is given it should not be misleading. It does not, however, require that a price indication be given. The Price Marking Order 1991 implements EC Directives on the indication of the prices of foodstuffs and non-food products. The Order requires traders to show clearly the selling price of the goods they sell to private consumers. In some cases (e.g. for goods sold from bulk or prepacked in variable quantities) the unit price is also required.

Further, the Price Indications (Resale of Tickets) Regulations 1994 are also now in force. They require that those reselling tickets, other than within packages to which the 1992 Package Travel etc. Regulations apply, have to disclose certain details before selling them. These include the original price and any known information such as the location and quality of the seat or space. It is to be hoped that this brings down the curtain on the triple price, back-of-the-arena practices of the past.

# FALSE OR MISLEADING STATEMENTS AS TO SERVICES

## 16. Services

Section 14 of TDA provides that it shall be an offence for any person in the course of any trade or business:

**(a)** to make any statement which he knows to be false; *or*
**(b)** recklessly to make a statement which is false; as to any of the following matters, namely:

(*i*) the nature or provision of any services, accommodation or facilities provided in the course of any trade or business, or the time or manner of their provision, or their evaluation by any person.

(*ii*) the location or amenities of any accommodation provided in the course of any trade or business: s. 14(1).

Anything likely to be taken as a statement as to any of the foregoing matters is deemed to be such a statement: s. 14(2)(*a*).

Note: For the purposes of s. 14, 'false' means false to a material degree, and 'services' does not include anything done under a contract of service: s. 14(4).

There are two offences created by s. 14. Offences under s. 14(1)(*a*) require knowledge by the maker of the statement that it was false. Offences under s. 14(1)(*b*) require recklessness (*see* **19**) in the making of the statement. The knowledge or recklessness must be that of the defendant himself, and not that of an employee. In the case of corporate defendant this means that it must be the knowledge or recklessness of one of the directors or other persons identifiable with the directing mind or will of the company (cf. *Tesco Supermarkets Ltd* v. *Nattrass* (1972) HL: *see* **21**).

The offence under s. 14(1)(*a*) – making a statement knowing it to be false – is, in regard to the actual making of the statement, an offence which is committed merely if a statement is made on a person's behalf in the course of a business and its content is false to the knowledge of the person carrying on the business; it is irrelevant that the defendant does not know that the statement has actually been made (*Wings Ltd* v. *Ellis* (1984) HL), though if the defendant were innocent of fault that might in appropriate circumstances amount to a defence under s. 24 (*see* **21**).

## 17. Scope of s. 14

Section 14 does not cover a false statement about the price at which services, accommodation or facilities are provided, nor does it cover statements relating to the supply of goods. Section 1, which is concerned with goods, and s. 14, which is concerned with services, are mutually exclusive.

> *Westminster CC* v. *Ray Alan (Manshops) Ltd* (1982): traders displayed a sign at their London branch saying, 'Closing Down Sale'. This was false – the traders continued to trade at the shop. HELD by the Divisional Court: No offence had been committed under s. 14 TDA, which did not deal with the supply of goods. The term 'facilities' in s. 14 meant something akin to services and accommodation, and did not cover 'shopping facilities' such as a closing down sale. (NB: Another point arising in this case is mentioned in **13** above.)

> *Newell* v. *Hicks* (1983): motor dealers advertised that a video cassette recorder would be given 'absolutely free with every X-registration Renault' ordered from them within a specified period. Customers discovered that the recorders were not free because the trade-in allowances on their old vehicles were correspondingly reduced if they sought to take advantage of the offer. HELD by the Divisional Court: No offence had been committed under s. 14, because a false statement offering to supply a free gift related to the supply of *goods* and not to the provision of services or facilities; further, the statement referred to the price of the recorders and for that reason also did not fall within the scope of s. 14, which did not cover a false statement about price. (NB: The traders in this case might have been successfully prosecuted under s. 11(2): *see* **14**.)

> *Note:* Similarly, it has been held that an offer to 'refund the difference if you buy cheaper locally' is not concerned with the provision of services or facilities and does not come within the ambit of s. 14: *Dixons Ltd* v. *Roberts* (1984) DC. In *Kinchin* v. *Ashton Park Scooters* (1984) DC, a helmet, suit, gloves and boots offered free with a motor cycle did not fall within the ambit of s. 14; but it was held that an offer of one year's free insurance was a 'facility' within s. 14.

On the other hand, in *James Ashley* v. *The London Borough of Sutton* (1995) where a book was sold which promised success on the football pools and came with a 'money back guarantee' a conviction under s. 14 was upheld. It was, of course, argued that the deal was for goods (the book) not services, but the court said that it was necessary to 'look at the essential nature of the transaction and what in reality it was that was being provided to the customer'. Here the cost of the book was 'grossly inflated' and the promise of a refund was not honoured.

Whilst the result in this case may be considered correct – the 'money back' promise was broken – the law here remains unclear and therefore unsatisfactory on the proper distinction to be made between the supply of goods and services.

## 18. Professional services

It seems that misdescriptions made in the course of providing professional services are within the scope of s. 14.

*R.* v. *Breeze* (1973): an architecture student falsely represented himself to be fully qualified, and in consequence his services were employed to draw up plans. HELD by the Court of Appeal (Criminal Division): A false statement as to qualifications or experience amounted to a statement about the provision of services within s. 14, since it affected the likely quality of the services. Further, whether or not s. 14 applied to professions, it was not for the defendant to argue that he was providing professional services since he was in fact unqualified.

## 19. Recklessness

The commission of an offence under s. 14(1)(*b*) requires recklessness. A statement made regardless of whether it is true of false is deemed to be made recklessly, whether or not the person making it had reasons for believing that it might be false: s. 14(2)(*b*). Recklessness does not necessarily involve dishonesty or even deliberate disregard of the truth or falsity of the statement (*MFI Warehouses Ltd* v. *Nattrass* (1973) DC, *see* below).

If a statement is made without recklessness, subsequent recklessness (e.g. failure to check that customers are in the event provided with the promised hotel accommodation, as in *Sunair Holiday Ltd* v. *Dodd* (1970)), will not involve a criminal offence under s. 14. Subsequent recklessness in the sense of recklessness occurring subsequent to the making of a false statement must, however, be distinguished from the reckless making of a statement subsequent to the provision of the promised services (*Breed* v. *Cluett* (1970): *see* below).

*MFI Warehouse Ltd* v. *Nattrass* (1973): the defendant mail order form advertised louvre doors on fourteen days' free approval, thereafter a specified price plus carriage charge being payable. The same advertisement offered 'Folding Door Gear (Carriage Free)'. The defendant's intention was that carriage on the folding door gear would only be free if the customer also ordered a louvre door. So a customer who ordered only the folding door gear was charged with the carriage. The justices found as a fact that a reasonable interpretation of the advertisement was that it offered folding door gear for separate purchase carriage free and on fourteen days' approval. On appeal, a Divisional Court held that the appeal would be dismissed. The word 'recklessly' in s. 14(1) did not require that the advertiser must have deliberately closed his eyes to the truth, or that he was dishonest. It sufficed for the prosecution to show that the advertiser did not have regard to the truth or falsity of his advertisement.

*Breed* v. *Cluett* (1970): twenty days after making a contract to sell a bungalow the builder falsely stated that the building was covered by the National House-Builders' Registration Council's ten-year guarantee. HELD: This was a recklessly made false statement as to services and was caught by s. 14. It did not matter that the statement did not induce the contract. (Cf. the position relating to the supply of goods – *Wickens Motors (Gloucester) Ltd* v. *Hall*: *see* **3**.)

## 20. Statements as to the future

Section 14 does not apply to promises as to the future, which cannot be either true or false, even if breach of such a promise involves breach of contract. The problem, familiar enough in civil law, is to determine when a promise as to the future also involves a question of past or present fact. A promise may involve by implication a statement of fact, for example that the promisor has the present intention, or the means, of performing the promise. Brochures and advertisements by package holiday firms often give rise to this problem of determining whether statements involve questions of fact or merely promises about the future.

*Beckett* v. *Cohen* (1972): a builder agreed to build a garage 'as the existing garage' and 'within ten days'. He fulfilled neither promise. HELD: The Act was never intended 'to make a criminal offence out of what is really a breach of warranty' (per Lord Widgery CJ). A Divisional Court accordingly upheld the magistrates' court's dismissal of the prosecution's case. The decision would have been different if the builder had never had the intention or the means of fulfilling his promises.

*British Airways Board* v. *Taylor* (1976): this case concerned the overbooking policy considered prudent for major international airlines to operate in order to counteract 'no-shows', i.e. those passengers who fail to turn up having made flight reservations. Occasionally intending passengers have to be off-loaded because of overbooking. The Board were prosecuted in respect of one such off-loading incident by BOAC. The intending passenger's booking of a specific flight had been confirmed by letter from BOAC. At the time of writing the flight had not been overbooked. A prosecution was brought in respect of the false statement about services contained in the written confirmation. The case eventually reached the House of Lords. HELD: The justices were entitled to find that the confirmatory letter was a statement of fact (i.e. the fact of a certain booking on a specified flight) and not a mere promise as to the future, which statement was false, contrary to s. 14 of the TDA, having regard to the overbooking policy exposing the passenger to the risk that he might not secure a seat on the flight. However, the British Airways Board could not be prosecuted for criminal offences by BOAC (BOAC had been dissolved by Order in April 1974).

*R.* v. *Avro* (1993): here a return flight ticket was issued for a flight that had never existed. The customer was issued with another ticket to fly a little earlier with a different airline. An appeal against conviction was dismissed because the statement about the return flight was made when the ticket was read and remained so so long as it remained uncorrected. It was wrong and Avro knew that. No contractual right to make changes could affect this.

# DEFENCES

## 21. Due diligence defence

Despite the fact that the offence created by s. 1 is one of strict liability (that in s. 14 requires *mens rea*) certain defences do exist within the TDA. The main defences are to be found in s. 24, namely: 'In any proceedings for an offence under this Act it shall . . . be a defence for the person charged to prove:

**(a)** that the commission of the offence was due to a mistake or to reliance on information supplied to him or to the act or default of another person, an accident or some other cause beyond his control; *and*

**(b)** that he took all reasonable precautions and exercised all due diligence to avoid the commission of such an offence by himself or any person under his control': s. 24(1).

The defendant has to prove that he comes within the terms of both paragraphs **(a)** and **(b)**. Moreover, if the defence involves the allegation that the commission of the offence was due to the act or default of another person, or to reliance on information supplied by another person, the defendant must at least seven days before the hearing serve the prosecutor with written notice giving such information identifying or assisting in the identification of that other person as the defendant possesses: s. 24(2). That other person may then be charged with and convicted of the offence: s. 23. Indeed, it has been held that in order to prevent the administration of the Act becoming slipshod, a defendant seeking to rely on s. 24 must do all that can reasonably be expected in the way of inquiry and investigating as to the identity of the defaulting party (*McGuire* v. *Sittingbourne Co-operative Society* (1976) CA).

Finally, in any proceedings for an offence of supplying or offering to supply goods to which a false trade description is applied, it is defence for the defendant to prove that he did not know, and could not with reasonable diligence have ascertained, that the goods did not conform to the description or that the description had been applied to the goods: s. 24(3).

> *Note:* Cf. the 'due diligence' defences under the Consumer Credit Act (*see* 14:**4**); the Fair Trading Act (*see* 20:**15**); and the CPA Part II (*see* 21:**17**).

> *Tesco Supermarkets Ltd* v. *Nattrass* (1972): one of Tesco's stores displayed a poster offering a 'flash' offer for Radiant washing powder. When the packets to which the offer related were sold out ordinary packets were sold, but the poster was not removed, the store manager failing to carry out the daily check of special offers as required by his superiors. Tesco were prosecuted for committing an offence under s. 11 of the TDA. The case reached the House of Lords. HELD: The offence was due to the default of 'another person', i.e. the store manager, and the company had taken all reasonable precautions and exercised all due diligence in setting up, as they had, a chain of command which in its detailed operation was an effective system of control to avoid the commission of offences under the Act. The store manager was 'another person' because, unlike the directors and others in top management positions,

he could not be identified with the controlling mind and will of the defendant company; nor had the company delegated powers of control to the manager, who was merely one of many store managers directed through the chain of command to take precautions against mispricing. The manager had no delegated powers of independent action in this respect. Tesco accordingly succeeded in their defence under s. 24(1).

*Note*: The TDA does not impose vicarious liability on an employer for the criminal acts or omissions of its employees. But where the commission of an offence under the Act is due to the act or default of some other person, that other person may be charged with and convicted of the offence whether or not proceedings are taken against the first mentioned person: s. 23. It follows that the store manager in the *Tesco* case could have been charged with the offence.

In any proceedings for an offence under s. 20(1) CPA, it is a defence for the defendant to show that he took all reasonable steps and exercised all due diligence to avoid committing the offence: s. 39 CPA.

## 22. Innocent publication of an advertisement

Where proceedings under s. 20 CPA arise by virtue of the publication of an advertisement, then publishers, advertising agents and others whose business it is to arrange for the publication of advertisements have a similar defence under s. 24(3) CPA to that contained in s. 25 of the Trade Descriptions Act 1968, that is to say the defendant in such a case must prove:

**(a)** that he received the advertisement for publication in the ordinary course of business; *and*

**(b)** that at the time of publication he did not know and had no grounds for suspecting that the publication would involve the commission of the offence.

Furthermore, in any processings for an offence under s. 20(1) CPA involving a recommended price, it is a defence for the person giving the misleading indication to show:

**(a)** that the indication did not relate to the availability from him of any goods, services, accommodation or facilities

**(b)** that the price had been recommended to every person from whom the goods etc. were indicated as being available

**(c)** that the price indicated was misleading only because of a failure by any person to follow the recommendation

**(d)** that it was reasonable for the defendant to assume that the recommendation was for the most part being followed: s. 24(4) CPA.

# SANCTIONS AND ENFORCEMENT

## 23. The enforcement authority

Enforcement of Part III of the CPA is the duty of the local weights and measures authority: s. 27(1) CPA. A duly authorized officer has powers for enforcing Part III of the CPA similar to those available under the TDA (ss. 26–29). Accordingly, he may make test purchases (s. 28 CPA), enter any premises used for business to inspect goods, and if necessary seize and detain goods or records required as evidence: s. 29 CPA. Intentional obstruction of an enforcement officer is an offence: s. 32 CPA.

## 24. Sanctions

Contravention of ss. 1 or 14 TDA or s. 20 CPA is triable either summarily or on indictment and punishable by a fine (not exceeding £5,000 if tried summarily, unlimited on indictment where up to two years' imprisonment can also be imposed).

> *R.* v. *Hewitt* (1991): here the defendant had been convicted on eight counts of 'clocking' Land Rovers and Range Rovers. He was sentenced to jail, but the term was reduced to two months with a £500 fine on each count on appeal. The court did note, however, Parliament's concern that goods which were offered for sale should be honestly described, and that this was likely to be a frustrated concern if those who engage in dishonest practice could take comfort in the fact that, in the not very likely event of detection, they could expect to be dealt with by the courts in a way which left them with their liberty.

Contravention of any provision made by or under Part III of the CPA does not confer any right of civil action in respect of any loss or damage suffered in consequence of the contravention: s. 41(2) CPA.

The penalties imposed in practice by the courts, even in cases of multiple prosecution, can be of considerable magnitude (cf. *R.* v. *Thompson Holidays Ltd* (1974), *see* 24:3). They can also be so small as to attract the DGFT's comment, that they are 'laughably inadequate'. He was referring to small fines imposed upon 'car clockers'.

It should be noted that a contract for the supply of goods is not void or unenforceable by reason only of contravention of the Act: s. 35. A compensation order may, however, be available to the consumer at the discretion of the criminal court following conviction of the trader (*see* Chap. 24).

## 25. Dealing in property: at last the Property Misdescriptions Act

The ideas within the Trade Descriptions Act were extended to property in less-than-swift response to the 1976 recommendations by the then DGFT when the 1991 Act came into force on 27 June 1991, although even then it had no practical significance until 4 April 1993 when the Property Misdescriptions (Specified Matters) Order 1992 came into effect.

The Act is designed, in its long title, 'to prohibit the making of false or misleading statements about property matters in the course of estate agency business and property development business'.

The basic offence is set out in s. 1(1). Where a false or misleading statement about a prescribed matter is made in the course of an estate agency business or a property development business, otherwise than in providing conveyancing services, the person by whom the business is carried on shall be guilty of an offence under this section.

Broadly, the scope and nature of the offence and the manner of enforcement of the law resembles that of the TDA. The 'prescribed matters' were set out in the subsequent Order, and include a predictable list including the location and address of the property described, its aspect, view, outlook or environment, the availability and nature of services, facilities or amenities, accommodation, measurements or sizes, fixtures and fittings, and so on.

One of the central ideas, of course, is to reduce the flowery nature of estate agents' 'particulars', and to require specific measurements of, say, the third bedroom to be accurate. There is the familiar 'due diligence' defence.

## Progress test 22

1. Does the TDA 1968 control statements which are:
   (a) made by a consumer to a dealer;
   (b) made by one dealer to another;
   (c) made by the bartender at a tennis club;
   (d) made by a buyer of goods?

2. Why was the TDA 1972 repealed?

3. What offences does s. 1 of the TDA 1968 create? How does statute law deal with false or misleading statements about land?

4. After carrying out a MOT test for a motorist a garage refuses to give him a MOT certificate, the vehicle tester stating falsely that the car's brakes do not conform to the requirements. Does this statement constitute an offence within s. 1 of the TDA 1968? (Cf. *Wycombe March Garages Ltd* v. *Fowler* (1972).)

5. Consider whether the following statements are trade descriptions within the TDA: (a) 'hand-made'; (b) 'all wool'; (c) 'showerproof'; (d) 'one-owner'; (e) 'extra value'?

6. When is a trade description 'false' for the purposes of the TDA?

7. A typing agency is selling off some electric typewriters, having replaced them with word processors. The typewriters are described as 'beautiful', but several of them do not function properly. Has the agency committed an offence under s. 1 of the TDA?

8. D, a trader, advertises in a newspaper in the following terms: 'drip-dry all cotton shirts, sky blue, £10 each. State collar size . . .' The shirts which D had in stock to supply to customers placing orders in response to the advertisement are sky blue and all cotton, but require ironing if they are to be free of creases after washing. Is D guilty of offering to supply goods to which a false trade description is applied contrary to s. 1 of the TDA? Would customers have any remedy if D were found guilty?

9. E, a second-hand car dealer, does not wish to cover over his vehicles' mileometer readings, but at the same time E does not wish to incur liability under the TDA should the reading in any particular case turn out to be incorrect. What must E do in the circumstances?

10. What goods have to be marked with or accompanied by an indication of their country of origin?

11. F, a window cleaner, falsely claims that his window cleaning services are patronized by Buckingham Palace. Is this an offence?

12. Can a hotelier be convicted under the CPA Part III of knowingly making a misleading statement as to the price of accommodation?

13. Does the same strict liability basis apply to misdescribed services under s. 14 TDA as to misdescriptions under s. 1?

14. A company publishes a brochure containing a photograph of a named hotel which shows it as having a sandy beach. Someone in the company has made a mistake, however, as the photograph is of a different hotel. The named hotel had a pebble beach. Is the prosecution likely to be able to secure a conviction in relation to this error against the company, assuming that none of the directors was aware of the mistake?

15. K undertook to install a burglar alarm system 'within one week of the customer placing the order'. The job took K one month. Has K committed any offence under the TDA? Would it make any difference to your answer if a strike were causing a shortage of materials at the time that K gave the undertaking, so that K was aware that the job could not be completed within the stipulated time?

16. What are the special defences afforded by the TDA? How 'strict' is the liability of a trader who is charged with applying a false trade description to goods, or (as the case may be) with supplying goods to which a false trade description is applied? Is the position of a publisher who publishes an advertisement which contravenes the Act, without knowing that such is the case, any different?

17. Which authorities are responsible for enforcing the TDA? What sanctions may be imposed on conviction of an offender?

18. Sharpe is the proprietor of a small car hire firm. From time to time he sells off vehicles at the prevailing trade price and pays the proceeds of sale back into the business for the purchase of new vehicles. Recently he advertised one such vehicle for sale in the local press, as follows:

   '1988 Cavalier 2.0 CDi, one owner from new, absolutely 100 per cent, £8,995.'

   The car's odometer reads 12,200 miles, whereas the true mileage was 112,200 miles, because the mileage had gone right round the clock on the five-digit odometer, such was the extent of the use to which Sharpe's customers had put the vehicle. Unknown to Sharpe, the Cavalier's engine had caught fire at his supplier's before the car had come into his (Sharpe's) possession; but his supplier had fully restored the engine at considerable expense. The form of contract used by Sharpe on sale of vehicles includes this clause in small print, viz.:

   'The seller is not answerable for the mileage shown on the vehicle's odometer.'

   Sharpe duly sold the Cavalier from his private residence (which was the address given in his advertisement).
   What criminal offences (if any) has Sharpe committed?

# 23

# FOOD

## 1. Introduction

The law relating to the consumer and his food is a complex matter. Of course, the general law of contract and the applied contract law relating to the sale of goods (*see* **1–8**) applies to the sale of food. Furthermore, the general law of product liability, the tort of negligence (*see* **11**), and so on apply too, as does the recent addition to the armoury – CPA Part I (*see* **11**).

The Trade Descriptions Act 1968 applies to food. Furthermore, there is a body of criminal statute law which is especially designed for food. It is very complicated and detailed, and only the barest of outlines is possible here. The temptation to start at the beginning – with the Assize of Bread and Ale in 1266 – will be resisted! The history of food law, particularly regarding the adulteration of foods such as beer, tea, coffee and bread, extended over the years to the first generalised statute: the Adulteration of Food or Drink Act 1860. There were several amending and consolidating Acts, ending with the Food Act 1984 which, as will be seen, has itself largely been repealed and replaced. The spring of 1990 saw an important step in the development of this law – the Food Safety Act 1990.

## 2. Composition

The contents of some foods are precisely stipulated by the law. This is done by way of regulations made under the Food Act and its predecessors. For example consider the simplicity of the regulations (*see* the Soft Drinks Regulations 1964, as amended) concerning fruit drinks: 'juice' must be pure fruit juice, 'citrus squash' must contain at least 25% fruit juice before it has been diluted, 'comminuted citrus drink' must contain approximately 10% processed fruit if it is to be drunk undiluted, or 2% if it is to be drunk straight from the container, 'citrus crush' which is to be drunk undiluted must contain at least 5% citrus fruit juice, except lime crush, which only needs 3%, and 'orangeade' and 'lemonade' need not contain any fruit juice at all!

## 3. The Food Safety Act 1990

The name of the statute may appear misleading – the Act covers far more than just the safety of food. The earlier legislation (e.g. the Food Act 1984) has, for all practical purposes, been repealed by this Act. Nevertheless, the many and various Regulations which were made under the previous legislation remain in force until replaced. This Act is 'EU compatible' in the sense that it provides the authority for the relevant Ministers to implement EU legislative requirements without further primary legislation.

The Act applies to the 'supply' of food in virtually all circumstances. That is not only restaurants but also canteens, schools, hospitals, clubs and so on. There is no need for the outlet to be profit-orientated. For the first time water is classified as food, and unless the contrary is proved, all food ingredients, raw materials and so on that are found upon business premises are assumed to be intended for human consumption.

## 4. Food injurious to health

It is an offence to render food injurious to health by the addition or subtraction or the use of any process or treatment: s. 7.

## 5. Nature, substance and quality

It is still an offence to supply to the prejudice of the purchaser food which is not of the nature, substance or quality demanded by the purchaser: s. 14. So cases such as *Smedleys* v. *Breed* (1974) (the caterpillar in the peas) and *Greater Manchester Council* v. *Lockwoods* (1979) (the beetle in the strawberries) will still be instructive.

## 6. Food safety requirement

An entirely new concept of a generalised food safety requirement has been introduced by this Act, s. 8. It is an offence to supply food which is unfit for human consumption, which is injurious to health or which is contaminated beyond the extent at which it would be reasonable for use for human consumption. This provision is wider than those which were found in ss. 1 and 8 of the Food Act 1984, but falls short of a general duty to supply safe food. This was the subject of some criticism, but the recently implemented European Directive on Product Safety includes food (*see* 21:**19**).

## 7. Powers of 'authorised officers'

The previous powers to inspect, seize, detain and condemn all or part of batches of food were strengthened and extended: ss. 29–33. 'Improvement notices' (s. 10) can be issued which might require specified steps to be taken to comply with Regulations concerning the condition of premises, equipment, the control of processes and treatments, materials, substances, and so on. Should there be a conviction, a court can issue a 'prohibition order' (s. 11) concerning the use of premises and/or equipment. In extreme cases an authorised officer can issue a notice to the effect that he intends to apply for an emergency prohibition order. This takes effect on one day's notice, but a court must act within three days to confirm it.

## 8. Emergency control orders

The Minister can make an emergency control order (s. 13) which would have effect beyond a single business enterprise. This is the legislative reaction to recently reported widespread food safety scare stories. There is no provision for compensation should such an order be made in error, although one was proposed in the Lords' debates.

## 9. Food labelling

Apart from the many and various regulatory requirements about the labelling of foodstuffs, it is an offence to use a label or advertisement or presentation which falsely or misleadingly describes the nature, quality or substance of food: s. 15.

The most important of the Regulations here are the Food Labelling Regulations 1984 (as amended), under which food must not be presented such that 'a purchaser is likely to be misled to a material degree as to the nature, substance or quality of the food.' There is an overlap of provision here. Furthermore, the application of the Trade Descriptions Act 1968 to food probably gives a three-layered protection for consumers against the misdescription of food, and this without taking into account the impact of the European Union and its work on regulating 'food claims'.

For example, there is currently a draft proposal for a Directive 'on the use of claims concerning foodstuffs'. This envisages banning false or misleading advertising or marketing claims about foodstuffs, banning 'medical' claims, requiring clear and concise explanations of any claim that is made and finally requiring that those making claims must be able to prove their accuracy and truthfulness.

## 10. Further steps forward

Food premises either have to be licensed or registered, in accordance with Regulations: s. 19.

Those who are employed as food handlers have to be trained: Sch. 1 para 5.

There are Regulations to cope with 'novel foods' (s. 18), and special food treatments and processes such as irradiation (s. 16), although it is interesting to note that, despite all the fuss that had been made about this process, the word 'irradiation' does not appear in the Act. This term 'novel foods' caused some puzzlement. It seems that such foods are those which have never been used for human consumption in Great Britain before. So they could include those which have been eaten elsewhere for centuries – such as some bizarre fruit from a jungle. It also includes something like 'state-of-the-art' foods such as the fancy slimming products that we hear so much about.

## 11. Defences

In s. 20 there is the defence that the offence was 'due to the fault of another person'. That person can be prosecuted instead – or as well. There is a due diligence defence: s. 21. It is intended that offences should be strict but that those who have done all that they could reasonably have been expected to have done to avoid the commission of strict liability offences should be able to defend themselves.

Naturally, the extent of the precautions necessary to satisfy the requirement of 'due diligence' will vary depending upon such factors as the size and resources of the business enterprise.

One aspect of the Act which caused a little alarm in the food industry was the removal of the 'written warranty' defence. This was available to a defendant who could establish that the food in question was within the law and that he had a written promise to that effect and that he had no reason to believe otherwise, and that the food was in the same state as it had been when he bought it in. This is no longer good enough.

There is also the defence of 'innocent publication' available to those who are charged with offences connected with food advertising but who published in the course of their business and had no reason to suspect that the copy would infringe the Act.

## 12. Penalties

Offences under the Act such as obstructing an officer in the course of duty and so on carry a maximum of £2,000; food-related offences are subject to a maximum of £20,000: s. 35.

## Progress test 23

1. Outline the general law which relates to food.

2. Describe the compositional requirements which relate to soft drinks. From your own research describe those which relate to another common food product.

3. List the various offences which relate to food which are to be found within the 1990 Act.

4. Describe the defences which are available to those accused of these offences; and the penalties which might induce them to seek the protection of those defences. What was the 'written warranty' defence? What justifications can you think of which might have supported its removal?

5. List the powers of authorised officers. Does the Minister have any further powers?

6. What are 'novel foods'?

# 24

## COMPENSATION ORDERS

## THE DISCRETIONARY POWER

### 1. Power to make compensation orders

A court on convicting a person of an offence, instead of or in addition to dealing with him in any other way, may make a compensation order requiring that person to pay compensation 'for any personal injury, loss or damage resulting from that offence or any other offence which is taken into consideration by the court in determining sentence': s. 35 Powers of Criminal Courts Act 1973 (as amended by the Criminal Justice Act 1988, ss. 105–106).

This wide power, introduced by the Criminal Justice Act 1972 and re-enacted in the 1973 Act, while not confined to benefiting consumers, is of great significance in consumer protection. It must be remembered that consumer protection measures imposing criminal law sanctions generally afford no direct remedy to the individual consumer suffering loss, who is left to his civil law remedies (cf., for example, s. 26 of the Fair Trading Act (*see* 20:**14**) and s. 35 of the Trade Descriptions Act (see 22:**24**)). Even the Consumer Safety Act only envisages an action for breach of statutory duty in respect of a breach of an obligation imposed by safety regulations (*see* 21:**20, 21**). Accordingly, the discretion given to the court by s. 35 of the Powers of Criminal Courts Act 1973 is an important addition to the consumer's remedies. The courts are prepared to exercise their discretion, particularly in trade descriptions cases.

### 2. Limitation on the s. 35 power

There are two points to note:

**(a)** No compensation order may be made for loss to dependants consequent on death; nor for injury, loss or damage due to a road accident (except that in the case of a Theft Act offence a compensation order may, in road accident cases as in other cases, cover damage to the property occurring while the property was out of the owner's possession): s. 35(2), (3).

**(b)** The compensation ordered by a magistrates' court cannot exceed £5,000 in respect of each offence for which the offender is convicted: Magistrates' Courts Act 1980, s. 40. In the higher courts there is no financial limit.

**(c)** In 1993–94 there were some 1,286 cases brought under the Trade Descriptions

Act. Those convicted faced fines totalling over £1 million. The total compensation ordered was only around £95,000.

## 3. Exercise of the discretion

Section 35 provides that in determining whether to make a compensation order, and the amount of any such order, the court must have regard to the defendant's means: s. 35(4).

The compensation will be such amount as the court considers appropriate, having regard to any evidence and to any representations that are made by or on behalf of the accused or the prosecutor: s. 35(1A). When the court considers that it would be appropriate both to impose a fine and to make a compensation order, but that the offender has insufficient means to pay both, the court must give preference to compensation (though it may impose a fine as well): s. 35(4A).

Decided cases have shown that s. 35 is only intended for simple cases. A compensation order is appropriate only where the legal issues are quite clear. However, with the 1988 CJA an attempt was made to (in the words of the Home Secretary) 'mark the great regard which society now pays to the position of victims of crime'. In 1993–94 traders convicted under consumer legislation were ordered to pay compensation totalling over £100,000. Nevertheless, the court will hesitate to embark on any complicated factual investigation. The fact that the loss is not precisely quantifiable is no bar to the making of an order. Finally, it should be noted that compensation orders may be made even in circumstances where the hope of compensation may act to encourage multiple prosecutions.

R. v. *Thomson Holidays Ltd* (1974): the defendants issued two million copies of their 1971 holiday brochure. One of the advertised hotels was falsely described as having certain amenities and on summary conviction under s. 14 of the Trade Descriptions Act the defendants were fined £450. A subsequent complaint by another member of the public who had been on holiday at the same hotel led to a second prosecution, this time on indictment. The defendants were fined £1,000 and ordered to pay the prosecution costs plus the sum of £50 compensation to the complainant. On appeal against conviction, sentence and compensation order, it was HELD by the Court of Appeal (Criminal Division) that each communication of the false statement in the brochure was a separate offence; so that the defendants could not plead *autrefois convict*. The present proceedings were not an abuse of process (though the Court did accept that a time might come when further prosecutions would be oppressive and either would have to be stayed or nominal penalties only would be imposed). The compensation order was therefore properly made. The loss could fairly be said to have resulted from the offence of failing to provide the advertised amenities. (The fine of £1,000 was also held not to be too severe in the circumstances.)

Note: In *Wings Ltd* v. *Ellis* (1984) HL (*see* 22:16), it was pointed out that for the purposes of s. 14 TDA a statement can be 'made' not only on communication to the ultimate recipient but also at earlier stages in the chain of distribution, such as when the brochures are first posted or published in accordance with the original intention of the issuing house.

# PROCEDURE

## 4. Making application for an order

The legislation lays down no express procedure governing an application for a compensation order. In practice if the consumer indicates to the justices' clerk or the prosecutor his wish for a compensation order, the court will consider the matter, whatever the consumer's theoretical lack of *locus standi*. The court may make a compensation order even though no express application for one has been received.

## 5. Subsequent civil proceedings

If damages are awarded in subsequent civil proceedings, any amount paid by the offender under a compensation order is deducted from the assessed damages: s. 38. The court may discharge or reduce a compensation order if the injury, loss or damage in respect of which the order was made is held in civil proceedings to be a lesser sum, or if lost property in respect of which the order was made is recovered by the victim: s. 37.

> *Note*: Under the Civil Evidence Act 1968 a conviction of a criminal offence may be used in evidence in subsequent civil proceedings: s. 11.

## Progress test 24

1. What is a compensation order? Why is it significant in consumer protection?

2. What financial limits (if any) are placed on the court's power to make a compensation order?

3. What factors must the court take into account in determining whether to exercise its discretion to make a compensation order?

4. What is the procedure for making application for a compensation order?

5. Can a consumer in whose favour a compensation order has been made acquire compensation twice over by bringing civil proceedings in respect of his loss?

6. In what circumstances may the court discharge or reduce a compensation order?

# 25

# THE SETTLEMENT OF CONSUMER DISPUTES

## SOURCES OF ADVICE

### 1. Consumer advice centres

If a direct approach to the trader does not result in a satisfactory solution to a consumer complaint, the consumer may turn to a solicitor for advice and assistance. Alternatively the consumer may turn, at least in the first instance, to other – generally free – sources of help. One such free service is available through consumer advice centres. Initially established and funded with the aid of substantial government grants, consumer advice centres, now funded by the community charge, are run by some fifty local authorities under powers derived from the Local Government Act 1972. Besides giving pre-shopping information and literature, consumer advice centres are often instrumental in helping consumers to resolve disputes with local traders. Sometimes the consumer advice centre will assist the consumer in litigation against a recalcitrant trader.

> *Note*: Pre-shopping information is of course also available to subscribers to *Which?* and other publications of the Consumers' Association. Moreover, subscribers to the *Which? Personal Service* have access to a service assisting with individual consumer complaints. The Consumers' Association, a non-profit company limited by guarantee, speaks and campaigns for consumers. In this connection there may also be mentioned the National Consumer Council (successor to the Consumer Council, abolished in 1971), an independent but government-funded body established in 1975. The National Consumer Council does not take up individual consumer complaints, but represents and articulates the interests of consumers to government, commerce and industry, including nationalized industry.

### 2. Citizens' advice bureaux

The citizens' advice bureau service is a voluntary agency consisting of a network of some 800 autonomous bureaux, which are largely financed by local authority grants. Local bureaux are represented through area committees on the registration and policy-formulating authority of the movement, the Council of the National Association of Citizens' Advice Bureaux.

Up to 20 per cent of all inquiries concern consumer matters. Staff (whose training includes instruction in consumer law) or volunteer lawyers in attendance will advise the consumer and may negotiate with traders on the consumer's behalf. They may refer the consumer to a local solicitor. Many bureaux operate a rota scheme, whereby volunteer solicitors attend at the bureau to give free advice to clients, complex problems being transferred to the solicitor's own office with fees charged to the legal aid fund where appropriate. Some bureaux now have their own salaried solicitors.

### 3. Neighbourhood law centres

Neighbourhood law centres, which owe their inspiration to experience in the United States, may be characterized as providing in deprived neighbourhoods a comprehensive legal service, including court representation, for groups as well as for individuals. It should be understood that advice on consumer problems forms a relatively low percentage of a law centre workload, problems of more pressing social urgency, such as housing, being given priority. Law centre clients are generally expected to fall within the ambit of the legal aid scheme, and may have to pay a contribution in accordance with the scheme's provisions. Subject to this, the legal service is free to clients. Adequate funding of a law centre often proves difficult, though funds can come from a variety of sources including the local authority.

> *Note*: Unlike neighbourhood law centres, *legal advice centres* do not provide a comprehensive legal service but instead give free legal advice, referring anything requiring protracted correspondence or court proceedings to a local solicitor or appropriate social agency. Legal advice centres are typically open for a few hours each week, staffed by volunteers.

### 4. Consumers' or consultative councils

It should not be overlooked that the consumer with an unresolved complaint against one of the public utilities may put the complaint before the appropriate consumers' or consultative council. The Acts setting up the utility companies of closest concern to consumers also set up these consumers' or consultative councils. Apart from considering complaints from the public, the councils act as consumer watchdogs and advise the company in question on general policy matters. How many teeth the watchdogs have is, however, somewhat problematical. Privatization of nationalized industries has spawned a number of new agencies (e.g. OFTEL, OFGAS, OFWAT) which are charged with protecting consumer interests.

## SOURCES OF FINANCIAL ASSISTANCE

### 5. Legal aid

Legal aid under the Legal Aid Act 1988 is available in principle for the litigation of consumer disputes as for the litigation of other disputes, provided of course that the applicant falls within the limits of financial eligibility. But legal aid will not be granted for a case which is automatically referred to arbitration under the small claims procedure in the county court (*see* **10**), and in practice legal aid seems rarely to be obtained in consumer cases. Moreover, even if legal aid is obtained there is often a statutory charge in favour of the legal aid fund, whereby money or property recovered or preserved for the client goes first to pay such costs as have not already been recovered from the other party or defrayed by any contribution payable by the client under the financial eligibility requirements of the scheme.

*Note*: The Law Society publishes 28 regional directories (known as The Solicitors' Regional Directory) which are distributed free to public libraries, citizens' advice bureaux, consumer advice centres and other agencies. The directories indicate the categories of work, including legal aid work, which local solicitors are respectively prepared to undertake. One of the specified categories is consumer problems. Details are also given of legal advice centres, law centres and citizens' advice bureaux providing legal help.

## 6. The green form scheme

Of greater utility for consumers is the 'green form' scheme, so called on account of the form to be filled in by an applicant for financial assistance. It operates as follows: a solicitor may, without needing authority from the legal aid office, incur up to the cost of 2 hours work at prescribed rates by way of giving advice, writing letters, negotiating and settling claims, even helping the consumer prepare for a court case. But the solicitor may not himself take steps in court proceedings.

An applicant under the green form scheme has to meet certain financial eligibility requirements. There are limits on the amount of disposable capital and disposable income (i.e. income after deduction of tax, national insurance and allowances for dependants) which an applicant may have. Applicants whose disposable income falls within the limits but exceeds an amount specified by regulations will be liable to pay a contribution towards the solicitor's costs in accordance with a sliding scale. Where the costs exceed the contribution (if any) payable by the client, there is as regards the balance a charge in favour of the solicitor on any money or property recovered for the client (cf. **5**).

*Note*: Consumers ineligible for legal aid or legal advice and assistance might feel inclined to take out an appropriate legal expenses insurance policy against the risk of future problems.

## 7. The fixed fee interview

Until quite recently, solicitors who participated in the fixed fee interview would charge the client not more than £5 including VAT for an initial interview of up to half an hour but the scheme died a natural death. Often a brief preliminary interview will not attract a charge from a solicitor anyway.

# SMALL CLAIMS

## 8. Action in the county court

The normal county court procedure is applicable to consumer matters as to other matters within the county court's jurisdiction. With the implementation of the Courts and Legal Services Act 1990, the margin between High Court and County Court jurisdiction has been both narrowed and clouded. In general the presumption is that cases in contract and tort with a value up to £50,000 will be tried in the County Court.

Since 1 July 1991 the Small Claims Service covers claims up to £1,000. In June 1995 it was suggested by Lord Woolf in his interim report on access to justice that the limit be raised to £3,000 and later to £5,000. A description of county court procedure is beyond the scope of this book, but attention is drawn to the booklet, *Small Claims in the County Court*, issued as a general guide for litigants in person and subtitled, *How to sue and defend action without a solicitor*. A revised edition of this clear and informative booklet may be available free from county court offices, citizens' advice bureaux and consumer advice centres – if you can get a copy. It has been replaced by a series of leaflets.

That the ordinary county court procedure was inappropriate for small claims was demonstrated in *Justice out of Reach*, a report published in 1971 by the Consumer Council. The county court was shown to be used largely as a debt-collecting agency by traders and finance houses. The court procedure discouraged private consumers from bringing claims by being too complex, intimidating and expensive. The government responded by rejecting the proposed establishment of a separate system of small claims courts, but it did introduce two significant reforms, namely:

**(a)** the pre-trial review was instituted

**(b)** the small claims arbitration scheme was set up.

## 9. Pre-trial review

The pre-trial review is designed to be an informal and usually private hearing before the county court registrar. The object is to enable the registrar to elicit the real issues, to ascertain what measure of agreement exists between the parties, and to fix a convenient date for the hearing of the action, if indeed the dispute is not settled by the parties at the pre-trial review itself. Some guidance as to the evidence needed to prove a claim may be given to the litigant in person. Non-appearance by the defendant allows judgment to be entered for the plaintiff on proving his case; non-appearance by the plaintiff may lead to the action being struck out.

## 10. Arbitration in the county court

Section 7 of the Administration of Justice Act 1973 (now s. 64 County Courts Act 1984) may be regarded as an important piece of consumer law reform because it enabled County Court Rules to provide for the reference of cases to arbitration, thus leading to the introduction of the small claims arbitration scheme in the county court. The arbitrator will usually be the District Judge, but on the application of any party he may refer the proceedings for arbitration by an outside arbitrator. The District Judge, may, on the application of any party, rescind the reference to arbitration if he is satisfied:

**(a)** that a difficult question of law or a question of fact of exceptional complexity is involved; *or*

**(b)** that a charge of fraud is in issue; *or*

**(c)** that the parties are agreed that the dispute should be tried in court; *or*

**(d)** that it would be unreasonable for the claim to proceed to arbitration having regard to its subject-matter, the circumstances of the parties or the interests of any other person likely to be affected by the award.

The advantage of arbitration is that it is an informal hearing usually held in private. The strict rules of evidence do not apply. Under the Lay Representation (Rights of Audiences) Order 1992 an individual can generally be represented by someone other than a lawyer, such as a CAB worker. The arbitration may be decided on a documents only basis if the parties consent. Whether such arbitration is a satisfactory method for determining small claims depends in large measure upon the readiness of the particular District Judge to adopt a more interventionist, inquisitorial approach than the traditional adversarial system characteristic of English law.

There is no right of appeal from the arbitration award but the award may be set aside in very limited circumstances, e.g. error in law on the face of the record or misconduct by the arbitrator. The award is enforceable as a judgment of the county court: s. 64(3) County Courts Act 1984.

## 11. Safeguarding as to costs

The County Court Rules 1981 (as amended) provide that where a small claim is automatically referred to arbitration, solicitors' costs as between party and party are not allowed except for the amount stated on the summons, the costs of enforcing the award, and such further costs as the arbitrator may direct where there has been unreasonable conduct by the opposite party in relation to the proceedings or the claim.

In practice, the unsuccessful litigant will rarely be ordered to pay the winner any costs where the claim does not exceed £1,000. The 'no costs' rule thus makes small claims less hazardous to litigate. Naturally the rule discourages the consumer from being legally represented at the hearing.

*Note*: Court fees (e.g. about 10% of the claim up to £1,000), witness expenses and out-of-pocket expenses will be recoverable by the successful party.

## 12. Voluntary arbitration

It has been noted already that the Office of Fair Trading, besides being a source of information and advice for consumers, approves voluntary codes of practice providing for the arbitration of consumer disputes (*see* 20:5).

## 13. The European dimension to the settlement of consumer disputes

Membership of the European Union has brought about changes to the rights of consumers within the UK. It has had far more impact upon the consumer law of other member states, such as Spain, Greece and Portugal. The future looks productive. Referring to the various Directives, K. Van Miert, a European Commissioner, said at a conference on Consumer Access to Justice:

> 'These Directives have given or will give the consumer a set of important minimum rights. Thus the European consumer, aware that he has the same rights in all member states, will be more prone to benefit from the big market. He will buy beyond the present borders, having a wider choice and raising competition level among suppliers. However, experience has shown us that the establishment of statutes providing consumer rights is insufficient if individuals do not have adequate procedural mechanisms to defend them'.

## Progress test 25

1. Where do consumer advice centres fit in the general structure of consumer advice agencies?

2. Why is legal aid of little practical use to consumers who contemplate taking or defending court proceedings?

3. Explain the 'green form scheme' as it operates in relation to consumers.

4. Explain the fixed fee interview scheme.

5. What is the extent of the county court jurisdiction for actions in contract or tort? Why is the normal county court procedure not thought to be suitable for the determination of small consumer claims?

6. What is the object of the pre-trial review?

7. When will reference of a county court case to arbitration be automatic? In what circumstances may the arbitrator rescind such a reference? What are thought to be the advantages of arbitration?

8. What is the 'no costs' rule and what are the exceptions to it? What effect is the rule likely to have on legal representation of the parties?

9. How is an arbitration award enforceable? On what grounds may an appeal against an arbitration award be brought?

# APPENDIX 1
## DISCUSSION QUESTIONS

1. It was market day in Perranaworthal. . . .

Denzil had gone to buy a shirt. He stopped at a stall which was advertising '100% cotton shirts – never need ironing – all sizes – £5.99'.

In fact, the shirts were 65% cotton and 35% polyester, they would remain badly creased if unironed, and the stall had no shirt to fit Denzil's ample frame.

Janner, meanwhile, was watching and listening to a fast-talking salesman doing his 'patter' to sell jewellery. After about five minutes of high praise and low price, Janner felt that he would like to buy a pair of cufflinks. The trader had described them as 'rolled gold', and an absolute 'giveaway' at only £4. In fact, the cufflinks were made of a base metal which had been sprayed with a thin layer of gold.

Denzil had moved on to look over the stand which displayed a famous brand of double glazing units. Denzil asked the salesman to describe how the units might look in his old granite cottage. He was shown a picture in a catalogue, and told that the units would make the cottage look just like the one in the picture. Denzil signed up for the work, but when it had been completed, some weeks later, the effect was not as he had been promised.

While Denzil was discussing double glazing, Janner was at the clothes stall. He examined a pair of jeans labelled 'Levis'. Even with his untrained eyes, he could see that the label had been stitched in by a clumsy hand, and that the colour of the thread used differed from that used elsewhere on the jeans. He also examined a jacket from a pile of similar jackets near which was a sign saying 'Wrangler – Style'. Janner read the label inside the jacket. It said 'Wrongler'. He tried it on. It fitted him well. It also seemed to be of good quality.

Denzil was now at the jewellery stall. The trader was not demonstrating at that time, so Denzil asked him for a Swiss watch. Without a word, the trader handed him a watch from underneath the counter and pointed to the price tag. It read £10. The trader was talking to another customer so Denzil just placed a £10 note on the counter and put the watch in his pocket. In fact, the watch was not from Switzerland. It was a cheap imitation made in the Far East.

By now Janner was talking to the man on the stand about double glazing. Janner asked how much warmer a room would be if the units were fitted. The trader said that 15% warmer would be a safe estimate. Having seen the manufacturer's advertising campaign on television, Janner also asked about noise reduction. He was promised that the noise in his home from traffic passing by outside would be at least 75% eliminated. The trader was aware that these were exaggerated claims, but he thought that Janner was a likely customer, and he was paid only by means of commission on the sales he arranged.

Discuss the legal position.

**2.** It was a busy day in the 'Down Home DIY Centre'. . . .

Several people were waiting in a line to see the Manager:

One had been given a 'two-speed hammer drill' as a birthday present. The moment he plugged it in to use it there was a flash, and the fuses in his house blew. When he checked the wiring in the plug, which had been supplied attached to the drill, he found that the wires had been put into the wrong places.

Another man waiting there was bandaged heavily. He had been badly cut when using a chain saw that he had purchased by credit card from the store only a few days earlier. 'I just started the thing up and it flew out of my hand and cut me, look', he said, waving his bandaged arm for all the customers in the store to see.

A lady was waiting to complain about some paint she had bought. It was described as 'a subtle shade of delicate green'. When she applied it to her bedroom wall it looked blue. She asked some of her neighbours and friends for their opinions. They were split about the matter, but several did agree that the colour was more blue than green.

Another lady was unhappy about some wallpaper. She had scanned the catalogues and carefully chosen a woodchip paper so that she could redecorate a replastered wall in her old granite cottage. She had employed a local decorator to hang the paper for her. He had charged several hundred pounds for the job. When he had finished, she was disappointed. All the joints between the rolls of paper he had put on the wall showed prominently. She had complained to him, but he had blamed the materials she had supplied. Now she intended to take the matter up with the store manager.

Towards the end of the line waited an elderly man who had bought, some five years ago, a set of patio furniture. He is complaining today because, as he placed it out for the summer, two of the chairs fell to pieces in his hands. The plastic seems to have become brittle.

At the end of the line stood a man with a brick and a box containing glue in one hand and a piece of iron in the other. He had asked a member of the staff to advise him as to which glue he should use to stick the brick to the metal. He had bought the glue as advised, but it had not worked. Incidentally, he had noticed, whilst waiting in line, that on the box for the glue it listed many of the purposes for which the glue could be used – but sticking bricks to metal was not included on the list.

Discuss the legal position.

**3.** Susan is a shorthand typist. In her lunch hour she visited the local 'Interstellar Store'. She wanted to buy a dress for a party. She is 'size 12'. She chose a dress labelled 'size 12'. She did not try it on. The dressing rooms were large and communal. Susan is shy. Wandering around the store, she picked out a pair of bright yellow jeans. She did not try those on either. On her way towards the cash desk, she noticed the 'bargain counter'. She chose a blouse which was labelled 'shopsoiled', and a set of hair rollers marked 'price was £20, special clearance offer £10'. The last item she chose was from the 'megahealth' counter. It was a 'crunchybake' cottage cheese and pineapple crispbread 'lunchpack'. She paid and went into the park.

She noticed that the crispbread was soggy, and it showed marks which could easily have been teethmarks, perhaps made by mice. When she arrived back at her flat that evening she tried on the dress, it did not fit. When her boyfriend Sebastian came around later she showed him the jeans. He said that he thought they were revolting. The next evening she said that she could not go out with him. 'She had', she said, 'to wash her hair'. The hair rollers did not work. The heater stayed cold. She tried on the blouse. It had a hole in the cuff.

In an advanced state of feeling fed up, she returned to the store. She asked to speak to the manager. She laid the blouse, the jeans and the dress on the counter. She showed him the remains of her 'lunchpack', which she had kept in her handbag. She also produced the hair rollers. She demanded all her money back, immediately.

The manager simply pointed to a sign on the wall which said 'no refunds'. He walked away.

Discuss the legal position.

**4**. Dryden, the travelling salesman, is staying at Peter's Moorside Retreat, a highly recommended hotel.

At the end of a long day, Dryden is attracted towards the swimming pool which he has seen advertised in the tourist board brochure, and on the signs outside the hotel. He changed into his swimming costume in his room and walked to the pool, only to find that it was empty. When he complained at the reception desk, he was told that the pool had been drained because there was no demand for it in the wintertime. Dryden pointed out that it was springtime, but to no avail.

The restaurant was open, so he went in for dinner. He was pleased with the quality of the meal, but when the bill arrived he noticed that a 15% service charge had been added. He questioned this with the waiter because no mention of the charge had appeared on the menu, but the waiter said that it was added to avoid customers having to worry about how much to tip the staff and mentioned that a tip on top of the bill would not be unwelcome.

After his meal Dryden, wandered into the hotel shop. He decided to buy a tape to play in his car the following day. He noticed one entitled 'John the Fish – live in concert'. Dryden is a fan of this artist and so he bought the tape. He also noticed a red tie. It was described as 'finest quality, silk-style fashion tie – Italian made'. On closer inspection he noticed that the tie was made of a shiny polyester, and on the inside of the label he saw the words 'made in Hong Kong'. He decided not to buy the tie.

Much later that same evening, having been chatting with other guests and enjoying their hospitality, Dryden ordered a round of drinks from the waiter. He had anticipated that the price would be around £8. In fact the waiter asked for £11. He complained, but he was told that the prices increase after one in the morning because the staff are paid overtime to serve late-night drinkers. Dryden pointed out that it was only 12.15. The waiter said that it was 1.15 because the clocks had gone forward that same evening.

He did not sleep well that night. The disco stayed active all night. He had not expected the hotel to have a disco. In fact, when he asked the tourist board for their suggestions as to where he might stay he had asked for a quiet hotel.

When he drove away the next morning he found that only one track on the tape he had bought involved John the Fish. The other artists were also recorded live, but he had not heard of any of them.

Discuss the legal position.

# INDEX